THE
HUNTER
HUNTED

THE
HUNTER
HUNTED
Submarine versus Submarine
Encounters from World War I to the Present

Robert C Stern

NAVAL INSTITUTE PRESS
Annapolis

Copyright © Robert C Stern 2007

First published in Great Britain in 2007 by
Chatham Publishing,
Lionel Leventhal Ltd,
Park House, 1 Russell Gardens,
London NW11 9NN

Published and distributed in the United States of America and Canada by the
Naval Institute Press,
291 Wood Road, Annapolis,
Maryland 21402-5034

Library of Congress Control Number: 2006938918

ISBN-10: 1-59114-379-9
ISBN-13: 978-1-59114-379-6

Printed and bound in Great Britain

Contents

Acknowledgements

A BOOK LIKE THIS could not be completed without the help of many people. I have been collecting the materials used in this book for more than 30 years, so I hope I will be excused if the source of some materials and the names of some of the kind individuals who helped me obtain them have slipped my memory. Those who have helped me recently enough for me to recall include:

Capitaine de vaisseau Jacques Favreul – son of the captain of *Doris* – who kindly responded to questions I had regarding the loss of his father's submarine and allowed me to reproduce two photographs from his collection. Captain Favreul kindly read over Chapter 10 and kept me from making several significant errors. (As with all others who have so kindly helped me on this project, his help was invaluable, but he is not responsible for any errors of fact or analysis that crept into this text. That responsibility is entirely my own.)

Vanessa Salazar de Ingardia and her father, Wilfredo Jesus Salazar, who graciously provided translations from Spanish into English for Chapter 6.

Paul Wittmer, who runs the excellent site www.subvetpaul.com, for permission to quote from the recollections of *Besugo* veteran John Geck.

Ken Macpherson and John Albrecht, who made photographs available to me over the years.

The research staff at a number of institutions, including, but not limited to: the US National Archives (NARA), College Park, MD; the US Navy Submarine Force Library and Museum, Groton, CT; the British National Archives and the US Naval Historical Center (NHC), each of whom supplied valuable primary documentation without which this book would be far less accurate and interesting.

And, last but not least, my wife, Beth, whose patience and support during this process is nothing short of astounding. She had the charity to act interested as I talked on and on about the writing of this book, and she had the courage to read these chapters in draft form and made many invaluable suggestions that made them more readable.

Robert C Stern
Cupertino, CA
August 2006

Illustrations

Introduction

UNLIKE ARMIES, WHICH FOR MUCH of history could be created as needed at short notice, naval forces took planning and long periods of time to bring into being. Not only was it necessary to build a ship, but it had to be manned and the crew trained to react instinctively in bloody battle. And that process then had to be repeated for as many ships as it might take to defeat an enemy's fleet. Small wonder then that for much of history, only a few nations 'ruled the waves'. For nearly 300 years, from the seventeenth century up to the beginning of the twentieth century, one nation – Great Britain – held virtually uncontested mastery of the world's oceans.

Unable to stand against Great Britain in a conventional fleet engagement, her enemies often looked to marginal encounters and unconventional means to challenge British dominance. The newly minted Americans used both tactics. They built a small number of novel 'super-frigates' and won some important single-ship duels in the Revolutionary War and War of 1812. An even more portentous attack on Britain's control of the seas took place in New York harbour on the night of 7 September 1776. Sergeant Ezra Lee of the Continental Army navigated an egg-shaped contraption under the water to its target, Lord Howe's flagship, HMS *Eagle*. This strange vessel, the *Turtle*, designed and built by Irish-born David Bushnell, was intended to drill a hole in *Eagle*'s hull, attach a 250lb (113kg) black powder charge and then escape to a safe distance before a fuse detonated the charge. This first attempt at submarine warfare failed because *Turtle*'s drill was unable to penetrate *Eagle*'s hull in two attempts. Despite this lack of result, a new age of warfare had begun.

It took more than 100 years for the necessary technologies to mature to the extent that safe and practical submersibles were entering service in the major fleets, but, once that point was reached, it was inevitable that the numbers of submarines in service would increase rapidly. By the time war broke out in Europe in 1914, the four combatants with significant navies (Britain, France, Germany and Italy) had almost 200 submarines in service and many more being built. This number included many old boats, already obsolete compared to new construction, and numerous new boats not yet ready for combat. The number of effective boats was certainly less than half of that total. Nevertheless, with that number of boats blundering about in the confined waters of the North Sea and the Mediterranean, it was inevitable that submarines would encounter each other. In fact, it took just a few months for the first such engagement to take place and the first blood to be drawn.

The subject of this book is just such encounters, in which submarines battled submarines. Given the immensity of the world's oceans and the relative smallness of a submarine, it is surprising how often submarines found each other. In almost all cases, it was nothing more than a sighting. One boat sees another, tries but fails to gain an advantageous firing position and the intended victim sails on, as often as not completely unaware of her near brush with the enemy. The incidents reported in this book are drawn from the far rarer cases when fate or luck allowed an attack to be made.

In these cases, the stories are often quite similar, at least until the advent of the Cold War when the rules of engagement changed dramatically. One boat would spot the other, make a short approach, fire torpedoes and hope they ran true. With a decisiveness rarely seen in warfare, in these engagements there was almost always a winner and a loser. The winner lived to fight another day; the loser most often sank. The engagements were generally brief and violent. Survivors from the losing boat were the rare exception.

Thus it is frequently impossible except in the imagination to recreate the events on the losing boat that led up to the fatal encounter. I have refrained from trying to depict for the reader the shouted orders and chaos of those last moments. On the occasions when I have indulged in speculation as to what was going on in the doomed boat, I make it clear that that is what I am doing. When I do so indulge, it is in an attempt to explain actions on the victim's part, never for dramatic effect. Because of the brevity and uniformity of many of these stories, I have, of necessity, spent time describing the events that preceded and followed the actual engagement to put it in context and give some life to the people who acted out these small dramas.

The incidents reported here date from 1914 up to the year 2000. Not surprisingly, information on the most recent encounters is the hardest to obtain. Only in the last few years have some official documents been declassified and some veterans come forward with accounts of their experiences. Despite the demise of the Soviet Union, there is still considerable sensitivity on the Russian side concerning what exactly happened in the Cold War. In a number of cases, there is disagreement as to the basic facts, including whether submarines were lost in these encounters and why. Where there is disagreement, I present the 'facts' as put forward by both sides.

While this is not a technical history of submarine development, nevertheless, some familiarity with the technology that enabled the battle is useful to understanding what happened. I have attempted to find a balance that provides enough of this background without detracting from the main narrative of this book.

I have tried to keep the story focused on the boats and the brave men who served in them. Whether the motivation was patriotic fervour, a quiet sense of duty or simply fear of letting down their shipmates, these men went under the waves in slivers of steel searching for the enemy. Sometimes they found another sliver with its own complement of dedicated men. These encounters are the subject of this book.

Note on units of measurement (and a few other things)

IT IS DIFFICULT, WHEN LOOKING THROUGH historical documents and reference works from any time period, to find a consistent set of units by which ships and everything related to them were measured. Further, being an American author writing in 2006, it is impossible to ignore the fact that every other developed country besides the US has adopted the metric system, at least officially.

Given all this, I have been forced to make decisions about which units to use in this book and have tried my best to stay consistent with these decisions. There are two places where my best efforts have been most challenged. One is in the area of gun calibres. I have decided in this case to simply use the designation system(s) of the nation whose weapon is being described and have added an appendix to explain as best I can how the various systems correspond. The other case is when I am quoting a source which used a measurement system other than the one I adopted for this book. In those cases, I have retained the original measurement system used by the author. The only exception to this is I did change the 12-hour clock time references in German logs from the First World War to the more standard 24-hour clock. In all other cases, I have attempted to use the following units consistently:

Distance/length – In general, distances are given in nautical miles. Historically, a nautical mile is 2,000 yards; in metric terms, it is 1,852 metres. Whenever I use the word 'mile', even when not preceded by the word 'nautical', I mean a nautical mile (nm). Shorter lengths, typically those less than one mile, I give in metres (m). The only exception to these rules is when I am giving a distance that is purely a measure of travel on land, such as the distance from Paris to Berlin. In these cases, I use kilometres (km).

Time – I use the nautical 24-hour clock throughout. Keeping track of time zones is next to impossible, as it was almost always true that when one submarine sighted another, their clocks would not have agreed any more than their politics. In general, I have used the time zone of the first boat mentioned in the narrative and adjusted the other boat's to agree.

Displacement – In this matter, I have made no attempt to reconcile long tons, short tons and metric tonnes, since knowing the exact displacement of a boat never alters the outcome of the stories. In most cases, the sources do not specify which 'ton' they are using. (Displacement is normally, but not always, given in long or English tons.) I give standard displacement when it is distinguished from other displacements (*eg*, normal or full load). I make no attempt to reconcile the various interpretations of what standard displacement means in different navies. In general, I try to find a consensus between sources before giving a displacement. I always give submarine displacement as surface displacement (meaning the displacement of the boat at normal surface trim). Merchant ship displacements are given as GRT (Gross Registered Tons), which is actually a unit of volume (1 GRT is 100 cubic feet or 2.83 cubic metres).

Speed – Always given in knots (nautical miles per hour).

Weight – I use kilograms (kg) and tonnes whenever possible.

Place names are also a problem, in that the two World Wars took place at a time when many of the locations of the action in these stories were under colonial administration. Colonial powers tended to either give new names to the places they 'administered' or give the local names new pronunciations and spellings that fitted the language of the administrators. As a result, many of the place names used by the combatants in these wars would not be found on a map today. I have opted to use the names and spellings of the period and power in question and to give the contemporary name in the footnotes.

When writing Japanese personal names, I use the traditional form which is surname first.

Finally, a note about the charts included in this book. With the exception of the chart showing HMS/M *Venturer*'s attack on *U-864*, these were found among the logs and reports of the U-boat campaigns captured and microfilmed by the British after the Second World War. The originals were hand-drawn, sometimes on paper of poor quality or on the back or in the margin of other documents. They were then microfilmed along with tens of thousands of other documents. The result often was rather poor-quality reproduction, exacerbated by then printing them on paper with vintage microfilm viewers. In this form, they were unfit for use in this book. One option was to leave them out, but that would mean losing valuable first-hand documentation by the participants in some of these events. Another option was to have them redrawn; this was rejected because new drawings would lose the immediacy of the originals, drawn within hours or days of the event. It was decided therefore to digitize the paper charts and attempt to clean them up. The results have been successful to an unexpected degree. We were able remove enough of the background noise and clutter introduced by multiple stages of reproduction that the original drawing stood out clearly.

CHAPTER 1

First Blood

U-27 and HMS/M *E.3*, and the '*Baralong* Affair'

WHEN WAR BROKE OUT IN Europe in August 1914, no-one foresaw the bloodbath that was to follow. Expert opinion believed it would be a reprise of the most recent major European conflict, the Franco-Prussian War of 1870–1. They expected a short and bloody war of movement, like before, except that the French and their British allies hoped for a different outcome. But the universal adoption of magazine rifles, machine guns and rapid-firing field artillery in the interim tipped the scales in favour of the defenders and guaranteed a stalemate in the west that would last until 1918.

Naval forces had played only a minor role in 1870, but with the realisation that there would be no quick resolution to the land war, the British implemented a strategy of naval blockade that had served them well for centuries in their wars with continental enemies. The Germans had the second largest navy in the world, but Britain's Grand Fleet was that much stronger that the Germans wisely declined to risk their fleet in a head-on engagement. There was a stalemate in the North Sea no less dispiriting than that in Flanders.[1]

Almost the only option the Germans had left to challenge the Royal Navy's stranglehold was submarine warfare. The first patrol line of ten old U-boats left Helgoland on 6 August 1914 searching for the British blockade. Two of those boats never returned; the eight that did reported no success. These losses brought home the reality that making war with these primitive early submersibles was going to be dangerous and often frustrating. Nevertheless, a second patrol line went out after the first and a third after that. On the afternoon of 5 September, Otto Hersing's *U-21* found the small, old light cruiser HMS *Pathfinder* in stormy conditions north of St Abb's Head on the east coast of Scotland. Due to the rough seas and the ship's poor endurance at any higher speed, *Pathfinder* was patrolling the southern approaches to the Firth of Forth at only 5 knots. That slow speed made her an easy target for *U-21*, which, despite the weather, managed a 45-minute submerged approach that put her in firing position 1,600m off the cruiser's beam. *U-21* put a single torpedo into *Pathfinder*'s side, igniting a magazine and sending her to the bottom with almost her entire crew. (Some accounts say there were three survivors; others say there were eleven.) *Pathfinder* had the sad distinction of being the first ship to be sunk by a modern submarine.[2]

The British had no intention of ceding the initiative to the U-boats. The Royal Navy started the war with more submarines than the Germans and put them to work immediately scouting the German fleet and the coastal shipping from Scandinavia on which German industry depended.[3] *E.9*, commanded by Lieutenant Commander Max Horton, evened the score by sinking the old German light cruiser SMS *Hela* south of Helgoland barely eight days after the loss of *Pathfinder*.

With submarines of both sides regularly sweeping the North Sea in those early months of the war, it was inevitable that there would be encounters. On 9 October, *E.10* rose to periscope depth and found a U-boat passing a mere 50m off her bow. At that range, a torpedo would not arm and *E.10*'s submerged speed was too slow to allow her to manoeuvre into a better attack position.[4] Her captain could only watch in frustration as the unidentified U-boat went on her way, unaware of the danger narrowly avoided. On 18 October, the roles were reversed and the outcome very different.

His Majesty's Submarine *E.3*, under the command of Lieutenant Commander G F Cholmley, departed Harwich on 16 October in the company of *E.8*. Both were assigned patrol areas near the island of Borkum, looking for any German warships coming out of the Ems. The two boats parted company at approximately 2200 that night. It was the last friendly sighting of *E.3*. On the morning of the 18th, *E.3* was patrolling on the surface south of Borkum. *U-27*, under the command of *Kapitänleutnant* (Lieutenant) Bernd Wegener, was heading towards the U-boat base at Emden. She was submerged, transiting north to south through the same waters. At 1125 that same morning, lookouts sighted what Wegener took at first to be a buoy, but it was moving and it was where no buoy should have been.[5] Wegener recorded the events in his *KTB*.[6]

18.X.

1100	5 nm NW Ems Buoy, NW 3–4, Sea NW 3, cloudy, partially sunny[7]	Smoke at 140° My course 180°
1125		At 320°, an object that looks like a buoy sighted. I turn on a course of 255° in order to get a look at the object from the side.
1140		Object is determined to be a submarine on a course approximately in the bearing direction.
		Remain on course 255°, attempting to gain a position upwind and up-sun; it was taken as given, that an underwater attack should be

executed. Throughout we went with both motors full speed, periscope retracted. Only every 400–500m was the periscope raised to get a bearing. Reduced speed to one motor at slow speed.

1205   Go to course 285°, separation is now approximately 2nm and we should soon nearly catch up with the enemy. This distance of 2nm is necessary to make a very good reconnaissance of the trimmed-down boat. I can see that there are six men in the tower watch.

Even with that many eyes on the bridge, *U-27* was able to approach completely unobserved. The sea state was such that the short choppy waves might have effectively hidden *U-27*'s periscope when Wegener made his periodic observations.

1245   Turned somewhat and then with a harder turn put us in front of the enemy – my course 50° – starboard bow tube with 1.5m depth setting made ready to shoot. On this course, we have with confidence concluded the target is an <u>enemy</u> submarine:

   1) It is missing any periscope support and breakwater from its tower structure.

   2) On the fore and aft ends of the tower – which can be made out despite the bearing of the target and its trimmed-down condition - there is a 2–3m long pole, apparently an unretractable mast.

   3) While observing the target during the brief time we had the periscope up, my WO said with confidence that he had seen: Black "83" on the tower.

Certain that he was tracking an enemy submarine, Wegener adjusted his course 3° to starboard and then turned again to aim his bow at the target as he was firing. (In these early days of submarine warfare, torpedoes could only run a straight course and were aimed by pointing the torpedo tube at the target.)

1322   Position of enemy 5–6° to port, in my
estimation 300m away. I go therefore
with starboard motor, previously running
at slow speed, now to AK ahead and turn
hard to port to make the shot.[8] Aiming
point: middle of the target. After maybe
12 seconds an explosion was heard, a tall
column of water with much debris was
observed; the boat broke apart in the
middle; bow and stern separated. As the
column of water fell back to the surface,
the boat disappeared.

Four of the six lookouts ended up swimming in view of *U-27*'s periscope,
but Wegener was as cautious as he was methodical:

> Four men can be seen in the water, which
> I have chosen not to rescue at this time,
> because of the risk of attack by another
> enemy submarine. Intentionally, I attempt
> the rescue only after a half hour has
> passed. After making two wide circles
> around the site of the sinking, I briefly
> surfaced and opened the tower hatch to
> see if anyone was still swimming. There
> were only pieces of cork, some bread and
> a wooden box to be seen.

   U-27 was the first submarine to sink another, enough to earn her and her
commander a place in the history of submarine warfare. Their career after
that only added to their fame. Under Wegener, *U-27* sank nine merchant
targets totalling 29,402 tons in ten patrols, as well as the old converted
seaplane tender HMS *Hermes* and the auxiliary cruiser HMS *Bayano*.
Wegener was noted for his correctness in following prize law, always
allowing merchant crews adequate time to get into lifeboats before sinking
their ship, up until the day his boat was herself sunk on 19 August 1915.
On that day he approached a steamer and forced her to stop by firing across
her bow. He was relatively unconcerned when his lookouts sighted another
small steamer approaching, flying an American flag and with standard
neutrality markings painted on her sides, which included her name and
nationality: '*Ulysses S. Grant* – USA'. She raised the international signal
flag indicating she intended to rescue the steamer's crew. Wegener allowed
her to approach unmolested.
   Ulysses S. Grant was in fact a British auxiliary, HMS *Baralong*, under the
command of Lieutenant Commander Godfrey Herbert.[9] She had three old
12pdr guns hidden under canvas disguised to look like deck hamper.[10] The
U-boat never stood a chance. *U-27* only got off one round in the general
direction of *Baralong* and then was silenced. *Baralong*'s gun crews got off

thirty-four shots in the minute it took to sink the U-boat.[11] About a dozen of *U-27*'s crew found themselves in the water, the men who had been on deck manning the guns or directing the action. The rest went down with the U-boat. But the men in the water, including Wegener, were no luckier than their mates. The Germans began swimming towards the still-floating steamer, which was the closest refuge for these men suddenly thrown into very cold water. At least half of the swimmers reached the steamer and began climbing up the pilot's ladder and the lifeboat falls. At some point, Herbert ordered his contingent of a dozen marines to open fire on the survivors.

In his official report, Herbert claimed that he did so because he believed that the Germans intended to commandeer the now-abandoned steamer and scuttle the ship along with her valuable cargo.[12] Regardless of the reason, several of the men climbing up the steamer's side were shot, but four (or six) appear to have reached the deck. The seas being dead calm, Herbert brought *Baralong* alongside, close enough that his marines were able to jump over to the steamer. According to Herbert, their instructions were to prevent the Germans from taking control of the ship. Some American muleteers who had been on the steamer and were now nearby in lifeboats said they were later told that Herbert gave explicit instructions that all the Germans were to be shot.

Regardless, everyone agrees that the marines started shooting. One version of the story states that Wegener was one of the men who made it to the deck and was hiding there when the marines boarded the ship. He attempted to surrender, but the marines kept firing. He jumped overboard in a last futile attempt to save his life, but several of the marines shot down from the deck at him as he tread water. Hit twice, he died in the water. Another German may have been shot on the deck. What is certain is that four fled below decks, finally being cornered in the engine room. There they were killed. Most accounts say that the marines shot them even as they were trying to surrender. Herbert's version is that they were actively attempting to scuttle the ship and the marines shot them when they refused to stop.

The British at first attempted to keep the affair a secret. *Baralong*'s civilian crew was sworn to secrecy, as was the crew of the steamer. This attempt at secrecy failed because the American witnesses were not subject to the strict British Official Secrets Act and some of them chose to tell their story to the press. The German government understandably declared the incident an atrocity, demanding that Herbert be tried for war crimes. The British refused, saying that Herbert had acted only to prevent the sinking of the steamer. The Americans protested that their flag and markings had been used improperly to trick the U-boat, but the British claimed that *Baralong*'s actions were consistent with the long tradition of using false colours as a *ruse de guerre* and that protest also came to nothing. The war continued with unabated ferocity for three more years, allowing the whole incident to fade from memory.

Lieutenant Commander Herbert, who had come to *Baralong* from command of the submarine *D.5*, returned to submarine duty again after leaving the Q-ship. He was in command of *H.8* in 1916 and then, in January 1917, he had command of the new, steam-powered *K.13* when she sank during a test dive. Remarkably, he survived the war and went on to become Managing Director of BSA Ltd in 1921.

Bernd Wegener died in the *Baralong* incident, but lived on in a sense. He became something of a martyr to the many Germans looking for excuses for losing the Great War. Wegener represented the chivalric Teutonic warrior betrayed by the treacherous enemy. As Nazi Germany prepared for war, Wegener's name was given to the 7th Flotilla of U-boats, which was formed at Kiel in June 1938 and moved to St-Nazaire after the fall of France in 1940. Its symbol, the 'Bull of Scapa Flow' was probably the most famous U-boat emblem.

CHAPTER 2

Fratricide I

U-7 and *U-22*

'FRIENDLY FIRE' IS A EUPHEMISM, one of those terms used to try to cover up a horrible reality. As rare as it was for a submarine to sink another, the odds that one submarine would sink another from the same navy should have been vanishingly small. Nevertheless, it happened, whether through a failure of drill, communications or just terribly bad luck.[1] And it happened more than once. The first time it happened was 21 January 1915, when two U-boats met in the North Sea.

One of those boats, *U-7* was already hopelessly obsolete, but as 1915 began Germany needed every U-boat it could deploy. So *Kapitänleutnant* Georg König was unsurprised when he received orders in early January to transfer his boat from Emden to the new Flanders Flotilla. His boat was so short-ranged that she would likely be far more effective operating from Zeebrugge, where the Flanders squadron had been established the preceding November. Short range had limited her first two patrols to the Helgoland Bight and the vicinity of Horn's Reef, where she had had no success. Of course transferring to Zeebrugge would not solve her other big problem, which was the tell-tale plume of white smoke left by her heavy-oil Körting engine whenever she navigated on the surface. Whether it was with hope or resignation that König nosed his boat out of the Ems in the evening on 20 January and headed west along the Dutch coast, we will never know.

That same day, *U-22*, a much newer and far more capable boat under the command of König's good friend, *Kapitänleutnant* Bruno Hoppe, broke off her patrol off the east coast of Britain and headed home. Hoppe still had torpedoes in his tubes, but the patrol had been long and frustrating and he decided it was time to head back to Emden. The weather had been horrible, with dense fog and rough seas, exactly the kind of weather that made patrolling in a U-boat an exercise in pure misery. He took his boat southeast across the North Sea, hoping to find some shelter from the waves under the Dutch shore. He made landfall shortly after dawn on the 21st, north of the island of Ameland.

The story of what happened next was the subject of much after-the-fact analysis – not only by the participants, but also by higher levels in the U-boat command. The responsible flotilla commander, in true military fashion, held a formal inquiry and issued a report which included a useful synopsis of the incident:[2]

> On 21 January 1915, *U-22* was steering 115° towards the Ems on return from an eight-day patrol and was at 0900 approximately 10nm distant from the marker buoy. That same morning at daybreak, *U-7* left the Ems en route to Zeebrügge. The weather was hazy, wind south 6–7, sea state 5.

At 0912, *U-7* was seen from *U-22* 4–6 points to starboard.[3] *U-7* was to the windward, so that from *U-22* the view to the south was so strongly impeded by wind and sea that Hoppe assumed that *U-7* must have seen him already. That *U-7* nevertheless continued on, without taking notice of *U-22*, made the captain of *U-22* immediately suspicious.

It was impossible to tell whether the boat was friend or foe.

> *U-22*, soon after sighting *U-7*, fired the prescribed signal flare 'B'; this was answered by *U-7* by a flare fired so low that it never separated into individual stars.[4] The same was true on the second attempt. On the second attempt at a recognition signal, the captain of *U-22* again hoped to see the correct response.

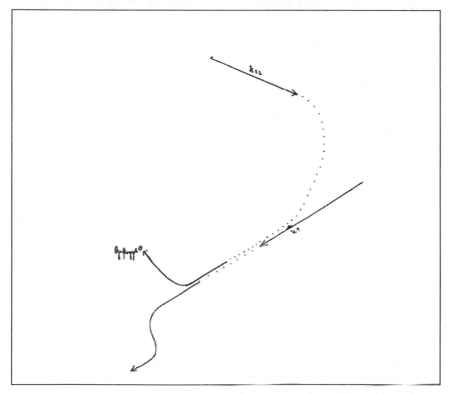

This is the first of two drawings included in the flotilla chief's report to show the positions of *U-22* and *U-7* during their encounter. The boats' original positions and courses are shown by the solid lines at the top and right. The dotted lines show *U-22* swinging behind *U-7*. The solid lines to the left show their turns away from each other.

The conclusion was reached that the signal was deliberately fired so low as to disguise an incorrect response.

U-22, which had been heading roughly ESE now turned sharply to starboard and swung around into the wake of *U-7*, which did not alter course.

> As *U-22* now turned towards *U-7*, *U-7* now was 1–2 points to port and only increased the suspicion on *U-22* that it was trying to flee. This suspicion became even greater because – as a result of the sea state – the breakwater typical of our boats wasn't seen and, further, they'd apparently lowered the exhaust pipe that was required for half or greater speed, and that it was running without making any smoke, whereas normally a dense white exhaust was produced.[5]

The other boat continued on a southwestward course and seemed to have increased speed because the distance between the boats grew. Hoppe responded by increasing his own speed to his boat's maximum 15 knots and began to close the range again. It seemed incredible to Hoppe that the other boat could be unaware she was being followed. She should have dived or turned to face her pursuer, but she did neither.

After several minutes like this, the other boat suddenly began to manoeuvre.

> *U-22* remained aft and to starboard relative to *U-7*, when *U-7* turned four points to port.[6]

Hoppe saw this turn, but apparently in the haze thought *U-7* was turning on the reciprocal course, because *U-22* now turned sharply to starboard. Very quickly, Hoppe must have realised his mistake, as *U-22* now turned back on a course to follow *U-7*. After less than a minute on her new course, *U-7* returned to her base course of approximately WSW. *U-22* continued to swing back to *U-7*'s course, eventually crossing her wake.

> *U-22* now stood in *U-7*'s wake and about 2 points to port, confident that this gave it no chance for a shot. It was quite likely at this point that neither boat would get a chance to fire a torpedo and, against the possibility of a close engagement, the captain of *U-22* armed his crew with pistols.

The two boats again settled into a stern chase. With the range down to 900m, Hoppe again tried to communicate with *U-7* and this time got no response at all.

> *U-22* then tried to communicate via signal flags; the message flew from the tower for between 4 and 15 minutes – the accounts differ – with no response from *U-7*.
> One more final attempt at the star signal was tried; if there was no valid response this time, the captain and all the bridge personnel of *U-22* would be convinced that they were following an Englishman. Not much was expected of this attempt, as the red and green stars can hardly be seen by day, especially in hazy weather.

The chase continued until *U-7* once again turned to port.

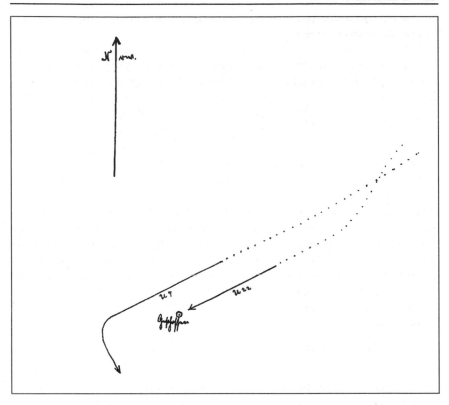

Having crossed *U-7*'s wake (dotted line), *U-22* fell into a pursuit that lasted
until *U-7* again turned left, setting up the fatal shot.

After about 5 minutes, *U-7* turned sharply to port and gave rise to the certainty,
that given the lack of other options, this was the time to fire a bow-shot.

U-22 fired both bow torpedoes when *U-7*, in turning, passed across her
bow. Actually, *U-7* appeared to be stopping in this position and had thus,
most unfortunately, denied herself the opportunity to manoeuvre to evade
the oncoming torpedoes.

At this point, it is possible that König finally realised that he was being
followed. We will never know for sure. What appears certain is that
Hoppe's decision to fire was made before it was noticed that *U-7* was
slowing. The first torpedo missed; the second, tragically, ran true, hitting its
target just forward of the conning tower. The submarine exploded in a huge
ball of smoke and flame and disappeared rapidly beneath the waves.

In less than a minute, *U-22* was in the middle of a large oil slick in which
there was a single survivor struggling in the water, shouting for help in
perfect German. It took only a few more minutes for the full force of the
tragedy to strike home. Not only had he sunk another German U-boat, but
worse it was the boat commanded by his dear friend, Georg König. With

the heaviest of hearts, he turned *U-22* back on to a course for Emden and the inevitable reckoning.

The commander of *U-32*, *Kapitänleutnant* Spiegel von und zu Peckelsheim, who had docked at Emden just an hour before *U-22*'s arrival, later described in detail the grim Hoppe, who brushed aside the normal dockside greeting for a returning U-boat and headed straight for the office of the flotilla commander. The reaction of the flotilla leadership was immediate. For many reasons, it was important that the cause of the tragedy, if possible, be found. If it was due to procedural problems or poor training, then those issues would need to be addressed immediately, before another similar error occurred. If the fault was Hoppe's, then he would need to be punished to serve as an example for others. A Court of Inquiry was convened the next day, which lasted until 2 February. Testimony was taken from the survivor and from the others who had been on the bridge with Hoppe during the pursuit of *U-7*. Ultimately, they were forced to conclude that *U-22* had followed correct procedure from start to finish. Multiple sets of eyes had observed *U-7* and none had been able to identify the other boat as German. They had tried several times to establish contact, but *U-7* had failed to respond in the prescribed manner. *U-7* had continued on her course and had stopped responding in any way to *U-22*'s presence, which had led to the suspicion and finally the certainty that *U-22* was following an enemy boat. Hoppe's superiors had to conclude that it had been an accident. Tragic, but unavoidable. All they could do was urge greater caution and hope that it did not happen again.

Hoppe remained in command of *U-22* for more than a year, before being relieved on 22 August 1916. He commissioned a new boat, *U-83*, on 6 September 1916. In two patrols, she sank five ships of more than 6,000 GRT of shipping. On 17 February 1917, *U-83* torpedoed the steamer *Norge* and then surfaced to finish her off with her deck gun.[7] But the *Norge* turned out to be the Q-ship *Farnborough*, which sank the U-boat with gunfire. Hoppe was killed by *Farnborough*'s first shell.

U-22 survived the war. Under three commanders, she sank thirty-six ships totalling more than 46,000 GRT. She surrendered to the Royal Navy on 1 December 1918.

CHAPTER 3

U-boat Traps

HMS *Taranaki*, HMS/M *C.24* and *U-40*

THE ROYAL NAVY'S BLOCKADE OF Germany began to have immediate effect. Before the war, Germany had a large and modern merchant fleet, but it was quickly driven from the seas – captured, sunk or forced into neutral harbours where the ships were interned. According to the rules of war, neutrals could trade with either side in the conflict, but contraband (meaning any materials that could aid the prosecution of the war) could be seized along with the ship carrying it. The British interpreted the rules quite broadly and let very little through; for example, they included foodstuffs in their definition of materials of war. Neutrals soon learned that trading with Germany meant a high likelihood that cargo and ship would be seized and, at best, tied up in lengthy litigation. It was far easier for neutrals to trade only with the British.

Despite Germany's land area and great industrial capability, shortages began to appear almost from the beginning. The Germans were dependent on imports of food, oil, nitrates and many other materials of war, and the blockade soon reduced the flow of these vital supplies to a fraction of what they had been before the war. Nitrates in particular, essential in the production of munitions and fertilisers, were soon in critically short supply.

Most frustrating was the fact that Germany could do very little about this situation. Nothing could be done about the fact that Great Britain sat astride Germany's access to the open ocean. Even worse, the British did not have to maintain a close blockade, as they had been forced to do in the interminable wars with the French in the eighteenth and nineteenth centuries. Any ship trying to enter or leave Germany from the Atlantic had to pass through the English Channel or the narrows between Norway and Scotland, which could be mined and patrolled by small craft. Early German attempts to attack the blockade had predictably proved futile. It was like punching air. There was simply no effective way for the Germans to attack the blockade.

The only way the Germans could effectively respond was to attempt to cut Britain's own seaborne lifelines. If anything, the British were even more dependent on imports to fight the war. Compared to Germany, Great Britain had few natural resources and an inadequate land area to feed its war industries or population without a continual flow of goods of all types from overseas. The very effective blockade by the Royal Navy would eventually starve Germany, but the process would be slow, taking a number of years. A far less complete blockade of the British Isles would have had a far more immediate effect.

So the Germans put their own blockade into effect, using the only weapon they had available, their U-boats. In February 1915, they announced an exclusion zone around the British Isles.[1] Inside this zone, shipping of any type and nation could be sunk without warning. The claim was that the announcement of the zone was the moral equivalent of the strict stop-and-search prize rules. Whether this was truly legal depended on which side of the war the observer was on. In practice it lasted only until May, when *U-20* sank the Cunard liner RMS *Lusitania* without warning. The outcry at the resulting loss of life, particularly of the 128 Americans who died in the sinking, forced the Germans into an awkward position. Although they did not call off the campaign officially until September, U-boat commanders became so cautious about sinking any vessel with a neutral flag that for all intents, the old prize rules came back into effect after the *Lusitania* was sunk.

Even before the sinking of the *Lusitania*, the Germans tried a new approach to attacking the British food supply, one with fewer risks of international repercussions. Like any island nation, Great Britain depended heavily on the sea for food. In 1915, she had a large fleet of trawlers that worked the rich fishing banks around the island, particularly in the North Sea. The catch from Britain's trawler fleet was already well down compared to before the war, because the North Sea had become a war zone and because most of the younger crewmen had gone into the Royal Navy. In May 1915, the Germans added a new reason for smaller catches. In the first weeks of that month, at several points along the North Sea coast, U-boats surfaced near working trawlers, forced the crews to abandon ship and proceeded to sink the ships. These were not isolated incidents; rather, they were the beginning of a systematic attack on the trawler fleet.[2] To the British public, these attacks were portrayed as yet another atrocity by the barbaric Huns, as attacks on 'innocent' fishermen by the cruel enemy. To the Germans, these attacks were fully justified, both as economic warfare (remember, the Royal Navy was stopping food imports to Germany) and because trawlers were being regularly requisitioned by the Royal Navy to act as patrol boats and netlayers.

To the Royal Navy, this attack offered a unique opportunity to counter the U-boat threat. If U-boats were going to attack trawlers, then why not use trawlers to attack U-boats? The small size of most trawlers gave the idea some plausibility. Early German U-boats carried very few torpedoes. Until *U-43* entered service in 1915, no U-boat carried more than six torpedoes total, including reloads. Thus it was highly unlikely that a U-boat would waste one of her precious 'eels' on a target as tiny as a trawler.[3] Far more likely, she would surface and attack with her deck gun. This led logically to the idea of arming some trawlers as U-boat traps, known also as Q-ships.

But the small size of most trawlers was also a problem. Often displacing as little as 100 tons, trawlers had trouble mounting the big, old 12pdr guns the Royal Navy had in surplus, and smaller guns were less likely to be effective. A submarine trap had to disable a U-boat immediately or the submarine could dive and gain the advantage.

Nevertheless, the Royal Navy did arm some trawlers and one of them had an early success, though it was hardly a validation of the concept. At 0745 on 5 June 1915, *U-14*, one of the old boats, approached the trawler *Oceanic II* on the surface not far from the Scottish coast between Peterhead and Aberdeen. The U-boat had been seriously damaged in a bombing raid on Zeebrugge in February and had been sent back to Germany for repairs. Before she was ready to rejoin the fleet, *U-14*'s original captain and most of her crew had been reassigned to new boats, so the old boat was now back in service but with a largely inexperienced captain and crew. So green was *Oberleutnant zur See* Hammerle that the half-flotilla commander, *Kapitän-leutnant* Mühlau, went along on his first patrol as an observer.

Hammerle did everything by the book.[4] He ordered demolition charges brought on deck and the deck gun manned.[5] The charges would be used to sink the trawler once she had been stopped by gunfire. *U-14*'s gun, probably a 5cm short-barrelled naval rifle, was simply too small to sink even a trawler. The gun would be used only to fire warning shots and, if necessary, a few shots into the deckhouse. That should have been sufficient to convince the fishermen to abandon ship, after which the charges would be planted and the trawler scuttled. This should have been easy pickings for *U-14*, except that *Oceanic II* was armed and opened fire with everything she had as soon as Hammerle fired his warning shot.

Hammerle's reaction was instantaneous and correct. He ordered *U-14* to dive. But that was when the problems started. The correct drill at this point was to open the rapid venting valves of the four main ballast tanks (two forward and two aft) and allow them to flood. This should have caused the boat to submerge on an even keel, but almost immediately it became apparent that, while the stern was submerging normally, the bow was not. The IWO was sent forward to find out what was going wrong. He rapidly discovered that inexperienced crewmen had failed to open the vent valves on the forward tanks. The valves were immediately opened, but not before the upward angle of the boat had reached 20°. The boat's bow was now sticking out of the water and the trawler was hitting it repeatedly with shells. So far none had penetrated the pressure hull, but that did not mean *U-14* was undamaged. The captain ordered the aft ballast tanks closed and blown and this brought the boat back to the surface on an even keel. Confident that the situation was under control, Hammerle again ordered a dive; again the stern dropped rapidly, but not the bow. This obviously shouldn't have happened, raising the possibility that the forward vent valves had been damaged by the shelling and were now jammed closed. The only option was to surface the boat again.

With the trawler approaching with obvious intent to ram, Hammerle once more ordered a crash dive. This time, by flooding only the forward trim tanks, something resembling an even keel was achieved. The diving-plane motor and the main bilge pump chose this moment to fail almost simultaneously, and now with no ability to adjust trim and only enough air pressure available to empty his ballast tanks one more time, the boat was essentially uncontrollable and Hammerle had run out of options. He decided to surface the boat one last time and let the crew attempt to escape. In the event, everybody got off the boat except for Hammerle, who stayed behind to open the seacocks. Whether he intended to escape and ran out of time or he had decided to go down with his boat will never be known. What is known is that he alone failed to get off the sinking U-boat. The rest of the crew was rescued by *Oceanic II* and other trawlers in the area.

The British were smart enough to realise that the sinking of *U-14* had been the result of luck and hardly an indication that arming trawlers was an effective anti-submarine tactic. Well before the sinking of *U-14*, an alternative plan had been proposed. Vice Admiral David Beatty's flag secretary, Acting Paymaster Commander Frank Spickernell, came up with the idea of teaming a submarine with a trawler to make a better U-boat trap. The idea was that the trawler would tow a submerged submarine into an area where a U-boat attack might be expected. The towline would include a telephone cable so that the two boats could communicate, since the submarine would be essentially blind. When a U-boat was sighted, the trawler would alert the submarine, which would then drop the tow and make a submerged attack on the U-boat, which would be unaware of its danger until the torpedoes struck. One aspect of the idea was particularly appealing to the Royal Navy; it provided a way to make use of some of the numerous obsolescent 'C' class submarines that were by 1915 considered too slow and short-ranged to send on regular offensive patrols. Towing the submarine into combat allowed her to carry out her attack with fresh batteries. The idea was received enthusiastically and immediately put into operation.

Captain Haggard of the 7th Flotilla at Rosyth was ordered to put the scheme, soon dubbed 'Tethered Goat' by the participants, into effect. By May 1915, he was ready to give it a try. The trawler *Taranaki*, under Lieutenant Commander Edwards, teamed up with the submarine *C.27* under Lieutenant Commander Claude Dobson to patrol an area off the Scottish coast. On 8 June a U-boat was sighted and *C.27* dropped the tow and lined up a shot just as planned, except that the torpedo missed and the target ran out of range before a second shot could be set up. The U-boat most likely was completely unaware of the danger she was in, since this incident was not reported in German histories of the naval war and the identity of the intended victim was thus never established.

The identity of the next U-boat to encounter *Taranaki* is well known. *U-40* was one of the new U-boats that men like *U-14*'s original crew were bringing into service. She was one of the last of the final series of pre-war boats to enter service, being commissioned on 14 February 1915. These boats, including *U-19* to *U-41*, were large, well-armed and long-ranged, especially when compared to *U-14*. *U-40*, under the command of *Kapitänleutnant* Gerhard Fürbringer was on her first patrol when she approached a seemingly unarmed trawler off Aberdeen right after 0930 on 23 June 1915. The trawler was *Taranaki*, this time towing the submarine *C.24* under the command of Lieutenant F H Taylor. *Taranaki* sighted *U-40* well astern. Using the telephone link to the submarine 12m below the surface, Edwards told Taylor the location and distance of the U-boat and ordered the submarine to engage.

This order set off a sequence of missteps that would nevertheless end with the sinking of the U-boat. Almost from the beginning things went wrong. *C.24* was supposed to drop the towline from her end, but the release gear failed to budge. Taylor called up to the surface, hoping perhaps to abort the operation, but found out that *Taranaki*'s panic crew was already rowing away from the trawler and the U-boat had taken the bait. Calling off the operation was no longer an option. The only alternative was to drop the line from *Taranaki*'s end: hardly an ideal solution, but the best one available. Should *Taranaki* be sunk with the line still attached and the release jammed at *C.24*'s end, the submarine would be dragged down by the trawler – a rather unappealing prospect. Edwards ordered the line released.

Suddenly weighed down by 180m of 20cm hawser and 9cm wire cable, the submarine's bow immediately dropped. The normal response would be to blow the forward ballast tanks, but Taylor reasoned that the U-boat could not fail to notice the air bubbles that would inevitably result, spoiling the surprise on which the whole plan depended. Using only his hydroplanes and motors, he was able to restore trim as long as the boat was moving at its best underwater speed. Circling around into attack position, the periscope was raised, revealing the U-boat pumping 88mm shells into the wallowing trawler. It took only a few more minutes to line up the boat and launch a torpedo. This time the shot ran true, striking *U-40* under the conning tower and sinking the U-boat instantly. Amazingly, there were three survivors; Fürbringer, *Oberleutnant zur See* Stobbe and *Bootsmann* Beizen, all of whom had been on the bridge, were blown clear and were picked up by the British.[6] *Taranaki*, somewhat battered but in no danger of sinking, and *C.24*, still trailing the hawser, returned to port in triumph.

This success was repeated once more. On 20 July, the trawler *Princess Louise* under Lieutenant Colin Cantile and the tethered submarine, once again *C.27*, sank *U-23* off the entrance to the Fair Island Channel. Once again, the plan failed to follow the script. This time, the telephone link went dead right after the trawler reported the sighting to the submarine. The plan called for the submarine to wait for further word from the trawler before actually dropping the tow, but the dead link meant that Dobson had to decide on his own when to begin his approach. The sound of shells hitting the water convinced him that the time was right, and *C.27* slipped its tow and made an approach on *U-23* at periscope depth. This time, the U-boat's lookouts sighted the periscope's wake and *U-23* began to turn away just moments after *C.27* launched her first torpedo. Just like before, Dobson watched in agony as the torpedo missed the turning U-boat. Determined to make sure this one did not get away, Dobson rapidly lined up his second (and last) shot. This torpedo hit *U-23* aft of the conning tower and U-boat sank quickly. There were ten survivors, all picked up by the British and interned for the remainder of the war.

Despite these successes, the scheme was not without its risks, as soon became clear. The normal practice, if a sweep by a trawler-submarine team did not attract a U-boat within the rather limited span of the submarine's endurance, was for the pair to separate and a new submarine to join up with the trawler. That happened on 4 August 1915, when *C.33* separated from the trawler *Malta* after two days of patrolling and headed back to port while the trawler remained off the Norfolk coast awaiting the arrival of *C.34*. *C.33* never arrived at Harwich and, after several days of fruitless searching, it was concluded that the submarine had strayed into a defensive minefield laid off Smith's Knoll and had run into a mine. No evidence has emerged since that offers a better explanation for *C.33*'s loss. A similar loss occurred on 29 August while the trawler *Ariadne* was towing *C.29* near the Outer Dowsing lightship, about 25 miles southeast of the Humber. This was in an area marked as clear on Admiralty charts. Nevertheless, an explosion occurred aft of the trawler and the towline went slack. *Ariadne* had apparently strayed into a minefield which was not yet marked on the navy's published charts. *C.29* was lost with all hands.

The Royal Navy reacted to these two incidents by ordering that all towed patrols occur further from shore. However, this safety measure proved unnecessary as the time of the towed submarine tactic was coming to an end. Inexplicably, the British had allowed the survivors of *U-23* to mingle in a transit camp with interned merchant sailors on their way back to Germany. When the sailors were repatriated in August, they brought with them word of the 'Tethered Goat' scheme. When the Royal Navy found that details of their secret ploy were showing up in German newspapers, they cancelled any further use of towed submarine traps. Under any circumstances, they had already decided to supplement the trawler-sized Q-ships with larger, better-armed, steamer-sized decoys like the *Baralong*. The decision to abandon submarine traps in no way diminished the Royal Navy's determination to combat the U-boat threat by any and all means.

Of the participants in the sinking of *U-23*, the one to go on to the greatest success was Lieutenant Commander Dobson. Not only was he awarded the DSO for his efforts against *U-23*, but he was also later awarded the Victoria Cross, the highest award for valour in the United Kingdom, for actions in the Gulf of Finland against the Bolsheviks in 1919.[7]

CHAPTER 4

Almost an Ace

Heino von Heimburg

THE CONCEPT OF AN 'ace', a fighter of such skill that he is able to destroy an unusually high number of the enemy in individual combat, seems to have originated among fighter pilots in the First World War. It appears the French first established a semi-official system to recognise the exploits of pilots, including the use of the term 'ace' ('*as*' in French) and the setting of five kills as the level of accomplishment necessary to achieve that status. There never has been an equivalent system of recognition of submariners in any navy, especially not in regard to the closest equivalent of aerial combat, the hunting of one submarine by another. No submariner ever claimed the sinking of five enemy submarines, but the man who undoubtedly came closest was the German, Heino von Heimburg.

The story begins with the need of the Austro-Hungarian Navy to obtain more modern and capable submarines. They started the war with only six small and old U-boats. Five larger boats had been ordered from the 'Germania' yard in Germany in 1913, but they were sold to the Germans in 1914 while still under construction, because it was determined that they were too big to be transported to the Adriatic by rail, even in sections, and the voyage by sea was considered too dangerous given that war had in the meanwhile broken out.[1]

The Austrians decided that the best solution was to acquire some of the new small 'UB'- and 'UC'-series boats being designed in Germany.[2] They would be more capable than any of their current U-boats and would be small enough to transport from Germany by rail. The first batch of five UB-I boats was ordered in March 1915. The type was known to the Austrians, since the Germans had already transported *UB-3*, *UB-8* and *UB-9* by rail to Pola, where they had been reassembled and were operating against Allied shipping in the Mediterranean under German command.[3]

The Germans were eager to sell the boats to their ally, both because it would bring in needed cash and because they were having difficulty finding crews to man all the new boats they were now building. So when the Austrians asked that a 'sample' boat be made available for training purposes, the Germans selected the already completed *UB-1*, disassembled her into three sections and sent her by rail to Pola. There she was reassembled and reported ready for her first patrol in the Adriatic on 4 June 1915. She was nominally in Austrian service, but for this first patrol, she went out with a German captain (*Oberleutnant zur See* Wäger) and crew, due to the somewhat tricky handling characteristics of the 'UB' boats.[4] After that shake-down, she was commissioned as the Austrian *U-10* on 2 July 1915.[5] A second boat, *UB-15*, followed immediately and was commissioned as *U-11* at the same time as *U-10*. Similarly, she had a German captain and crew for her first patrol. The captain was *Oberleutnant zur See* Heino von Heimburg. *UB-15/U-11* was von Heimburg's first command.

Von Heimburg took *U-11* out on patrol just four days after she was recommissioned, heading north from Pola to sweep the waters around Venice.[6] The first day out, *U-11* found an Italian submarine on the surface at dawn but was unable to engage and returned to a course towards Venice. There, two days later, after a swing towards the southwest and back again, von Heimburg sighted the Italian coastal submarine *Medusa*, under the command of Alessandro Viturri, on the surface off Porto di Piave Vecchia along the Adriatic coast northeast of Venice. (*Medusa* was quite small at 250 tons surface displacement, but was still almost twice the size of the truly diminutive *U-11*.) He described the encounter in an addendum to his KTB:[7]

At 0620 on 10.VI. a submarine was sighted aft. *U-11* was steering 200°.

I turned to starboard towards the submarine, which had stopped to let a patrol boat pass.

A single torpedo dispatched the Italian submarine.

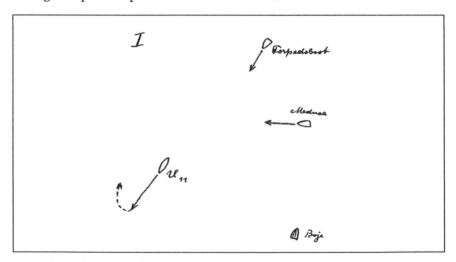

This chart, labelled 'I' by von Heimburg, was drawn in the margin of the addendum to *U-11*'s KTB. It shows *U-11*'s course and those of the torpedo boat and *Medusa* at the time that von Heimburg sighted the Italian boat and began to turn back towards *Medusa*. *U-11* was submerged throughout this engagement; *Medusa* was on the surface. The buoy referred to several times in this account is marked '*Boje*' and is in the bottom right corner of this chart.

At 0630 the torpedo boat passed in front of the submarine. Its course now approximately 270°, speed 10kt. I continued to the north. The sea was perfectly smooth, so that I was forced to use the periscope very cautiously.

As I raised the periscope, there was the target directly in the crosshairs. I went from slow speed to AK and turned hard to port.

Torpedo range 150m, depth 1.5m. The detonation was barely felt in the boat. After the shot, the boat took a dive, so that I was unable to observe the hit.

The detonation was reported by the prisoners as being very powerful. The boat's stern was lifted out of the water and it sank bow-first in just a few seconds.

UB-I boats were notorious for losing trim after a torpedo was fired. When a U-boat fired a torpedo, such as the 45cm C/06 torpedoes carried by the UB-Is, she instantly lost considerable weight. *U-11*'s torpedoes each weighed 773kg (1,704lbs). This weight had to be replaced immediately by an equivalent weight of water or the submarine could lose trim. Being at periscope depth, her bow could break the surface or, as happened in this instance, if too much weight is taken on, the bow could plunge. U-boats such as *U-11* had a compensating tank under each bank of torpedo tubes that was supposed to flood automatically when a torpedo was fired, but that sometimes did not work correctly on UB-Is. That was exactly what went wrong this time; *U-11*'s bow dived as soon as the torpedo was fired. It took rushing the crew into the aft compartment to restore something like correct trim, after which the compensating tank was pumped out manually and the crewmen were able to return to their stations. Only then was von Heimburg able to bring the boat back to periscope depth in stable trim and take a look around.

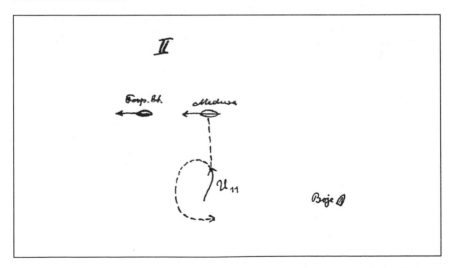

U-11 fired a single torpedo at *Medusa* (shown by the vertical dashed line). The torpedo boat had turned to the west and the submarine had followed along the same course. After firing, *U-11* then looped 270° while von Heimburg fought to regain control of his boat.

I remained at 15m for 10 minutes, while in the direction of the submarine, grenades were being launched. A small explosion was heard.

At the site of the sinking, there was nothing to be seen. A destroyer of the *Artigliere* class, that I had not at first seen, was heading away to starboard on a southerly course.

After an hour I headed towards the buoy, to search for debris.

At 0820, I saw five men hanging on to the buoy, waving at my periscope.

As there was no other vessel in sight, I surfaced near the buoy and took the men onboard. It was the second officer and four seamen from *Medusa*. One man was badly wounded. The officer had towed him to the buoy.

The prisoners said that the torpedo's wake had been seen when it was 100m from the boat. That hard rudder had been applied, despite which the torpedo had struck in the middle of the engine compartment.

The heavily wounded stayed with the boat and many were thrown into the water as it sank.

After the rescue of the five men, I headed for Salvore and handed the blindfolded prisoners over to the signal station there.[8]

After another day of patrolling, *U-11* returned to Pola where, on 19 June 1915, von Heimburg and the German crew turned the boat over to an Austrian captain and crew. *U-11* remained in Austrian service in the Adriatic for the remainder of the war.

For most commanders, sinking an enemy submarine would be the highlight of their naval career, but Heino von Heimburg was just getting started. Another new UB-I boat, *UB-14*, was disassembled in Germany, arriving at Pola on 12 June 1915. While still being reassembled, von Heimburg assumed command of the boat on 21 June and recommissioned her on 24 June with the same crew he had commanded in *UB-15/U-11*. Unlike the previous boat, *UB-14* would remain in German service throughout the war, though she carried Austrian markings and the Austrian designation *U-26* when she operated in the Adriatic. On her first patrol, von Heimburg once again headed towards Venice and once again had a resounding success on what was now only his second in command of a U-boat. On 7 July 1915, he torpedoed and sank the Italian armoured cruiser *Amalfi*. Having returned to Pola, *UB-14* departed on 15 July this time heading for Constantinople.[9]

The route called for a stop at the Turkish port of Bodrum to refuel, but even that was beyond the rather limited range of a UB-I boat, so the first part of the trip was made under tow from an Austrian destroyer.[10] *UB-14*'s engine and compass both broke down off Crete, but the tiny crew, just fourteen officers and men, were able to patch them up sufficiently to allow the boat to make Bodrum on 24 July. A repair crew was dispatched from Constantinople, a journey that required travel by train and camel. *UB-14* was repaired in time to leave for the Dardanelles on 13 August. That same evening, having barely cleared the island of Kos at the mouth of the bay on which Bodrum is located, she encountered several inviting targets sailing unescorted in the naïve belief that there were no U-boats in the region. The first ship von Heimburg sighted was the hospital ship *Soudan*, which he allowed to precede unmolested. The second ship had no such immunity. He torpedoed and sank the troopship *Royal Edward en route* from Alexandria to Mudros with a full load of over 1,400 troops for the Gallipoli front, plus another 200 crew. Although the British only admitted to the loss of 130 men at the time, it appears that fewer than 500 were rescued. *UB-14* made no attempt to interfere with the rescue ships, which included *Soudan*, two French destroyers and some trawlers. While attempting to leave the area, *UB-14* again lost the services of her compass and had to return to Bodrum, where she arrived on the morning of 15 August.

Repaired again, *UB-14* set out again for Constantinople. On board this time was a passenger, *Oberleutnant zur See* Heinrich XXXVII Prinz Reuss zu Köstritz, a scion of German nobility in need of transportation to the Turkish capital. Yet again, *UB-14* suffered mechanical problems and had to put in at Chanak to await repairs.[11] Within days of arriving at Chanak, von Heimburg was relaxing in his bunk when news arrived that a submarine was snared in the Nagara Point anti-submarine net across one of the narrowest parts of the Dardanelles, just a few miles to the north. Von Heimburg, Prinz Reuss and Herzig, the U-boat's cook, immediately headed to Nagara to check out the situation. They took Herzig along because he had been a commercial fisherman by trade before the war and they thought his skills might come in handy. They arrived to find that the submarine, presumably British, was still tangled in the net. She had run into the net at around 0800 that morning, 4 September 1915.

The Allies had been running submarines up the Dardanelles and into the Sea of Marmara since April 1915. It was a difficult task and there had been losses at first. The straits are narrow, less than mile at their narrowest, 35 miles long and defended by numerous minefields, fixed torpedo tubes and forts with approximately 150 guns of 6in calibre or larger, but the biggest problem from a submariner's point of view was the steady current of between 2 and 5 knots that ran down the straits into the Mediterranean. The task was made even harder in mid-June when the Turks set up the anti-submarine net at Nagara Point. A loose and initially rather shallow steel mesh net suspended from mined buoys, the idea was that the mines would be dragged underwater if a submarine ran into it. The mines would then be detonated electrically from shore. A squadron of small boats equipped with sinker mines serviced the net; should a boat be snared and not destroyed by the net's own mines, the small craft would try to drop their mines on the submarine and set them off, destroying her or driving her to the surface.[12] A pair of torpedo boats was assigned to support the small boats in case the submarine tried to escape after surfacing.

The situation when von Heimburg and Prinz Reuss arrived on the scene

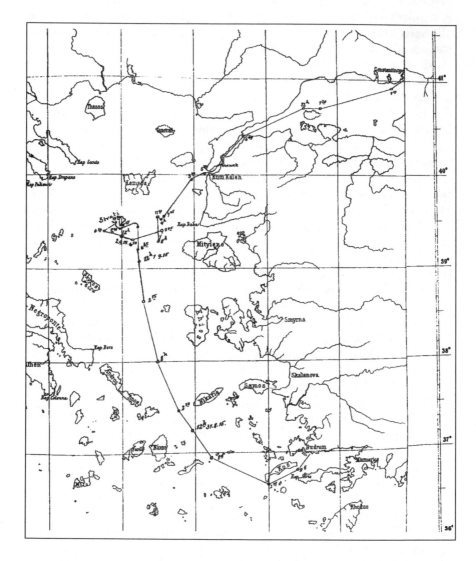

This chart, from *UB-14*'s *KTB*, shows her course from Bodrum (here spelled 'Budrum')
to Constantinople with a stop at Chanak in the Dardanelles, whose name is written
in by hand. The delay at Chanak is not indicated, but it was there that von Heimburg
was involved in the sinking of HMS/M *E.7*. Nagara Point is where the straits
take a sharp right turn just north of Chanak.

was something of a standoff. The submarine, the British *E.7* commanded by Lieutenant Commander Archibald D Cochrane, had been trying to free herself all day. Since the net was erected in June, several British submarines, including *E.7* on a previous patrol, had encountered it and had been able to force their way through or dive under the net. Cochrane tried the same tactic again, but this time it did not work.[13] Unbeknownst to the British, the Turks had replaced the original net with a stronger one that extended all the way to the bottom. *E.7* entered the straits at 05.00 and proceeded north submerged at periscope depth. The periscope was sighted and fired on from the fort at Kilid Bahr opposite Chanak at the Narrows, but the fire was inaccurate and the submarine continued on. At 0730, Cochrane sighted the net buoys and took his boat down to 30m, the boat's rated maximum depth, and increased speed to 7.5 knots, almost her greatest submerged speed, so as to strike the net with maximum impact. The manoeuvre very nearly worked. The boat tore a hole in the net and had made it almost all the way through when the starboard propeller got tangled in the netting, which wrapped around the shaft before the motor could be shut down. Maneuvering with only the port screw, the boat gradually swung around until she was caught in the net fore and aft. Repeated attempts to free the boat by switching between full forward and full astern managed to loosen the net's grip somewhat, but failed to free the boat.

The Turks were alerted to all this activity by the bobbing and spinning of the marker buoys and sent out a small boat to try mining the submarine. A single mine was detonated perhaps 100m away at 0830. When that produced no noticeable result, the Turks regrouped, trying again at 1030. This time, the charge exploded much closer to the submarine, rattling her crew, but again not causing any significant damage. Rather it appeared to loosen the netting a bit more, leaving Cochrane hoping that another try would do the trick. Unfortunately, that did not work, nor did repeated attempts after that. By 1400, however, he had depleted the batteries to the point where no more attempts could be made. Cochrane then announced to his men that they would wait until dark, surface the boat and see if they could cut her free from the netting. To the crew's distress, they watched him destroy the boat's codebooks and confidential papers and rig scuttling charges around the boat.

The waiting lasted until 1840, when an explosion close aboard shook the boat, shattered lights, ruptured fittings and sprang several leaks in the pressure hull. Heino von Heimburg, Prinz Reuss and Herzig, who had been watching the Turkish operation for much of the day, had finally decided to act. They had rowed out to the submarine's position and Herzig, who had brought along a plumb line with a lead weight on the end, began methodically searching for the submarine while von Heimburg rowed the small boat back and forth over her suspected location. After half an hour, the search was successful. Herzig felt his sinker hit metal. Now they knew *E.7*'s exact location and depth. With that information, they cut the fuse of one of the Turkish sinker mines, lit it, dropped it over the side and began rowing away as fast they could. Seconds later they were inundated by a column of water shooting up from below, followed by a large patch of oil bubbling up to the surface. This was the explosion Cochrane felt at 1840. It convinced him that escape was impossible and he gave the order to surface the boat.

No sooner had *E.7*'s conning tower broken the surface than gunfire erupted from the shore and the two torpedo boats. It is hard to determine who was more upset, the British sailors coming on deck hoping to surrender or von Heimburg, who was uncomfortably close to the target of the shelling. *E.7* was hit twice before the Turks could be convinced to stop, but it made no difference. *E.7* was already sinking. As the last of his men cleared the conning tower, Cochrane set the fuse on the scuttling charges, opened the seacocks and then followed the crew out onto the deck. He dived into the water and swam over to the nearest boat. He could hardly have been more surprised to find himself pulled out of the water by a U-boat commander who spoke passable English.

Cochrane now faced several years in Turkish captivity, much of it in rather harsh conditions. In March 1916, he escaped with two other submarine commanders, but was recaptured 17 days later. He escaped again in August 1918, this time with twenty-five other officers from a camp in Yozgat, 150km east of Ankara. All were recaptured except for a group of eight, led by Cochrane. This group covered almost 650km cross-country to the southern coast, stole a motorboat and landed in Cyprus. Cochrane was awarded the DSO for this and his other exploits. He retired from the navy in 1922 as a captain, was elected to the House of Commons, first from East Fife and then from Dumbartonshire, and was knighted in 1936. He served as Governor of Burma until the Second World War started, when he rejoined the navy and commanded an auxiliary cruiser protecting transatlantic convoys. Only at the end of that war did he retire from public life.

Heino von Heimburg, on the other hand, still had more fighting to do in the First World War. He commanded *UB-14* for another two months, conducting two patrols out of Constantinople. The first was in the Black Sea off Varna and the Crimea between 3 and 19 October 1915. At the beginning of November, he took the boat into the Sea of Marmara with a specific target in mind.

French submarines operated in the Dardanelles and the Sea of Marmara during this period as well as British, though the French had a far less consistent record of successfully passing through the straits. Nevertheless, the Allied naval command at Mudros planned for a combined operation in the Sea of Marmara, with the French *Turquoise* and the British *E.20* scheduled to rendezvous at 1600 on 5 (or 6) November.[14] The French submarine was to precede the British by more than two weeks and operate independently until the rendezvous. *Turquoise* managed the passage to the Marmara successfully, arriving on 22 October. Unfortunately, mechanical problems forced the French captain, *Lt. de vaisseau* Léon Ravenel, to abandon the mission on 30 October and attempt the passage back down the Dardanelles. Experience had shown that the return trip to the Mediterranean was generally easier than the passage up the straits due to the strong following current. Nevertheless, the French submarine was difficult to handle and got caught in the swirling currents around Nagara Point. She ran aground on the southern side of the point under the guns of a Turkish fort. While Ravenel was trying to manoeuvre *Turquoise* off the beach, the Turks opened fire and obtained a hit on the conning tower. Ravenel decided to surrender to save his crew.

So far the story of *Turquoise* is not much different from that of other submarines, British and French, that had similar problems in the Dardanelles, but Ravenel made several mistakes that had disastrous consequences. First, he had failed to report his abandonment of the mission, so that *E.20* continued to expect to rendezvous with the French boat. Secondly, in his haste to abandon the submarine, Ravenel failed to destroy his confidential orders, which included details of the planned rendezvous. (One report states that when the Turks searched the submarine, they found the lights still on and an alarm still sounding.[15])

E.20, under the command of Lieutenant Commander Clyfford Warren, successfully passed up the Dardanelles and headed to the rendezvous, expecting to find *Turquoise*. What she found instead was a watery grave. The Turks passed along the papers captured in *Turquoise* to the Germans, who immediately saw the opportunity to set a trap for *E.20*. But there was little time. The only boat ready to sortie was *UB-14*, still commanded by von Heimburg. He was preparing to set out on another patrol in the Black Sea, but plans were changed and the boat went south instead of north. The boat left Constantinople at 0010 on 5 November 1915, the scheduled day of the rendezvous. With not much time at his disposal, he set out at high speed on the surface, submerging at dawn as he approached the rendezvous point. *UB-14*'s *KTB* tells the story:

6.XI.15	Sea of Marmara	
0010	WSW 2 – later 0, Sea 0, very good visibility	I intend to head for the rendezvous directly and to wait there submerged during daylight for the enemy boat.
0545		Boat stopped, ventilated.
		Took sighting. Boat is 10–15nm from meeting point. To make sure I'm not sighted, I will proceed submerged.
0600		Dived 250° 1.8kt
1600		In the south, there came, maybe 5nm away, the tower of a submarine in sight. Because I'm assuming the boat is heading directly towards the rendezvous, I steer 90° 2.2kt.[16]

The boat approached without changing course and then stopped at the meeting place.

1628	185° 5.8 kt	Prepared to attack, from the west with the sinking sun behind me. The perfectly smooth water, like an oil slick, forced the extremely careful use of the periscope. As we get closer to the target, the periscope is raised more frequently. The attack became more difficult because the periscope enlargement failed. As I approached within 2000m, the boat gradually drew abeam of us.

I turn to 160° towards the boat. It is straight ahead as the range drops to 1200m. Before raising the periscope, the torpedo is made ready. After raising the periscope, I make the aiming point just aft of the tower, with that I order the torpedo fired. Range 500m, depth 1.5m. Because I'm only going half speed, my tower broke the surface of the water after the torpedo was fired. The wake of the torpedo was seen by the enemy too late.

Apparently when they saw our tower break the surface, they must have assumed this was the friendly boat surfacing.

1716   The torpedo was seen to hit the boat amidships. A weak detonation was heard in the boat. The enemy boat was totally hidden by the column of smoke and water and, when these had dissipated, had disappeared.

1720   Surfaced and fished out of the water the captain, two officers and six seamen. There was little debris to be seen. Headed back to base on the surface.

One group of six swimmers was rescued first. The second group proved to be Warren supporting two non-swimmers. All were taken below and

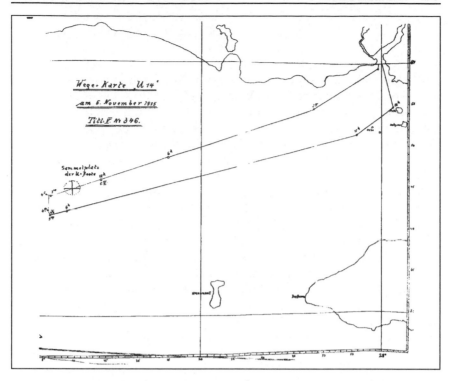

This chart, also from *UB-14*'s *KTB*, shows the path of the one-day patrol during which
von Heimburg claimed HMS/M *E.20* in the Sea of Marmara, 5 November 1915.
The rendezvous point (*'Sammelplatz der U-Boote'*) is marked by the circled-cross,
the actual site of the sinking by the crossed swords to the southwest.

given dry clothing and a hot drink. Twenty-seven of *E.20*'s crew went to
the bottom with their boat.

Interrogation of the captain: His boat, *E.20*, had been in the Sea of Marmara for 4 weeks. He had intended to remain longer. All prisoners appeared to be in good condition. The captain had mistaken our boat for the French boat, and when they sighted our torpedo approaching, tried to get underway. They were surprised our boat was so small. They had passed the net barrage at Nagara by running through it at full power. They wanted to know how our boats get through their nets in one try. The English obviously still believe that our boats run in and out of the Dardanelles. At the time of the

explosion, two of the men had been
inside the boat and had been hurled
out.

One story, apparently told by von Heimburg himself in later years, states
that when *E.20* was torpedoed, Warren had been brushing his teeth.[17] The
explosion stunned him to the extent that he was still dazed when pulled
aboard the U-boat. When asked what he needed by the obliging von
Heimburg in his halting English, Warren reportedly replied that he wanted
a toothbrush and, when given one, proceeded to continue his dental care
where it had been so rudely interrupted.

Turquoise was towed to Constantinople and repaired. She was given the
Turkish name *Müstecip Onbasi*, but she was never commissioned into the
Turkish navy.[18] She proved too hard to handle and was mechanically
obsolete, being powered by a petrol engine. She served out the war being
used only to charge the batteries of German boats operating out of
Constantinople. *UB-14* was taken over by *Oberleutnant zur See* von
Dewitz upon the completion of this patrol. Heino von Heimburg remained
at Constantinople and actually briefly resumed command of *UB-14*
between 12 February and 17 June 1916, before he returned to Germany
where he took over the newly built *UC-22* on 30 July.

UC-22 was a UC-II class boat. These were ocean-going minelayers
intended, like the several 'UB' series, to be produced in large number and,
like the 'UB' boats, were generally quite successful. *UC-22*'s assignment
was to operate in the Mediterranean, based at Pola. She was more than
twice as big as *UB-14* and, thus, could not be sent to the Adriatic by rail.
Rather, she would have to make the long trip around the British Isles and
through the Straits of Gibraltar. The UC-II boats had three torpedo tubes
(two forward, one aft) and six vertical mine shafts forward of the conning
tower, each of which could hold three mines. The mines could be laid while
the boat was submerged, making them excellent at laying minefields in
enemy waters.

Having completed working up, *UC-22* left Helgoland on 22 September
1916. She encountered the Russian three-masted schooner *Emma* near the
Shetlands and dispatched her with her deck gun. The rest of the passage
went without incident and *UC-22* arrived at Cattaro on 12 October. Von
Heimburg led *UC-22* on multiple patrols into the Mediterranean, laying
minefields off Malta, at numerous points along the coast of Italy and North
Africa and as far afield as Alexandria. On 19 June 1917, *UC-22* was
approaching Cape Bon off the coast of Tunisia with the intent of laying a
mine barrage when von Heimburg sighted a submarine moving at high
speed on the surface.

She proved to be the French *Ariane*, a relatively modern diesel-powered
submarine, launched in 1914. She had just completed some repairs and was
still working up again, when she was sighted by von Heimburg.[19]

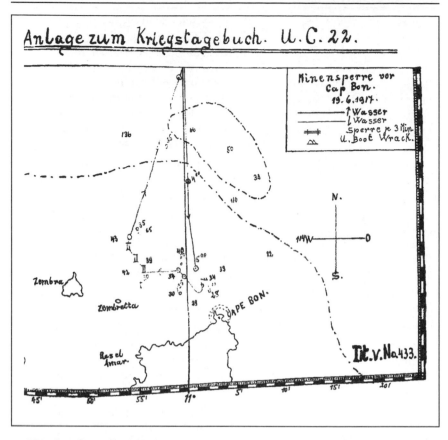

Anlage zum Kriegstagebuch. U.C.22.

This chart from *UC-22*'s *KTB* for 19 June 1917 shows the boat's track off Cape Bon. The approach and sinking of *Ariane* required almost no manoeuvring. The site of the sinking is indicated by the double-triangle symbol next to the numeral '34' north of the cape. Von Heimburg then resumed his original mission and laid three strings of mines (indicated on the chart by double lines) just east and a little north of the island of Zembra.

18.6.17	Sicilian Sea, very	Nothing is seen.
0800	clear, NW 2–3	
		Test dive.
		I intend to steer towards Cape Bon from the north.
19.6.17		
0200	SE 2–4, Sea 3	Lighthouse at Cape Bon in sight.
		A big convoy passes, two steamers with four escorts (three with stern lights ahead, one with dimmed light astern). Attack is not possible.
0450		As it starts to get light, submerge.

0545	37° 9' N; 11° 5' E	Large French submarine with a torpedo boat approach from the west. Stern attack rejected in favor of a bow-on approach. It is a new boat similar to the English 'H' class. Gun aft of the tower, 2 above-water torpedo tubes. Flag at the stern, painted dark gray, without any markings.
		Hit! Range 170m, speed 14kt.

Twenty-one of her crew went down with the boat.

After firing the torpedo, *UC-22* acted just as unpredictably as the 'UBs' had, suddenly diving out of control.

		Went to 50m. Boat hits the seafloor. Turn towards deeper water.
0620		At periscope depth.
		At the site of the sinking, there is a large trawler. The torpedo boat causes an empty steamer that was approaching from the east to turn away from the area.
		The French act as if they are in a minefield, therefore, I will lay my barrage further away from here. The course taken by the steamer supports this.

This was von Heimburg's fourth and final sinking of an enemy submarine, but he continued to wage war with great success. He gave up command of *UC-22* on 14 July 1917 and again returned to Germany. He commissioned *UB-68*, one of the UB-III class boats, at Kiel on 5 October 1917. Much was expected of these boats. They had the range and power of many of the largest U-boats, but they were smaller (just over 500 tons surface displacement) and were intended to be produced in sufficient quantities to influence the outcome of the war. While von Heimburg was waiting to put his new boat into service, he was summoned to Berlin and, on 11 August 1917, was awarded the *Pour le Mérite*, the famed 'Blue Max', Germany's highest award for valour.[20]

UB-68 proved to be even more difficult to master than von Heimburg's earlier boats. She was unstable and prone to excursions in depth with little or no warning. This characteristic was shared with the rest of the class of six UB-IIIs built by Germaniawerft in 1917, though *UB-68* appears to have been the worst of the group. It was not until 15 December that the boat departed Kiel for Pola, where she arrived on 5 January 1918. There, von Heimburg conducted four patrols in command of the boat, though he was never happy with her performance. Finally, in July, *UB-68* was docked for a major overhaul and he was allowed to relinquish command of this troublesome boat.

When *UB-68* was ready to return to service, she was taken over by a young *Oberleutnant zur See* named Karl Dönitz. He soon found out exactly why von Heimburg had wanted so badly to transfer out. Even though the pressure hull had been strengthened, the boat had been reballasted and the 10.5cm gun had been replaced with a lighter 8.8cm gun, she still handled poorly. On 4 October 1918, Dönitz, on his first patrol in command of *UB-68*, sighted a convoy of six steamers and an unknown number of escorts headed towards Malta. Determined to try out the new tactics he'd been pondering for attacking convoys, namely attacking from the surface at night, he slipped through the escorts in the darkness and found himself between the two columns of three ships each.[21] He succeeded in torpedoing one of the steamers and then had to dive to avoid an oncoming escort. Surfacing again a half-hour later, *UB-68* went on a long loop to get ahead of the convoy. As dawn was rapidly approaching, Dönitz got in position well ahead of the convoy and dived the boat to wait for the targets to come within range. He was just setting up his target when the boat lost trim without warning and started settling stern first. From then on, Dönitz was never in control of the situation. Eventually, *UB-68* hit the surface and settled in a bow-down attitude. The boat sank rapidly, so fast in fact that the chief engineer, who had stayed behind to make sure all the men were out, got caught in the hatch by the inrushing water and never made it off the boat. He was the only casualty. Dönitz spent the remainder of the war in POW camps, which gave him time to think about the tactics he had devised for attacking convoys and their potential to make a difference should U-boats go to war again. He would have a chance to test his ideas when he led Germany's submarine forces in the Second World War.

Heino von Heimburg, on the other hand, was still not yet done with his war. On 14 August 1918, he was given command of the most famous and most successful U-boat in the German navy, *U-35*. Under four commanders, *U-35* would account for 224 merchant ships totalling over 530,000 tons. Von Heimburg was the third winner of the *Pour le Mérite* to command this particular boat, having been preceded by Waldemar Kophamel and Lothar von Arnauld de la Periere. His tenure as commander of *U-35* was relatively brief; the boat was interned at Barcelona on 26 November 1918.

Heino von Heimburg remained in the navy after the war, but his post-war career did not match his wartime success. He commanded a torpedo boat in 1919–20 and thereafter held mainly shore postings of minor importance until he retired with the rank of *Vizeadmiral* in May 1943. In March 1945, he was captured by the Russians and, despite the fact that he was now retired, was sent to a POW camp near Stalingrad, where he died in October of that same year.

Some historians dispute whether he really should be credited with sinking *E.7*, but even without that 'kill' in his score, he was the most successful submariner ever when it came to sinking other submarines.[22] No doubt luck had as much to do with that success as any other factor, but, given a choice between serving under a lucky commander as opposed to one possessing great skill and bravery, a submariner will choose the lucky one every time.

CHAPTER 5

The Sound of Torpedoes?

ONE OF THE MOST POPULAR movies in cinema history is *The Sound of Music*. It is a wholesome musical from 1965 depicting a family of singers, led by their father, who escaped Austria one step ahead of the Nazi occupation. The father, played in the movie by Christopher Plummer, was a retired captain of the Austrian navy and something of a war hero. The story, as set out in the movie, is basically an accurate, if somewhat over-dramatised, depiction of historical fact. There really was a *Korvetten-kapitän* (Commander) Georg *Ritter* von Trapp and he was a *bona fide* war hero.

Having joined the navy of the Austro-Hungarian Empire in 1898 upon graduation from the naval academy, he was following in the footsteps of his father, who also achieved the rank of *Korvettenkapitän* and was also granted the honour of adding 'von' to his name.[1] He first earned recognition for his bravery under fire during the Boxer Rebellion in China in 1900, where he was on his first overseas cruise while serving aboard an Austrian armoured cruiser.[2] In 1908, Georg requested transfer to the recently created U-boat service and in 1910 he was given command of the newly built *U-6*. In 1912, he married Agathe Whitehead, the granddaughter of Robert Whitehead, the inventor of the submarine torpedo, and daughter to the owner of the Whitehead & Co. shipyard at Fiume.[3]

He commanded *U-6* until 1913 and then was assigned to shore duty. After war broke out the next year, he lobbied hard to return to sea, but had to wait until 22 April 1915, when he took over *U-5*. Older sister to *U-6*, *U-5* was a small, Holland-type coastal boat suitable only for short-range patrols from Pola or Cattaro.[4] Nevertheless, Trapp was highly successful in *U-5*. He conducted nine war patrols in the brief span of six months, sinking, among other victims, the French armoured cruiser *Léon Gambetta* just five days after taking over his boat. He found the cruiser patrolling at slow speed with no escort south of the Straits of Otranto at the entrance to the Adriatic and put two torpedoes into her. She sank with the loss of over 600 of her crew.

The tiny island of Pelagosa sits in the Adriatic midway between Italy and the Dalmatian coast.[5] As such it was considered strategically important in the First World War. It started the war in Austrian hands, but was captured by the Italians in July 1915. Later in that same month, the Austrians made an unsuccessful attempt to take it back. Worried that they might try again, the Italians continuously patrolled the waters around the island with several small submarines. At dawn on 5 August 1915, the Italian *Nereide* was moored inside the tiny harbour of Pelagosa when lookouts sighted an Austrian submarine surfacing just offshore. Caught at a disadvantage, the Italians could easily have abandoned the boat and followed the mooring cables to shore. Instead *Nereide*'s captain, *Capitano di corvetta* Carlo del Greco, ordered the lines cut and tried to manoeuvre his boat into attack position. He managed to fire one torpedo, which missed. His target was *U-5*, which, after turning to avoid the Italian torpedo, lined up the slowly submerging target and fired back with one of her own torpedoes. This shot found its mark. *Nereide* sank with her entire crew of twenty. For his sacrifice, del Greco was awarded the *Medaglia d'Oro al Valor Militare*, the first such award to a sailor in the First World War.

In October 1915, Trapp took over command of the newly acquired *U-14*. This boat had started life as the French *Curie*, one of a large series of medium-sized boats built by the French in the years leading up to the war. *Curie* was launched at Toulon in 1912 and was assigned to reconnoitre the Austrian navy when the war broke out. In December 1914, she was towed into the mid-Adriatic by the armoured cruiser *Jules Michelet* and then took up patrol position off the harbour at Pola. On the night of 12 December, *Curie* tried to sneak into Pola harbour, but got tangled in anti-submarine nets and was unable to extricate herself. After struggling for five hours, the air had become sufficiently foul in the submarine that it was necessary to surface. Quickly sighted by the harbour defences, *Curie* was engaged by a destroyer and a torpedo boat and subsequently sank with the loss of three of her crew. Work began immediately on raising the wreck, which was refloated on 2 February 1915. *Curie* was found to have sustained only minor damage and was rapidly repaired and commissioned into the Austrian navy as *U-14* on 6 June 1915. Under the command of Georg Trapp, *U-14* was quite successful. Trapp led her on ten patrols until he was promoted to *Korvettenkapitän* and given command of the base at Cattaro in May 1918.[6] Altogether, Trapp conducted nineteen war patrols and accounted for twelve cargo vessels, besides the two warships, making him the most successful and by far the most famous Austrian naval officer of the war. Along the way he was knighted and awarded the Knight's Cross of the Order of Maria Theresa, the highest award for military valour in the Austro-Hungarian Empire.

The end of the war left von Trapp unemployed and frustrated, cut off from the sea and denied any future in a navy that no longer existed. Unwilling to profit from his fame and not needing to work due to the wealth Agathe brought to the marriage, he eventually settled at Aigen near Salzburg, and set about fathering seven children. In 1922, Agathe died in an epidemic of scarlet fever. When one of his daughters caught the same disease several years later, von Trapp arranged with a local convent for a novice, Maria Kutschera, to nurse the sick girl. Maria stayed on after the girl recovered, becoming the family's governess and music teacher and eventually, in 1927, marrying Georg. With Maria, Georg had three more children.

The von Trapps lived well until 1932, when banks across Europe collapsed and wiped out the family's savings along with those of many others. Forced to look for means to supplement their now meager finances, Maria decided that singing, at which the family was now very good, was the answer. They received high honours at the 1936 Salzburg Music Festival and parlayed that into commercial success, singing at concerts across Europe.

The *Anschluss* – the annexation of Austria by Nazi Germany in 1938 – was a serious threat to the family because Georg was an unreconstructed monarchist and ardent anti-Nazi.[7] Fortunately, his birth in Zara qualified the family for dual Italian and Austrian citizenship and they crossed the border to Trieste by train, taking up residence in Italy until a concert tour brought them to the United States in the same year.[8] Georg von Trapp died there in 1947.

CHAPTER 6

The First 'Cold War'

U-34 and *C-3*

THE TREATY OF VERSAILLES ended the First World War and stripped Germany of its feared U-boat arm. The world took a deep breath and prepared for a new era of peace. Sadly, that dream lasted only a few years. The Communist Revolution in Russia, the rise of Fascism in Italy, the Nazis in Germany and the Great Depression, all conspired to keep tensions high and guarantee that Europe and then the world would be at war again in barely twenty years.

No sooner had the guns fallen silent in November 1918 than the admirals and analysts started trying to figure out exactly what had and had not happened in the late war. One thing should have been abundantly clear: the billions of pounds, marks, dollars, etc. spent on building more than 150 dreadnought battleships and battlecruisers had been effectively wasted.[1] Tons of steel and thousands of men had sat rusting and restless at opposite corners of the North Sea for four years, while the war at sea was being decided by much smaller boats. For all the grandeur and majesty of those battlefleets, it had been the relatively tiny submarines, built at a fraction of the cost, that had come closest to tipping the scales in the Great War. Despite Churchill's comment about Jellicoe, it had been Germany's U-boats, not the Kaiser's beloved dreadnoughts, that had posed the greatest threat to the British.[2]

Thus it was not surprising that the Treaty of Versailles specifically denied Germany the right to possess submarines and equally unsurprising that the Germans looked for a way around the ban almost from the first days of the post-war *Reichsmarine*. In 1920, an Inspectorate of Torpedoes and Mines was established at Kiel and became a centre for the clandestine development of U-boat designs and tactics. It provided employment for some of Germany's most experienced U-boat officers and designers and kept tabs on the whereabouts of the rest, should their talents be required in the future.

In 1921, retired *Korvettenkapitän* Karl Bartenbach, who had commanded the Flanders Flotilla during the war, was hired by the Argentinean navy to help them develop a modern submarine force. He proposed they build a force of ten submarines of several different sizes based on the types Germany had been developing at the end of the war. He approached the *Reichsmarine* in the name of the Argentines, requesting technical assistance in developing the designs. The *Reichsmarine* responded by secretly arranging the establishment of a naval engineering firm in the Netherlands named *Ingenieurskaantor voor Scheepsbouw* (*IvS* – literally 'Engineering Works for Shipbuilding'), which took on the task of designing ships of all types prohibited by the Versailles Treaty.[3] In the event, the Argentines changed their mind and decided not to build a submarine force at that time, but *IvS* continued working on submarine designs, eventually designing boats for Turkey, Finland and Spain.

By 1927, the *Reichsmarine* had established a U-boat Plans Office which took over responsibility from the Torpedo Inspectorate for planning the resumption of U-boat construction in Germany. While the political question of when Germany would begin building U-boats again was very much up in the air at the time, there never seemed to be any doubt that it would happen and the *Reichsmarine* intended to be ready. Plans were developed and, beginning in 1933, material set aside to allow the rapid construction of two new types of U-boat. Parts for the first eight boats were secretly assembled and stored at Deutsche Werke, Kiel. Three enclosed construction sheds were built, so the boats could, if necessary, be built in secret. Six of these boats were to be the small, coastal U-boats of Type IIA. These were based on the *IvS* design for the Finnish *Vesikko*. They were truly tiny boats, barely 250 tons, and capable of just over 1,000nm range, but they were state-of-the-art in terms of construction and technology. They were perfect for their real intended purpose, the training of a new generation of U-boat officers and technical petty officers, the core of a resurrected U-boat fleet. The other two boats were to be larger and in the event turned out to be less successful. They were based closely on another *IvS* design, that of the Spanish *E-1*.[4] This was a medium-sized boat of approximately 750 tons, with long-range and high speed, designated Type IA. Plans were drawn up in 1934 for six additional Type IIs to an improved design, though, as of yet, no construction had actually begun.

In the end, the Anglo-German Naval Agreement of 1935 obviated the need for secrecy. The fourteen new boats were assembled from the collected materials within months of the signing of the agreement. This pact, which effectively gutted the naval restrictions of the Versailles Treaty, was one of a number of attempts by the former Allies to appease Hitler's appetite. It was defended at the time as being an example of *realpolitik*, in that it bound the Germans to build a navy no more than 35 per cent as large as the Royal Navy. The fear in Britain was there would be another naval arms race such as preceded, and had a role in causing, the First World War. This was a race for which Great Britain was simply neither economically nor politically prepared. Agreeing to limit Germany to a fixed tonnage of prohibited weapons seemed a better alternative to having them simply ignore the old treaties and build without restraint.

In retrospect, it is clear that Germany never intended to build up a significant surface fleet.[5] The Naval Agreement served mainly to legitimise

Germany's determination to start building U-boats again. It is doubtful that Germany's actions would have been much different had the British not appeased Hitler's naval ambitions. The most significant effect of the Naval Agreement was to push the development of a new design of medium-sized U-boat. The U-boat Plans Office, which was not privy to Hitler's secret intentions, began to plan for the next round of construction to follow the first fourteen boats. It was agreed that a minimum of a dozen more Type IIs would be required to support the training of a cadre of U-boat personnel.[6] These, along with the boats already ordered, brought the tonnage of planned U-boats to 7,500 tons out of the 18,500 tons Germany would be allowed if it abided by the pending Naval Agreement. With the remaining 11,000 tons, the U-boat Plans Office wanted to acquire the maximum number of more capable boats. That meant they could order fourteen more Type Is or twenty-two of a hypothetical 500-ton boat, which would be twice the size of the Type IIs and roughly the equivalent of the 'UG' design that many First World War veterans in the U-boat Plans Office still favoured. The old designs were rapidly updated and orders were placed at the beginning of 1935 for ten of the new boats, designated Type VII.[7] The first of these boats to be started were *U-33* and *U-34*, on which construction began at Germaniawerft, Kiel in September 1935.[8]

The navies of the former Allies had no such constraints on submarine design and development, yet for many reasons, economic and political as well as technical, that development proceeded slowly and fitfully. Great Britain and the United States both studied the lessons of the First World War and the technology of the surrendered U-boats and drew similar conclusions – that the future of submarine warfare was in large, long-ranged 'cruiser-type' submarines, as opposed to the smaller types favoured by the Germans. This is easy enough to understand in the case of the United States, where war planners had to contemplate conflict in the Pacific, with its great distances and general lack of resupply facilities. In the case of the Royal Navy, the situation was more complex. At least at the beginning of the post-Versailles period, it was possible to hope that there was no longer a European threat to the Royal Navy's position. (Soviet Russia was clearly a potential enemy, but it was not, and had little chance in the short term of becoming, a naval threat. France and Italy were both now lesser naval powers and, more importantly, both at least nominally allies.) That left them to worry about threats to the more distant parts of the empire, such as India, Australia, Singapore or Hong Kong. Japan was an unknown; it had also been an ally of Great Britain in the First World War, but it was openly ambitious and was building up its naval forces at an alarming rate. The Americans certainly saw the Japanese as the greatest post-war threat. To defend Britain's distant possessions, the Royal Navy needed submarines with exceptional range as much as the Americans. Thus the trend in the development of submarines in the Allied countries in the 1920s was towards ever larger boats. Most were well above 1,000 tons displacement, some over 2,000 tons.

Smaller countries watched the war at sea play itself out in 1918 and drew their own conclusions. Obviously, to defend a coastline, much less to threaten any other nation, it was necessary to acquire at least a few modern submarines. Thus, after the end of the First World War, there was something of a rush among smaller navies to buy or build submarines of a type that could provide coastal defence and, at the same time, present a credible offensive threat if necessary. The extremely large boats being developed by the British and the Americans would clearly not meet those needs. A different kind of boat was needed.

Spain was typical of the smaller countries that had a strong interest in building up a submarine force in the years immediately following the end of the First World War. They had ordered two different submarine types during the war: three coastal boats of Italian Laurenti-Fiat design from the yard at La Spezia and one somewhat larger Holland-type from the Electric Boat Company in the United States. Initially, these boats were given names, but later the names were dropped and all four boats were given 'A' designations. The Holland boat, originally *Isaac Peral*, later renamed *A-0*, was the more successful design and the Spanish navy turned again to the Americans for their next design. Six 'B' series boats were ordered in 1919, very similar in design to *A-0*, derived from Electric Boat's *M-1*, a double-hulled boat of 488 tons. These came into service between 1921–3 and were quite satisfactory, leading the Spanish to return to Electric Boat for its next design as well. In order to promote a domestic shipbuilding capability, the Spanish required that the 'B' and 'C' series boats be built in Spain, at the SECN shipyard at Cartagena.

The design for the 'C' series was derived directly from Electric Boat's 'S' class boats being built for the US Navy, particularly the later boats in the series, completed between 1922 and 1924. They were the last of a class planned during the First World War and, as such, were not strongly influenced by the *U-Kreuzer* examined after the war. They were large boats, over 900 tons, but not the much larger type the United States turned to after 'absorbing' the lessons of the war. The Spanish boats differed from the American prototype by adding two stern torpedo tubes and a broader deckcasing. To make room for the additional torpedo tubes, these boats had reduced fuel storage which gave them less range than their American predecessors. *C-3* was the third of six 'C' class boats. She was laid down at Cartagena in May 1924 and completed five years later. (Five more years would pass before *U-34* was laid down and it was another year-and-a-half after that before she would cross paths with *C-3*.)

C-3's career was mostly uneventful, as might be expected from a submarine in a navy at peace. Her first six years of existence were spent training, punctuated only by the occasional fleet exercise or foreign port visit. That all changed in 1936. The end of the First World War had brought an effective end to the age of monarchies in Europe. The end of the reigning dynasties in Germany, Austria and Russia and the acquiescence of the king in Italy with the rise of Fascism had heralded the emergence of a new type of authoritarian, 'corporate' state in Europe.[9] As the world watched Mussolini consolidate power in Italy and Hitler rise in Germany, it barely noticed the equally extreme changes in government in Spain. There, the king Alfonso XIII supported his own fascist-style dictator, Primo de Rivera, beginning in 1923. Unlike his contemporary Mussolini, or Hitler who came along later, Primo failed to maintain popular support and was eventually driven out in 1930. The king followed a year later when the Second Republic was established in Spain.[10] The victory of the leftist Popular Front in the elections of 1936 led to a rising by the conservative Spanish military, nominally led by Francisco Franco. Despite the solid support of the Spanish army and air force, the rising failed to defeat the Republican government in the first days and the country settled into a brutal three-year-long civil war.

The Spanish navy was the least politically engaged of the three services and, when the rising took place in July 1936, the navy had for the most part remained loyal to the Republic. This included every submarine. In a process repeated in boat after boat, the crew spontaneously formed sailors' committees after the style of the soviets of the Russian Revolution, and voted on whether to retain their existing officers or elect new ones. As in most cases the officers would have supported Franco given the chance, the crews most often picked popular junior officers or even fellow crew members to take over the boats. This led to a serious dilution of the experience level of the officers running the submarine force and individual boats. The end result was the near-paralysis of the Republican navy, including the submarine *C-3*. (It should be noted that many of the junior officers promoted by their crews were just as reactionary as the senior officers they replaced, but they were sufficiently discreet or timid to have kept their views to themselves during the rising. Their silent support of the Nationalists no doubt contributed to the inertia of the submarine force.)

The rising found *C-3*, along with seven other submarines, in port at Cartagena. The events that occurred in *C-3* during the crucial early days of the rising were typical of what happened on most other units of the Spanish fleet. The submarine's commander was *Capitán de Corbeta* (Lieutenant Commander) Javier Salas Pintó. On the evening of 17 July, the day of the rising, *C-3* along with the other submarines at Cartagena received orders to deploy to the Straits of Gibraltar the next morning to enforce a blockade between Morocco and the mainland. Franco in fact had a serious logistical problem. His only good troops, the ones with the ability to crush any Republican resistance, were in the wrong place. They were all in Morocco when Franco desperately needed them across the Straits of Gibraltar on the Spanish mainland. His easiest recourse would have been to convoy the colonial troops and their equipment over the 16 miles that separate Ceuta in Morocco from Algeciras or Cadiz. He had more than enough drifters, trawlers and ferries to get the job done in a few days, except for that he needed control of the straits. Since the only ships to declare for the rising were far away in Galician ports, Franco was forced to wait several crucial days for an airlift to be arranged, during which time his chance vanished to sweep out the Republic in a swift decisive stroke.[11] Ironically, he in fact need not have feared the intervention of the Republican fleet. They were all, like C-3, too busy with internal squabbles to have done anything to stop a boatlift across the straits.

On the 17th, Salas was on leave in Madrid, where he was arrested on suspicion of supporting the rising. The next day, the flotilla chief formally removed him from command and promoted the boat's executive officer, *Teniente de Navío* (Lieutenant) Rafael Viniegra Pérez-Roldán to command the boat and the former third officer, *Alférez de Navío* (Sublieutenant) Luis Jáudenes Junco took over as second-in-command.[12] The vacant position of third officer was taken over another young *Alférez de Navío* Antonio Arbona Pastor, who had been second officer on B-5, which was then undergoing a refit. C-3 left port that morning along with C-1, C-4, C-6 and B-6 and the flotilla proceeded slowly across the western end of the Mediterranean to Melilla, where they took position on the 20th.[13] Blockading Melilla may have had symbolic value, but it had little practical effect on the Nationalist's plans to move troops across from Morocco. This was being done from Ceuta, 120nm to the west and 60nm closer to the Spanish mainland.

Once off Melilla, however, all thoughts of fighting the Nationalists were put aside. The sailors' committee on C-3 met and demanded that Viniegra declare his political leanings. A delegation of the committee attempted to confront the captain in his wardroom, but was intercepted by Jáudenes, who tried unsuccessfully to talk them out of it. The sailors instead arrested both the captain and second officer and turned to the relatively unknown Arbona, appointing him the new captain. Sailors on the remaining submarines in the group soon imitated those on C-3, until new captains had been appointed for all five submarines. The mission to stop Nationalist reinforcements from crossing the Straits of Gibraltar was now completely forgotten. C-1, C-3 and C-4 headed immediately to Málaga, where the flotilla commander and the arrested officers were turned over to authorities on shore. Henceforth, C-3 would operate from Málaga.

From this point on, C-3 only moved after a majority vote of the crew, which didn't occur very frequently. The first mission they agreed to was escorting a tanker to Tangiers and returning immediately to Málaga. On 15 August, it was agreed they would, along with C-6, run much-needed supplies to the northern zone.[14] They would then remain in the north in an attempt to break the blockade by Nationalist cruisers based at El Ferrol. A breakdown off the Portuguese coast forced C-3 to turn back, but after repairs, she again set out for the north on 25 August. She spent the month of September operating in the Bay of Biscay without sighting any Nationalist targets, until she was ordered back to the south again on 2 October. After another breakdown, which disabled one of her two diesels, C-3 put into Tangiers and then limped into Cartagena for repairs on 6 October. The shipyard there was unable to repair the broken engine.[15]

Still operating on one diesel, *C-3* left Cartagena on 10 December, made a brief stop at Almería and then headed for Málaga the morning of the 11th.

The trip from Almería to Málaga was made submerged. The situation in the Mediterranean had changed dramatically while *C-3* had been laid up in Cartagena. No longer was it just a fight between units of the Spanish fleet. Fascist Italy and Nazi Germany, despite going through the motions of 'non-intervention', were both moving rapidly to support Franco and the Nationalists. At first that support had been in the form of aircraft, particularly transports that allowed the movement of troops from Morocco across to the Spanish mainland, but Mussolini rapidly increased the level of Italian aid to include combat troops, armour and naval support. Italian submarines based at Majorca began patrolling off Spain's Mediterranean coast on 8 November, hunting for any ships bringing war materials to the Republican zone, as well as any Republican warships. *C-3* was warned to be on the lookout for submarine activity.

Compared to the chaotic career of *C-3*, that of *U-34* had been short and orderly. It had been less than a year before the rising in Spain when *U-34* had been laid down at Germaniawerft, but construction had gone rapidly and the boat was commissioned into the new *Kriegsmarine* on 12 September 1936. The crew that had assembled for her initial commission was among the best Germany could offer, with excellent young officers and a cadre of veteran NCOs. She was immediately assigned to the new *U-Flottille 'Saltzwedel'* at Wilhelmshaven.[16] Her commanding officer was *Kapitänleutnant* Hans-Ernst Sobe.

Sobe's tenure in charge of his new boat was to be interrupted almost immediately. On 4 November, he was informed that he and his watch officers were temporarily relieved. In their place, *Kapitänleutnant* Harald Grosse took over command and brought with him his two watch officers from *U-8*. Although Sobe had earned commendations while serving on Dönitz's staff prior to commissioning *U-34*, he was nevertheless considered too inexperienced for the special task to which his boat had just been assigned. Sobe had never commanded a U-boat before; Grosse had significantly greater experience. He had been one of the German officers in charge of the Spanish *E-1* before she was sold to the Turks. Besides this experience in one of the Type VII's design antecedents, his time in *E-1* had given him experience operating in Spanish waters, which, given *U-34*'s new assignment, was particularly useful.

Hitler's support for Franco was always reluctant. He found the Spanish *Caudillo* to be overly cautious and slow to push the advantages his experienced colonial troops and the extensive material support from the Germans and Italians gave him.[17] Mussolini's impetuosity regularly forced Hitler into moves he would have preferred to avoid. This included Mussolini's decision to deploy submarines, which seemed to Hitler to be reckless in the extreme. The main goal of the deployment was to block the flow of military supplies, mainly from Russia, to the Republican side. As much as Hitler agreed with this aim, he was terrified of being pushed into a war with the

French and particularly the British before he was ready. But Mussolini insisted that the British would do little more than go through the motions of protesting submarine attacks against neutral shipping in the Mediterranean and events were to prove him right.[18]

The decision to send U-boats into the Mediterranean in support of Franco came from Hitler, but the planning was left to the head of the submarine force, *FdU* Karl Dönitz.[19] He codenamed the operation 'Ursula' after his daughter. The idea was that two of the small number of long-range U-boats then in service would be sent to the Mediterranean coast of Spain.[20] There, they would patrol for as long as they were able and then return to Germany. Any decision on further patrols would be held off until the results of the first could be assessed.

While they were on patrol, their actions were to be strictly circumscribed. Every precaution was to be exercised to assure that German involvement was concealed. The Spanish were not to be informed of the operation at all and the Italians were told only the minimum required to co-ordinate patrols. The selected boats were to remain submerged during the day, surfacing only at night to charge batteries and communicate with home. If forced to surface during the day, they were to break out the Royal Navy's white ensign. If they needed repairs, they were to put in only at the Italian port of La Maddalena, fly the Italian flag and any crew on deck were to wear Italian uniforms. Attacks were to be made only on positively identified Republican warships, which meant that only daylight attacks could be made. To make sure these stringent rules were followed, the young commanders of both U-boats were replaced by older men. Grosse replaced *U-34*'s Sobe; *Kapitänleutnant* Ottoheinrich Junker of *U-33*, the other selected boat, was replaced by *Kapitänleutnant* Kurt Freiwald, who had commanded *U-7* for over a year.

Every effort was made to conceal the true nature of the operation, even from the rest of the *Kriegsmarine*, although the sudden and simultaneous replacement of two young captains must have raised some eyebrows in Wilhelmshaven. On the night of 20 November 1936, the two boats left port for what was publicly described as a training exercise. Once out of sight of land, the large black hull numbers carried on the sides of the conning towers were painted over and boats assumed the coded identities *Triton* (*U-33*) and *Poseidon* (*U-34*) for all radio communication. Their departure was timed to allow them to pass through the Straits of Gibraltar on a moonless night, 27 November. Since it had been agreed with the Italians that their submarines would vacate the Germans' designated patrol areas on the 30th, the two U-boats had to wait two more days once within the Mediterranean before they could take up their stations. For additional safety, they were warned to be doubly cautious before attacking any submarine, to avoid attacking an Italian boat.

The areas assigned to the two U-boats were adjacent stretches of water off the east coast of Spain, divided at 0°44'W, the longitude of Cape Palos. *U-33* was assigned the coast east of this line up to Cape Nao, a stretch of coast centred on Alicante; *U-34* was assigned the coast west of the line, including the main Republican port at Cartagena. They had every reason to expect a warm reception. Although Italian submarines had been patrolling these waters since the beginning of November, they had initially restricted their activities to stopping merchant shipping. The Republican navy, disorganised and in a state of near-paralysis, was content to ignore the threat, but that came to an end on 22 November. On that day, the Italian submarine *Torricelli* torpedoed the Republican cruiser *Miguel de Cervantes* at anchor off Cartagena. The cruiser was hit twice, but did not sink. She was towed into the port and docked, out of action for the remainder of the war. Thus, the two U-boats would be hunting an enemy now fully alerted to the danger and presumably on the lookout for enemy submarines.

In the event, they found no lack of targets. The Republican navy remained active and yet remarkably lax in their anti-submarine defence. On the first day of active patrolling, 1 December, *U-34* sighted a destroyer moving at high speed close in to the shore. Grosse fired one torpedo, which missed and exploded on the shore. Amazingly, neither the intended target nor anyone on shore showed any interest in the explosion. Four days later, another torpedo was fired at another destroyer, this one identified as *Almirante Antequera*, and on the 8th, another single torpedo was fired at another destroyer. Both of those torpedoes also missed, but at least they completed their runs without exploding. Freiwald in *U-33* sighted several targets but was unable to achieve a firing position. *U-33* had a good shot at a ship identified as the cruiser *Méndez Núñez* during the night of 5 December, but followed orders and did not make a night attack.

Each night, the U-boats surfaced to recharge batteries and make detailed reports by radio. The responses they got from Germany betrayed increasing nervousness at the risk of detection. The two boats received a strict order directly from fleet headquarters:

> Lack of visible success must not lead to such determined action that concealment and the avoidance of revealing German identity are not considered the highest priority.[21]

Finally, on the night of the 10th, the Nazi War Minister von Blomberg lost his nerve completely and ordered that the boats cut their missions short and return to Germany starting the next day.

U-34 followed orders, submerging at dawn on 11 December 1936 and setting a course westward along the southern coast of Spain. At 1400, hearing the sound of activity close by, Grosse brought the U-boat up to periscope depth to take a look around. What he saw was a submarine on the surface, moving towards the entrance of the harbour at Málaga. Broadside on, the silhouette was unmistakably that of a Spanish 'C' class submarine. The target was moving fast and would soon be out of range. Grosse had only moments to make a decision. He had every excuse to pass on the shot. The setup was not particularly good and was getting worse by the second. He was close in to shore and there were other ships in the vicinity, raising the risk of detection and making a clean escape more difficult. He had been warned about attacking submarines given the possibility that an Italian boat might have strayed into the area. Perhaps most importantly, the entire operation had already been cancelled and he was on his way home. But, on the other hand, here was a shot at a positively identified target. Who knew when such an opportunity would come again? It was simply too good to pass up.

The submarine was *C-3*. She had been running submerged all the way from Almería, but now that she was approaching Málaga, she had surfaced for the run into the harbour. She was making 11 knots, the best speed she could make on her one diesel, but otherwise Arbona had taken no precautions against attack. He was confident the short run into the harbour could be made without enemy interference. The captain was on the bridge along with merchant marine Captain Agustín Garcia Viñas, the navigator.[22] The crew had just finished the midday meal, a thick Galician-style soup followed by fried eggs with tomatoes, and two sailors were on the afterdeck dumping the food scraps overboard. The seamen, Isidoro de la Orden Ibáñez and Asensio Lidón Jiménez, were grumbling about having to handle this messy chore. The next watch, which should have had this duty, was lingering over their meal and was already almost 20 minutes late. The two men owed their lives to the tardiness of their replacements, because it was at just that moment, at 1419, that *C-3* shuddered violently, began to list to starboard and sank rapidly by the bow. In a matter of seconds, the two sailors and Garcia, treading water, were the only survivors of the crew of *C-3*.[23] A cloud of white smoke hung briefly over the site and then dissipated in the breeze.

Having made the decision to attack, the crew of *U-34* moved with well-practiced precision. As there were other ships in the immediate area, the risk of detection was high, so the periscope was raised only briefly to get bearings and angles and lowered just as quickly. Numbers were read off the periscope dials and entered into the attack computer. There would be time to fire only one torpedo. Grosse made a second quick observation to confirm that the target had kept the same course, lowered the periscope and, as soon as the torpedo's gyroscope matched the attack computer's settings, ordered: '*Rohr ein – Feuer!*' The U-boat lurched slightly as a ton and a half of torpedo left the tube. Then the waiting began. And seemed to last interminably, far past the length of time it should have taken the torpedo to reach its target. Grosse was starting to give orders for a course that would take the boat away from the coast when the radioman called him over and handed him the earphones connected to the GHG, the sound array located at the boat's bow.[24] In the earphones, Grosse heard the sound of a diesel engine running at high speed and, at the same time, the noise of collapsing bulkheads, an unusual and distinctive sound signature. As none of the other ships in the vicinity could have been in the path of the torpedo, the sinking ship could only be the submarine; however, he would not risk even a brief glance through the periscope. If the target was indeed sinking, the reaction from the port would be swift and angry. It was time to get *U-34* away from the area as rapidly as possible.

The reaction on the surface was anything but swift. It seems that not only did Grosse and the crew of *U-34* not hear an explosion but neither did most observers on the surface. The closest ships, two fishing trawlers (*Joven Antonio* and *Joven Amalia*), the patrol boat *Xauen* and the *Tabacalera* boat *I-4*, all reported having seen the submarine sink, with a small amount of flame and the cloud of white smoke or steam, but the witnesses either reported hearing no explosion at all or at most a very faint detonation.[25] A search of the site revealed, besides the three survivors, a large oil slick and some floating debris. The immediate conclusion was that *C-3* had been torpedoed and the initial public statement, released the next day, blamed a 'submarine, evidently foreign' for the loss. Since the Nationalists had no submarines and it was an open secret that the Italians were operating submarines in the area, the conclusion was obvious that the Republicans blamed the Italians for the sinking, though this was never explicitly stated in either the initial or final reports.

The Germans were just as happy to let everyone believe the Italians were to blame. Until the two boats returned to Wilhelmshaven on 21 December, all Dönitz or his superiors knew was what Grosse reported in two short, cryptic messages. On the night of the attack, Grosse radioed:

> From *Poseidon* – time: 1603 – location: AQ 1419 – sank 'red' submarine type C off Malaga.[26]

The next night, Grosse was urgently (and nervously) asked for clarification and responded, almost as briefly:

> From *Poseidon* – time: 0327 – it was confirmed definitely Spanish type C before firing – after the explosion submarine sank without a trace.

This last part was clearly embellishment on Grosse's part as he had neither heard an explosion nor confirmed that *C-3* sank without a trace, but it was sufficient to satisfy his superiors for the moment and, by the time he returned to Germany, it was obvious that no-one even suspected there had been U-boats in the Mediterranean.

On the Spanish side, there was confusion. The three survivors and eyewitnesses on the other ships and on shore gave differing and often contradictory accounts of what happened. No-one had seen *U-34*'s periscope or the track of her torpedo. The sole surviving officer, Garcia, claimed there had been a third man on the bridge responsible for watching the seaward side of the boat, though this was denied by the two surviving seamen and was probably invented by Garcia in an attempt at covering up his and the captain's negligent watchkeeping. What was clear was that there had been no big explosion, as there should have been if a torpedo had indeed detonated against *C-3*. Therefore, when the official report was released on 22 December, it backed off from the claim that *C-3* had been sunk by an enemy submarine. It also ruled out the possibility of a mine, as the area had been swept both before and after the sinking and no mines were found. The possibility of an explosion of 'battery gasses' was also considered unlikely, given that the boat was being ventilated with fresh air and the batteries were low on charge.[27] Therefore, it concluded that an internal explosion, either one of *C-3*'s torpedoes' air flasks or a low-order explosive smuggled on board by a saboteur, was the cause of the sinking.

This explanation satisfied no-one and was highly controversial, but the events of the war, including the capture of Málaga by Italian 'volunteers' fighting for the Nationalists in February 1937, soon overshadowed any concern about the true fate of *C-3*. To make the matter even more confusing, the Nationalists, who had 'bought' two modern Italian submarines in early 1937, painted them in the markings of *C-3* and *C-5* (another Republican submarine lost in December 1936) and spread the story that the crews of the two boats had rebelled and switched sides.[28] In fact the two transferred submarines were never officially named *C-3* and *C-5*, and no-one was really fooled by the deception, as the Italian boats looked quite different; but some official Spanish records reported that *C-3* was still in service as late as 1947.

As soon as *U-33* and *U-34* returned to Wilhelmshaven, the original commanders and their officers took the boats over again, as if nothing had happened. Grosse was commended and given command of a new boat, *U-22*. He was awarded a medal specifically created for Germans who served in Spain with particular distinction, the *Goldene Spanienkreuz* (Spanish Cross in Gold), though the secrecy of the affair was such that he was not actually given the medal until June 1939. In fact, the operation remained so secret that it was never officially acknowledged and might have been completely forgotten with the defeat of Nazi Germany, had evidence not been uncovered in German archives by a French researcher after the war. *U-34* went on to conduct seven combat patrols during the first year of the Second World War, before being reassigned as a training boat in the Baltic. She will appear again in these pages. Harald Grosse did not last as long as the boat he had commanded off the coast of Spain. After commanding *U-22* for less than a year, he was given shore assignments and a promotion to *Korvettenkapitän*, before he was given another boat, *U-53*, a Type VIIB, in January 1940. On her first patrol under Grosse, she was sunk on 23 February 1940 by depth-charging by the destroyer HMS *Gurkha* near the Orkneys. There were no survivors.

The actual cause of *C-3*'s sinking will never be known with total certainty, but it strains credulity to believe that *U-34* fired a torpedo that missed and at that same moment *C-3* suffered an unrelated internal explosion. Sonar images show the wreck of *C-3* on the seabed off Málaga broken in two sections forward of the conning tower. The lack of an audible explosion remains a mystery, but the most likely explanation would seem to be that *U-34*'s torpedo hit *C-3* forward of the bridge and either failed to detonate at all or exploded incompletely. It appears that either way, the impact was sufficient to punch a hole in *C-3*'s hull and, as the bow section filled with water, the still-running diesel drove the submarine to the relatively shallow bottom where the hull broke at the point where the torpedo had struck.

CHAPTER 7

First Shots of a Long War

ORP *Sep*, *U-14* and HMS/M *Spearfish*

ON 3 SEPTEMBER 1939, Britain and France reluctantly found themselves at war once again with Germany. Neither nation wanted this war, but found themselves pushed into it by Hitler's insistence on a rigid timetable for Poland to cede the corridor of land separating Pomerania from East Prussia. The refusal of the Poles to be dismembered the way Czecho-slovakia had been and the final realisation by the British and French that they had really only one more chance to stand up to Hitler's demands made war inevitable. When Hitler's ultimatum to the Poles ran out on 1 September, the *Wehrmacht* invaded. The British and French demanded the Germans withdraw no later than the 3rd. When that deadline passed, Europe again found itself at war.

This first day of hostilities was surprisingly busy, starting in the Baltic, where six U-boats had been deployed from their base at Memel on 30 August.[1] The Polish navy was tiny, but still of concern to the Germans. Its major units were four relatively modern destroyers, a minelayer and five submarines. Three of the submarines were of French design, ordered in 1926. The other two were brand new Dutch-built boats, having both joined the navy only months before the outbreak of war. The Germans were mainly concerned that Polish ships might escape the confines of the Baltic and they deployed units in the straits around Denmark, but the Poles had in fact moved faster than the Germans expected. Fully anticipating Hitler's intransigence, the Poles realised that their tiny navy had little chance of surviving against German air and naval superiority and decided to get as many of the larger units as possible out of the Baltic before the shooting started. *U-6* watched helplessly as three of the four Polish destroyers escaped at high speed through the Kattegat on 31 August, unable to shoot because war had not yet been declared.[2] Only the destroyer *Wicher*, the minelayer *Gryf* and the five submarines remained as effective units of the Polish navy in the Baltic, based at the port of Gdynia on the Gulf of Danzig.[3]

Just as was to be the fate of the country they served, the units of the Polish fleet that stayed in the Baltic did not last long. *Wicher* and *Gryf* were sunk at Hela on 3 September by German bombers.[4] That night, at 2022, *U-14* was patrolling in the Gulf of Danzig when she spotted an enemy submarine on the surface. The captain of the cramped little Type IIB, *Kapitänleutnant* Horst Wellner, judged a single torpedo to be sufficient for a boat of just over 1,100 tons. Carrying only six torpedoes in total, he was trained to use them sparingly. He lined up the shot carefully and fired at the slow-moving target. He was rewarded with a loud detonation, a brilliant flash and the sounds of a submarine heading to the bottom. He surfaced his boat and circled the area. He found floating debris and a large oil slick. He was convinced he had had a success and radioed that claim to *FdU Ost*. It was to be recorded in official German logs as the first attack of the war and the first sinking by one of the new generation of U-boats.

In fact, it was neither. The dubious honor of making the first successful U-boat attack of the war went to *Kapitänleutnant* Fritz-Julius Lemp's *U-30*, which torpedoed and sank the liner *Athenia* an hour earlier. So terrified were the Germans of a repetition of the controversies surrounding the sinking of passenger ships in the First World War that its boats had been explicitly ordered to follow prize rules for all except warships, and in particular to avoid sinking liners. Yet that was exactly what Lemp did on the first day of the new war. In his defence, Lemp later claimed he mistook *Athenia* for an armed merchant cruiser because she was steaming without lights and following a zigzag course. Regardless, he failed to inform Dönitz, so the Germans first heard of the sinking when it was announced by the Admiralty and labelled as yet another German atrocity. The German response was to deny all knowledge of the incident and to speculate publicly that it had been perpetrated by the British themselves to help whip up anti-German feeling. When Lemp returned to Wilhelmshaven on 27 September and Dönitz learned for the first time that *U-30* had indeed been responsible for the sinking, the captain and crew of the U-boat were sworn to secrecy and all mention of the incident was expunged from the boat's *KTB*.

Even had *U-30* not torpedoed *Athenia* before *U-14*'s attack on the Polish submarine, Wellner still could not have claimed the first sinking of the war, because his target did not in fact sink. The boat he was aiming at was *Sep*, one of the two new submarines in the Polish fleet.[5] *Sep*, under the command of Commander Wladyslaw Salmon, was making a sweep of the Gulf of Danzig when her lookouts were startled by the explosion of *U-14*'s torpedo close by. The detonation occurred close enough to *Sep* to rupture an oil tank and generally damage the external structures along the exposed side, but did not cause any damage to the pressure hull and the boat was able to dive and make good her escape. When Wellner surfaced, he found the oil slick and debris and drew the logical, but incorrect, conclusion. This kind of torpedo failure was to be a recurring frustration for the Germans, problems with the magnetic influence fuse leading to premature detonation or failure to detonate.[6] In both *U-14*'s attack on *Sep* and *U-22*'s later attack on *Zbik*, the torpedo detonated while it was still approximately 200m from the target. In both cases, this allowed the target to get away.

Escape for *Sep* was only temporary, however. With complete German mastery of sea and air, *Sep* was forced north towards Sweden, away from the Polish coast. When Salmon reached the conclusion that his boat and his crew were no longer capable of either fighting on or escaping to England, he headed towards the Swedish naval base at Stavsnas, near Stockholm, where the boat was interned on 17 September 1939. The boat remained in Swedish hands until reclaimed by representatives of liberated Poland on 5 September 1945. She served in the reconstituted Polish navy until decommissioned in 1969. *U-14* was withdrawn from combat operations in July 1940 and was used as a school boat until she was decommissioned in April 1945.[7]

Other attacks occurred that same night, equally without success. *U-18* engaged an unidentified Polish submarine, without obtaining a hit.[8] The Polish submarine *Rys* spotted a periscope and fired two torpedoes at it, also without result. In both cases, the target was apparently unaware of the attack, as records do not include any mention of boats on either side, other than *Sep*, having survived attack that night.

Interestingly, yet another submarine also claimed to have been unsuccessfully attacked by a U-boat on 3 September 1939. The Royal Navy submarine *Spearfish*, under Lieutenant J H Eaden, had deployed along with the rest of the 2nd Submarine Flotilla from their base at Dundee in late August to take up positions across the several exits from the North Sea. *Spearfish*'s assigned patrol area was in the Kattegat between Denmark and Sweden. On 3 September, barely minutes after receiving the ominous radio message 'TOTAL GERMANY', *Spearfish* was attacked.[9] According to Eaden's report a torpedo just missed his boat. He immediately submerged and then spent the next six hours trying to line up a shot on the enemy submarine, which was also submerged. Between sound bearings and occasional glimpses of the U-boat's periscope through his own periscope, Eaden tracked the quarry relentlessly. At one point, out of frustration at his inability to reach an acceptable firing position, he attempted to ram the U-boat with *Spearfish*, but seemed to pass above the enemy, which apparently was deeper underwater. After this, *Spearfish* lost track of the U-boat and returned to patrolling.

The only problem with this 'incident' is that no record of it can be found in any German source. It would be easy enough to put it in the same category as the *U-18* and *Rys* incidents, where the target was unaware of being attacked, except that Eaden claimed that the U-boat initiated the encounter by firing a torpedo at *Spearfish*. It is unlikely that a U-boat could engage in a six-hour 'dogfight' with a British submarine, one that included firing a torpedo, and not have some reference to it show up in official records. Either Eaden, suffering from understandable over-excitement after just learning that another war with Germany had begun, had just spent six hours chasing a non-existent enemy, or the German captain, perhaps ashamed at having missed an easy target, decided not to record it in his log or report it to his superiors and got the rest of his crew to go along with the cover-up.[10]

CHAPTER 8

Fratricide II

HMS/M *Triton* and HMS/M *Oxley*

IN THE FIRST WORLD WAR, the normal practice for both sides was to assign each submarine a set area within which to patrol. All other friendly submarines were supposed to stay well clear of other boats' areas for their own safety. This approach worked well enough when targets had been distributed more or less randomly in the seas around Britain, but after the introduction of merchant convoys by the British in 1917, the success rate of Germany's U-boats dropped off sharply. To the Germans, it became obvious that another approach was required. To Karl Dönitz and others, the idea of the wolfpack, a disciplined, co-ordinated concentration of submarines, was the answer. But even to the Germans, it was obvious that this tactic required both a concentration of targets, such as a convoy, and a sufficient number of submarines deployed, so that enough boats could be gathered to attack the well-defended convoys.

At the start of the Second World War, for different reasons, neither the British nor the Germans immediately adopted pack tactics. The only delay in the Germans' adoption of wolfpacks was the small number of available U-boats, given that this time around the British did not hesitate to introduce a convoy system. The first tentative experiments with packs would come in late 1939 and early 1940, but it really was not until June 1940, after the conclusion of the Norwegian campaign, before there were enough U-boats in the Atlantic truly to attempt pack attacks. The British, on the other hand, did not need to use this approach. The small German merchant fleet, which had never really recovered from the previous war, was again rapidly driven from the open ocean.[1] That left the *Kriegsmarine* as the only proper target of the Royal Navy's submarines and those targets moved unpredictably, unlike the regularity with which convoys approached the British Isles. The only practical tactic was to assign submarines to discrete patrol zones, concentrating them at the entrances to the North Sea and across the swept channels in the vast minefields that both sides laid in the first few weeks of the war.[2]

Thus it was that the Royal Navy sent two of its submarines to patrol adjacent zones off the coast of Norway in the first week of the new war. One was an older boat, HMS/M *Oxley*, under the command of Lieutenant Commander Harold G Bowerman. The other was the much newer *Triton*, under Lieutenant Commander H P de C Steel. Three other boats patrolled zones in line with these two, each zone 12nm wide, forming an east–west sweep line just south of Stavanger. All the boats complained that keeping within their designated areas was proving difficult due to rough seas and the frequency of German patrol flights. *Triton* had the easternmost zone; *Oxley*'s was the next zone to the west.

Both boats had interesting histories. *Oxley* had been built in England for the Royal Australian Navy and was commissioned into that navy in 1927. She sailed for Australia with her sister *Otway*, under orders not to dive during the voyage. This proved unfortunate, as diving would have allowed the boats to avoid a beating from storms in the Bay of Biscay. Arriving at Malta in March 1928, both boats were found to have sustained damage to their engine mounts and were laid up there for nine months before proper repairs could be completed. Finally arriving in Australia in February 1929, they were in service for less than a year before they were placed in reserve because the worldwide economic depression left the Australian government unable to afford to maintain them. By mutual agreement, they reverted to the Royal Navy in 1931, served in the Mediterranean until 1936 and were placed in reserve again in 1938. They were scheduled for disposal, but were reactivated when war approached in 1939.

Triton was completed in late 1938. It did not take long for the boat to gain a reputation as being accident-prone. In June 1939, while based at Portsmouth, *Triton* was loading practice torpedoes when one of those accidents occurred, damaging a nearby patrol vessel, HMS *Puffin*.

> The *Triton* was moored alongside the depot ship *Titania* when the torpedo, weighing over a ton, began to slide. Ratings tried to secure it, but being smothered in grease it was difficult to hold. As soon as the propellers touched the water the automatic starting mechanism was set in motion, and the torpedo, drenching the men who were trying to hold it, left the submarine at a speed of 45 knots.[3]

The torpedo ran true, slamming into the side of the patrol boat. Fortunately for *Puffin*, the warhead was a dummy, causing only minor damage.

This boat and *Oxley* were thus patrolling their adjacent sectors off the Norwegian coast as darkness fell on 10 September 1939, barely a week after the start of the war. *Triton* surfaced at 2004 and, trimmed with decks nearly awash, was heading south on her starboard engine at a speed of 3 knots, using the port engine to recharge batteries. Being close into the shore, just 8nm away, and Norway still at peace, *Triton* was able to take fixes on two lighthouses. This established her position as well within her assigned zone, so Steel went below, ordering the watch officer to continue heading south, but to swing further away from the coast to keep clear of a fishing trawler also heading south on a parallel course closer in towards the shore.[4] At 2055, lookouts on *Triton* sighted the silhouette of a submarine off to starboard. The watch officer turned the boat towards this sighting and called Steel up to the bridge.

Oxley, like *Triton*, had spent the day submerged. When she surfaced at 2030, she was also able to take sightings on two shore lighthouses, which should have been a tip-off that she was too far to the east and possibly out of her patrol sector, but this clue was apparently misinterpreted. There were reasons for this that seemed good at the time. The weather was misty and in those conditions at night, direct observation of a light can be mistaken for the reflection off the ocean's surface of a more distant light. Sighting the lights alone was insufficient to establish that *Oxley* was further east than Bowerman believed. He had communicated with *Triton* earlier in the day and was satisfied that she was more than 7nm away to the east.[5] Nevertheless, Bowerman concluded that he was too far south and turned his boat to a course of 330°. In fact, he was approximately 6nm further east than he believed, and was actually at that point to the south and east of *Triton*, which had swung to the west. This new course caused his boat to pass in front of *Triton* from southeast to northwest and she was off *Triton*'s starboard bow when she was sighted at 2055. *Oxley*'s lookouts did not see *Triton* in the haze.

Steel briefly considered that the boat he saw through his binoculars was *Oxley*, but he dismissed the thought because of the prior communication he had had with Bowerman, which should have warned *Oxley* away. Steel had the two external tubes at *Triton*'s bow, tubes 7 and 8, readied and the crew was ordered to diving stations. As a final precaution against the possibility that the boat he was now trailing might be *Oxley*, he ordered a signalman to the bridge and had him flash the recognition signal.[6] There was no response from the other boat, which continued on her previous course. This signed was repeated twice more with the same lack of response. As a final attempt to ascertain the identity of the boat, Steel ordered that a green flare be fired into the air. When, after 15 seconds, this also caused no response or change in the movement of the other boat, he then ordered that both bow tubes be fired. Just before the torpedoes struck the target, flashing was seen from the bridge of the target, but it was not a readable signal. A few seconds later, both torpedoes hit; the target was seen to explode violently and sink immediately. Steel headed for the site of the sinking and was appalled to discover that the three men in the water were all calling out in English.

Two survivors were eventually rescued, Bowerman and one of the lookouts. (The third swimmer apparently drowned in just the few minutes it took to get lines out to them.) The story that Bowerman told confirmed that the sinking had been the result of errors and bad luck on both sides. The lookouts on *Oxley* had not seen any of the three attempts to flash recognition signals, but had seen the green flare and only then realised that they were being trailed by another submarine. *Oxley*'s watch officer called Bowerman to the bridge and at the same time fired a flare in response but it failed to ignite. Bowerman, once he reached the bridge ordered that another flare be fired off and that signals be flashed at the trailing boat, which he assumed was *Triton*. There was time to do neither before the torpedoes hit almost directly below the bridge, throwing him and the two others into the water.

Steel was absolved from any blame for the sinking. *Oxley* had been within his zone when sunk and he had tried four different times to contact the other boat. All attempts to visually identify the boat were defeated by the misty conditions and the fact that *Oxley* was trimmed low in the water, which hid her distinctive bow shape.[7] It was determined that Steel had done all he reasonably could to identify the target before he fired. If there was any culpability, it would lie with *Oxley*'s lookouts, who failed to see *Triton* coming up behind them until it was too late. The bad luck of the failed flare could be blamed on no-one.

There were certain factors at work here, other than the basic question of whether Steel should have refrained from firing his torpedoes. It would have sent exactly the wrong message to the submarine force for a verdict of culpability to be handed down against a commander acting with some aggressiveness. Certainly, questions could have been asked, such as whether a U-boat would have acted as *Oxley* did had she seen the various recognition signals *Triton* sent. Nevertheless, the Royal Navy would certainly decide that it was better to accept the loss of a submarine than leave its captains questioning too much whether to shoot in cases when identification of the target was less than perfect. In the real world of 1939, precise identification would be rare.

But perhaps something can be read into the fact that, despite being cleared, Steel was replaced in command of *Triton* before her next patrol. He was posted as an instructor at Fort Blockhouse, where the Royal Navy trained prospective submarine commanders. Harold Bowerman went on to command a destroyer with success. *Triton*, along with a number of other 'T' class submarines, was transferred to the Mediterranean, where they suffered a high rate of loss due to their size. The Mediterranean was better suited for smaller, more manoeuvrable submarines. *Triton* operated out of Alexandria, using Malta as a forward base. Her last patrol started on 28 November 1940, with an assigned operating area in the southern Adriatic. The Italian merchantman *Olimpia* radioed a distress call on 6 December near Brindisi, in *Triton*'s operating sector, making it likely she was a victim of the submarine's torpedoes. This will never be known for certain as *Triton* was never heard from again. The Italians claim that *Triton* was sunk by the torpedo boat *Clio* on 18 December, but the Royal Navy believes this unlikely since *Triton* should have cleared the Adriatic several days earlier, being due back at Malta on the 17th. The British believe it more likely that she was mined in the Straits of Otranto sometime between 10 and 13 December. Either way the submarine was lost with all hands.

The relatives of the crew of *Oxley* were told that the boat had been sunk by an accidental explosion. After the war, the story was changed to the loss being due to a collision between the two boats. It was not until the mid-1950s that the true story was finally revealed.

CHAPTER 9

Tit for Tat

HMS/M *Thistle* and *U-4*

DÖNITZ'S PLANS FOR HIS U-boat campaign were well thought out. He realised that Germany, even more so in this second conflict than the first, would have absolutely no hope of challenging British dominance of the surface of the world's oceans. There was no way that the tiny *Kriegsmarine* could wrest control of the waters around the British Isles even temporarily from the Royal Navy. The U-boat represented the only chance Germany had to win the war, for as long as Britain was fed and supplied with raw materials, Germany would eventually lose the war through a slow process of strangulation. Only by reducing the inflow of those supplies to the point where Britain starved faster than the Germans could the war be won. It was a game of hard numbers. The British had a large merchant fleet to start with and the ability to build many more ships if their yards were supplied with steel. Further, the rapid victories of the German army meant that the merchant fleets of France, Belgium, Holland and Norway fell virtually intact into British hands. Plus, there would always be neutral shipping willing to join the Atlantic convoys, if the risks were not too great. To win the war, Dönitz figured in 1940, would take a monthly toll of 700,000 GRT of shipping sent to the bottom. Since the average freighter in 1940 was perhaps 5,000 GRT, that meant something like 140 ships would need to be sunk each month. He calculated that if that rate could be maintained for two years, Germany would win.[1]

This was easy enough to theorise, but much harder to put into practice. To accomplish this rate of success, Dönitz calculated he would need a minimum of 300 of the medium-sized Type VII boats to fight in the waters of the Atlantic around the British Isles, plus additional long-range Type IX boats for raids further afield, such as off the American coast, and then still more boats of the smaller Type II design to train the crews and officers the larger boats would need.[2] Plans were developed, but Hitler's interest in his navy was sporadic at best and construction proceeded far more slowly than Dönitz had hoped. Hitler had repeatedly told the *Kriegsmarine* that they had until 1946 before war with Britain would come again. In September 1939, when the war actually started, Dönitz had fifty-seven U-boats in commission, of which only twenty-seven were sea-going or ocean-going boats.

The conundrum facing Dönitz when war broke out so much sooner and with U-boat numbers so much smaller than expected was whether to leave his short-range Type II boats dedicated to training new crews or to use them in combat and accept the attrition that would entail. On the one hand, he needed the training to continue, but he equally needed to deploy as many boats as he could in those critical first days of the war. The deciding argument was the realisation that orders for new boats had been allowed to dwindle in 1938 and the first part of 1939. Only with war looming was Dönitz allowed to increase orders to the levels needed to fight a war. Unfortunately, from Dönitz's point of view, the small number of orders he had been able to place in the period before the war meant that only a small number of shipyards had experience building the new, more technically sophisticated U-boats and therefore the ability to ramp up production rapidly.[3] Suddenly able to order new boats by the dozens, he found that the capacity of the few experienced yards was soon filled and he had to turn to other yards, some of them quite small, and none of which had built a U-boat in over twenty years, if ever. These yards often took quite a bit more time delivering the first boats of their orders than did the more experienced yards. All these factors led to a period of over a year after the war began when there would only be a trickle of new boats, for which few crews would be needed. Dönitz thus reluctantly ordered that most of his small Type II boats be prepared for combat assignments.

So it was that the oldest and smallest of U-boats were sent out to wage war in 1939, among them *U-4*. After having spent four years as a training boat, she was made operational again at the beginning of September 1939 and sent on two short patrols in the Skagerrak. The second patrol was particularly successful. Under the command of *Oberleutnant zur See* Hans-Peter Hinsch, she sank three small steamers of just over 5,000 GRT. At the end of the month, *U-4* returned to training duties for five more months, until the plans for the German invasion of Norway were well advanced. Afraid the British would act before they were ready, the Germans deployed every U-boat they had in an attempt to disrupt the enemy's preparations. Radio intelligence indicated that the British had the same concern and reacted in the same way, concentrating as many as fourteen submarines in or near the Skagerrak, in an attempt to block any German move to the north. The Germans dispatched six Type IIB and IIC boats against this concentration on 14 March 1940, joined in the next two days by the four oldest boats in the fleet, *U-1*, *U-2*, *U-3* and *U-4*. These four boats, plus *U-21* and *U-22* were then diverted to the area of Lindesnes at the southern tip of Norway in response to a report that a large force of Royal Navy ships had been seen there. No sooner had they arrived there than all boats were ordered back to base in final preparation for the invasion ('*Weserübung*') scheduled for 9 April.

On 4 April, *U-4* left Wilhelmshaven again, this time under sealed orders which were to be opened only on the 6th. Those orders assigned *U-4* to the 4th Group of U-boats, along with *U-1*, with the task of protecting the passage of German troops along the coast between Egersund and Bergen. *U-4* arrived in position off Stavanger on the 8th. She attempted to contact *U-1* without success.[4] Reports the next day that the British planned on laying mines across the fjord leading to Stavanger caused *U-4* to be moved towards Skudenes at the northern entrance of the fjord.

Norway was neutral in early 1940, but was very much on the minds of both the Germans and the British. The Germans depended heavily on iron ore from mines in northern Sweden. In winter, the ore was shipped by rail over the mountains to Narvik on the Atlantic and then down the coast in freighters that stayed well-protected in Norway's territorial waters. (The more direct route, by water down the Gulf of Bothnia, was only navigable from May to October due to ice. Narvik and the Atlantic coast south of there stayed ice-free all year round.) The British considered a number of moves to disrupt this traffic. They tried diplomatic pressure on the Norwegians, but had little success.[5] The British finally settled on a complicated strategy that they hoped would provide the justification for the Allied occupation of the country, starting with mining Norwegian coastal waters (Operation 'Wilfred'). They intended to declare a 'danger zone' that included Norwegian waters, much like the zone the Germans declared around Great Britain in April 1915, and then use that as a pretext for the mining. They hoped this would take the Germans by surprise and cause them to mount a hasty, piecemeal invasion, which the British then planned to defeat with a counter-invasion (Operation 'R4'). The Germans, aware that the British planned to occupy Norway but not of the details of the plans, reluctantly organised their own invasion.[6] Unconcerned with diplomatic niceties, they intended to invade as soon as plans could be completed and the necessary ships and troops gathered. Their only fear was that the British would beat them to the punch.

The British indeed had scheduled Operation 'Wilfred' to start on 8 April and made the 'danger zone' announcement the previous morning, but realised before the mining started that major German movements were underway and cancelled most of the operations. Seventeen British submarines, along with three French and one Polish boat, were deployed along the coast to intercept German fleet movements. One of those boats was HMS/M *Thistle*. One of the early 'T' class boats, like *Triton*, she was a large boat intended for long-range operations, but was pressed into North Sea operations because she was one of the newest and most capable boats in the fleet. Her commander was Lieutenant Commander W F Haselfoot.

As with every other submarine available to the Royal Navy, *Thistle* was on patrol off the coast of Norway on 8 April 1940.[7] Late in the day, she received a signal ordering her to stand away from the coast and then, early in the morning of the 9th, another order directing her to head for Stavanger where German ships had been reported. Once there, she was to work her way submerged into the harbour, a dangerous assignment involving navigation more than 15nm up the narrow fjord just to determine if there were targets in the harbour worth the risk. *Thistle* was at least 50nm from the entrance to the fjord when she received the order. At best speed, staying on the surface until within sight of shore, it would be 1800 at the earliest before she would have the harbour in view.

In the event *Thistle* did not make good time. There was nearly constant air activity and Haselfoot kept his boat submerged for much of the passage. Thus, it was already nearly 1600 when *Thistle* was just approaching the mouth of the fjord. Submerged, close under the northern shore, Haselfoot swept the horizon through his periscope and sighted a U-boat approaching on the surface. A radio message sent back to Rosyth later that evening tells us all that is known for certain about *Thistle*'s actions on the afternoon of 9 April 1940:

> Expended six torpedoes on inward bound U-boat at entrance to Stavanger fjord at 1604. Result unconfirmed due to enemy air activity. Intend to carry out orders of 1249/9 tomorrow Wednesday with remaining two warheads, air activity permitting.[8]

The message to which Haselfoot was referring was a reiteration of the order to enter Stavanger fjord and search for German shipping there. Almost simultaneously, a message was sent to *Thistle*, rescinding those orders. Further reconnaissance had shown that there were in fact no German ships at Stavanger.[9] There is no evidence that Haselfoot ever received this later message.

It is not at all clear why *Thistle* fired six torpedoes at so small a target, especially when it would appear that there were only eight torpedoes remaining on board at the time.[10] The account left by Hinsch indicated that *U-4* first became aware of *Thistle*'s presence when the sound of torpedoes was heard approaching from the port side.[11]

9.4.		
1705		Torpedo sounds from the port quarter. Evasive manoeuvre with hard starboard turn and 12kt. A trail of bubbles passes within 1cm of the bow. Alarm! Go to 40m. During the dive a further three torpedoes were heard. Subsequently four explosions.

The two boats remained close for several hours before losing contact with each other.

| 2000 | Qu. 3131 | There were repeated electric motor sounds detected. Considered the following: in darkness, the coast offers a very good background, so that even a large boat can remain undetected. We would then have a better horizon looking out to sea. Moreover, I don't suppose the enemy |

		will remain as close to us at night.
2217		Surfaced.
2400	Qu. 3131 NNW 3, Sea 2, dark night, good visibility.	Nothing to report.

Hinsch ordered his boat to the surface in order to recharge batteries, despite being certain that a British submarine remained in the area. After almost four hours on the surface, *U-4*'s lookouts were startled to see a submarine surface close by.

<u>10.4.</u>

| 0157 | Qu. 3123 | Off the starboard bow, a submarine surfaces very near, so that I cannot immediately shoot. Bow to the right, bearing 140°. Turned to starboard with both engines ahead full and the enemy is now directly astern of us. Tubes I and III clear.[12] |

U-4 continued to turn until in position aft of *Thistle*, which, apparently completely unaware of her presence, had drifted to a stop. No explanation exists as to why Haselfoot would have stopped his boat in these waters, even if he had convinced himself there was no longer an enemy nearby.

After that manoeuvre, we are now 600m from the enemy's position. The enemy appears to have stopped. 1st torpedo (G7a) fired with no lead. Due to the drifting of the target, the trail of bubbles leads right past the target's bow. The 1st torpedo thus misses. 2nd torpedo (G7e) is fired at approximate range of 400m with lead for a target going 5kt and a course of 70°.[13] Hit in the middle.

Thistle sank quickly. Nevertheless, Hinsch approached cautiously. He noted the same thing described by many other captains: the overwhelming, often sickening, smell.

| 0213 | Qu. 2989 | Big oil slick, very strong stench of oil. In the darkness, no wreckage can be recovered. Remained at the spot only a little time, |

then left the site on a course of
330° at 5kt. Reported success by
radio, message not repeated.

Dönitz, who expected to receive radio reports of all U-boat activity, knew
nothing of this success until *U-4* showed up in port without warning on
14 April. His log entry for the incident was typically laconic:

> *U-4* returned to Wilhelmshaven unexpectedly. It was unable to report the return
> passage owing to W/T breakdown. The boat destroyed an English U-boat in its
> position.[14]

That was all to the good, as far as Dönitz was concerned, but looking at the
operation against Norway as a whole, the news was anything but
satisfactory. The worst of it was the devastation the Norwegian campaign
had caused to his plans for the Tonnage War (*Tonnageschlacht*) against
Great Britain. For the entire month of April 1940, his U-boats had achieved
eight sinkings, including *U-4*'s sinking of *Thistle,* totalling slightly over
32,000 tons. Excluding two warships from that total, because in Dönitz
strategy the sinking of warships was of secondary importance, total
sinkings of merchant shipping were six ships of less than 31,000 GRT. At
that rate, Germany had no chance of winning the war.

To make matters worse for his U-boats, numerous chances for success in
the opening months of the war were lost due to torpedo malfunctions.
German torpedoes in 1939 could be set to explode on impact or to run
under a target and be set off by the ship's magnetic field. Neither worked
well. The magnetic fuse was far too sensitive, frequently leading to
premature detonations.[15] The impact detonator, on the other hand, was
overly complex and failed seemingly randomly.[16] The frustration was
palpable in Dönitz's log entries. His staff strongly suggested withdrawing
his boats from combat until the problems were rectified.

> It is quite clear to me that I must expect a further considerable number of
> failures . . . , but I have no other choice, unless I withdraw the boats altogether.
> But I cannot lay up the boats now, of all times, without damaging the whole arm
> to an unpredictable degree. As long as there is the chance of a small percentage
> of success, operations must be continued.[17]

He would be faced with a crisis of similar scale exactly three years later, but
would reach a very different conclusion.

CHAPTER 10

This War was Anything but Phoney

Doris and U-9

UNLIKE THE WAR ON LAND, which, with the exception of the Norwegian campaign, had been largely static since the conquest of Poland, in early 1940 the war at sea maintained a steady intensity as the two sides struggled for control of the North Sea and the waters around the British Isles. That quiet period in the land war, which lasted seven months, became known in the West as the 'Sitzkrieg' or 'Phoney War'.[1] For those men at sea in submarines, the war was anything but phoney.

The British, with bases along the western side of the North Sea, had no problem getting boats to the fight. The French, the other main combatant facing the Germans, had no naval base on the North Sea except Dunkerque. (This was not a major base, lacking the repair and refit facilities necessary to support a combat deployment; the closest such base was Cherbourg.) According to the terms of an Anglo-French naval agreement reached after the war started in 1939, the North Sea and Baltic were exclusively the responsibility of the Royal Navy. This situation had changed sufficiently by the end of the year that, at the urging of their ally, the French agreed at the beginning of 1940 to second eight of their seagoing submarines to Harwich, on the Essex coast, and later four more to Dundee in Scotland. There they would operate under the tactical command of Vice Admiral (Submarines) Max Horton, who was at that time Flag Officer Submarines in the Royal Navy, the British counterpart to Karl Dönitz.[2]

Four of the first eight boats were from the 13th Division based at Toulon (*Circé*, *Thétis*, *Calypso* and *Doris*). They were part of a group of twelve collectively known as the '*600-tonne*' class.[3] By 1940, these were obsolescent boats, being an average of 14 years old at a time when a 'generation' of submarine development could be measured in half that time. *Doris* was laid down in 1923, launched in 1927 and not commissioned until 1930. In typically French fashion, the technical parameters were determined by the navy, but the actual designs were generated by the building yards. The twelve '*600-tonne*' boats were allocated to three different yards, which each produced four boats. Two of the four boats of the *Circé* group were built by Schneider at Bordeaux (including *Doris*). They were the smallest and probably the least successful of the three variants. As a group, the *600-tonne* boats were considered to be very manoeuvrable and well armed for their size. They had a complex arrangement of torpedo tubes. There were two internal tubes at the bow, along with five external tubes (two at the bow, one at the stern and two tubes in a trainable mount built into the deck casing just aft of the conning tower). The external tubes could be loaded only in port, but three reloads were carried for each of the internal bow tubes. Unfortunately, these boats also quickly developed a reputation for poor lateral stability underwater and were notoriously cramped inside, with poor living conditions for the crew. They also had a reputation for mechanical unreliability. They were often laid up due to faults in one or more mechanical systems. Compared to the similarly-sized German Type VII design, which came along ten years later, *Doris* was significantly slower and less reliable.

At the end of 1939, all four *Circés* were completing refit at their normal base at Toulon and then, in February 1940, began working up, based temporarily at Bizerte in Tunisia. The commander of the group of four submarines was *Capitaine de corvette* (Lieutenant Commander) Jean Favreul, who was also captain of *Doris*. The refit and training cycle was cut short by the orders to report to Harwich. At the end of March, they headed into the Atlantic via Oran, stopping in at Brest on 4 April. There they replenished and made final equipment checks. They then crossed the Channel to Harwich in the company of *Orphée*, one of the '630-tonne' boats. At Harwich, they found the other three boats and the tender *Jules Verne*, which flew the flag of *Capitaine de vaisseau* (Captain) de Belot, who had overall command of the twelve French boats. The eight boats at Harwich were organised into the 10th Flotilla, alongside an equal number of Royal Navy submarines forming the 3rd Flotilla. Each boat made a brief training patrol from Harwich to familiarise themselves with the port and Royal Navy procedures. They then reported ready for assignment.

Conditions for the crews on the submarines, particularly the '600-tonne' boats, left much to be desired. The British were unable (or unwilling) to provide shore accommodation for the French crews, so, with the exception of the few who were assigned berths on *Jules Verne*, the French sailors lived on board their submarines.[4] To make matters worse, due to repeated air-raid alerts and the periodic need to degauss the boats, they spent more time at anchor in the middle of the harbour where the boats rocked constantly, than they did tied up at the pier or alongside *Jules Verne*. When Horton gave the French boats their first operational patrols, they were hardly in the best of condition.

There was no time to wait for these problems to be solved. This was a time when Horton needed all the help he could get. At the beginning of May 1940, it was clear that the 'Phoney War' in the West was coming to an end. All the signs pointed to an imminent Nazi move on France and the Low Countries. Despite having seen a copy of the German attack plan, the Allied leaders continued to believe that the upcoming campaign would resemble the opening of the First World War in the West, with a wide swing through Belgium by the Germans in order to get around the French frontier defences.[5] Confident they could stop the Germans on land, they remained concerned that the enemy might attempt to move troops by sea around the advancing Allied lines.

Horton's plan was to maintain a continual submarine blockade of the Dutch and Belgian coasts with all the boats at his disposal. These included not just Royal Navy boats and the French contingent at Harwich, but also a pair of Polish boats, which had escaped in September 1939, also operating under Horton's orders.[6] To add to the confusion, the Dutch navy operated a small number of well-designed and well-manned boats for service in the North Sea.[7] The Dutch remained stubbornly neutral up to the moment the Germans crossed their border, despite months of increasingly clear signs that the invasion was coming. The presence of Dutch boats in these waters further complicated an already complex situation, since it meant that it would be possible to encounter a boat that did not know the Royal Navy's recognition signals but was also not German. This caused Horton to issue strict orders to all boats that no submarine was to be attacked unless she could be identified as German beyond any doubt. He wanted no repetition of the tragic sinking of *Oxley*. These orders were received without enthusiasm by his captains. To achieve the kind of certainty Horton was demanding would require that recognition signals be exchanged or that an unidentified boat be approached closely enough to allow definite visual identification. Either way, if the unidentified boat was German, she would have been given the initiative in any engagement.

Regardless, *Doris* was ordered out on her first operational mission from Harwich, setting out on 19 April 1940 for a patrol off Helgoland. Within days, the mission was aborted due to the breakdown of *Doris'* port diesel, the boat limping back into Harwich on one motor. The failure was particularly serious. These boats had two-cycle diesels built by Schneider.[8] Two-stroke engines require a separate blower to clear exhaust from the cylinders, and it was this blower that failed on *Doris'* port diesel. Back at Harwich, the mechanics on *Jules Verne* concluded that the blower was irreparable and would need to be replaced, which would require replacing the entire engine block of the diesel. No such part was available in England and could only be found in France at Toulon. It was judged to be too large for rail shipment and would have to be sent by sea, a process that would take more than a month. The best advice the naval constructors in France could come up with was to feed the output of the starboard motor's blower to both diesels. The net effect would be incomplete exhaust clearance in both engines, so that neither would produce more than about half the designed power. The necessary vents were rigged and *Doris* reported ready for her next assignment at the beginning of May.

Any thought of waiting for *Doris* to be fully repaired was out of the question as far as Horton was concerned. Two other French boats had also suffered breakdowns. *Circé* had returned early from patrol with diving-plane problems, but these were at least temporarily resolved and *Circé* also reported ready. *Orphée* had an electric-motor failure that rendered her unable to manoeuvre underwater. The number of breakdowns occurring to the French submarines deployed to England was such that Admiral Darlan, the head of the French fleet, ordered an official investigation into what he suspected to be communist sabotage.[9] Given the signing of the Non-Aggression Pact between Berlin and Moscow in August 1939, it was easy enough for the leaders of the French military to believe in the existence of a conspiracy in which leftist workers in shipyards acted to weaken the forces facing the German threat.

With the German attack appearing daily more imminent, there was no thought of keeping *Doris* in port. Therefore, at 1530 on 7 May 1940, Favreul put *Doris* out to sea again, in the company of *Amazone* and HMS/M *Shark*. Doris' assigned patrol sector was a narrow rectangle bordered on the north by the 53rd Parallel, which intersected the Dutch coast just north of Den Helder, and extended south only about 15nm, yet any Dutch boat on its way to or from port would have to pass through *Doris'* zone.[10]

On the German side, there was, in fact, no intention of using naval forces as part of the invasion of the West. This was in part due to the absence of any necessity for a seaborne invasion, there being a long land border between Germany and the intended targets, and in part due to the heavy losses in surface ships during the Norwegian campaign. From Dönitz's point of view, the Norwegian operation had been a dismal failure on every count. It proved yet again what Dönitz firmly believed – that U-boats made terrible scouts and even worse escorts. They were too slow and too vulnerable to play that kind of role. In the restricted waters of the North Sea, they had nevertheless had multiple opportunities to attack Royal Navy ships, but the continuing torpedo failures had frustrated attacks again and again.[11] Further, the intensity of operations in the North Sea in April and May had left a high percentage of operational boats in need of yard work, overloading the ability of German shipyards to perform the necessary refits. It would be late May before a substantial number of boats would be ready for operations again, and when they became available, Dönitz was determined that they would be sent out into the Atlantic to resume the war on merchant shipping.

For all these reasons, Dönitz assigned exactly two boats to patrol in the southern North Sea at the beginning of May in support of *Fall Gelb* (the invasion of the West). They were both old Type IIB boats, *U-7*, assigned a zone off Rotterdam, and *U-9*, assigned the waters further south off Antwerp. *U-7*'s patrol was uneventful and resulted in no sinkings; *U-9* had a more exciting time.

At that time, *U-9* was under the command of *Oberleutnant zur See* Wolfgang Lüth. He was to become a highly successful commander and more that a little controversial, but, at the beginning of May 1940, he was taking *U-9* out on his fifth and last patrol in command of this boat. In the previous four patrols, he had taken *U-9* twice to the Scottish coast to lay mines and sink shipping in the Moray Firth, once to the Skagerrak hunting British submarines and once to Bergen in support of the Norwegian campaign. In these patrols, *U-9* accounted for three steamers by torpedoes and another was sunk by a mine laid in the Moray Firth nearly three months earlier. Dönitz was quite impressed with this last sinking, noting it glowingly in his *KTB* (especially since his sources of information somewhat exaggerated the extent of the success):

> According to radio intelligence reports, two steamers, one a 6,000 tonner, have run into the minefield laid by *U-9* in the Firth of Moray. This is further proof of the fact that such minefields, laid with the mines far apart, are successful in the long run.[12]

U-9 left Kiel on this patrol on 6 May. Two days later, she was passing Den Helder on the surface just before midnight on her passage south towards Antwerp. Lüth kept a particularly detailed log of that evening's events:[13]

8.5.40		
2227	Qu. 8271, starry night, moderate visibility, Sea 2, E 2, new moon	Surfaced, towards shore to the east are the lights of ten to twenty trawlers.
2350	Qu. 8277, starry night, good visibility, sea sparkling, dark night with new moon	Submarine with dimmed lights sighted to port, east of us, against the lights of the fishing boats. Distance: 3,000–4,000m. Prepared to attack, unfortunately I have the bright horizon to the west. Enemy steers reciprocal course approximately 320°, then comes around on a parallel course 140° and temporarily increases speed, so that its bow-wave becomes visible. I turn in order to line up my shot, just as the enemy turned towards me. Turned away in order to gain distance. Enemy turns again to a northwesterly course.
9.5.40	North of Ijmuiden	
0014	Qu. 8511, strong reflections off sea	Double shot with G7e – depth 2m, G7a – depth 3m and speed 30kt, range 700m, target speed 5kt, gyro angle 80°, aiming point 20m from bow, 30m from stern.[14]
		Own speed: port motor at slow speed because a bow wave would be highly visible. After 52 sec (780m), a loud detonation. Both torpedo wakes are visible. The G7e's wake runs a corkscrew course through the water, the G7a's wake runs straight to the aft edge of the tower.

Explosion is followed by a second stronger one. The column of fire reaches 25m high, the base whitish, the upper part red. A rain of sparks reaches 30–50m higher, smoke rises to 100m high before dissipating. Debris falls within 50m of the boat. Can see an oil slick of maybe 500m diameter. We approach the site; nothing more to be seen. Strong smell of powder and oil. Boat appeared to be about 1000t, had a comparatively low but long tower, seen from the side. Perhaps *Grampus* class.[15] Didn't notice a gun installed on deck.

0026   A second explosion was heard, but wasn't visible. Must be the G7e at the end of its run after 12 minutes.

Set course for Scheveningen, to fix the boat's position.[16]

Forty-five men lost their lives in *Doris*, including three Royal Navy sailors, an officer and two signalmen on board for liaison and to assist with communication with Harwich.

The sinking of *Doris* was one of the few submarine-versus-submarine encounters that was witnessed by another boat. The French submarine *Amazone* was patrolling the next sector to the north of *Doris* and was also on the surface recharging batteries. At 2318 on the 8th, the watch on *Amazone* reported that it: 'observed an immense ball of flame rise at the horizon and heard three strong explosions'.[17] This could have been nothing other than the destruction of *Doris*. Late in the day on 9 May, the Germans announced the sinking of an enemy submarine in the North Sea. The broadcast was heard in Britain and noted, but followed as it was just a few hours later by the German invasion of Holland and Belgium, it was not investigated. Over the next several days, *Doris* and *Amazone* were ordered to patrol closer into the coast. *Doris'* silence was noted but not yet considered a cause for concern. On the 12th, *Circé* was scheduled to relieve *Doris* on patrol, and *Doris* was ordered to report her position and confirm that she was returning to port. On the 15th, when no word had been heard from *Doris* after repeated attempts to make contact, Horton listed the submarine as overdue and presumed lost due to torpedo attack by a German submarine.

U-9's patrol did not end with the sinking of *Doris*. She was still in transit to her operational sector off the Belgian coast. There she sank two ships over the next several days before she was forced to make for Wilhelmshaven to replenish torpedoes and other expendables.[18] The replenishment was carried out overnight on 15/16 May and *U-9* put out again immediately to resume her patrol. Off Zeebrugge on 23 May, she sank the German freighter *Sigurds Faulbaums* (3,256 GRT), which had been captured by the British and was on her way to England under a prize crew. After completing this dual patrol on 30 May 1940, *U-9* returned to a training role, operating out of Danzig and Pillau until May 1942.[19] She was the second U-boat, after *U-24*, selected for transport to the Black Sea. She was disassembled, transported by canal, road and river, reassembled at Linz and sailed down the Danube to Constantia, where she formed part of the 30th Flotilla. There, she conducted twelve patrols and sank at least one more ship. On 20 August 1944, she sank alongside a pier at Constantia as a result of an air raid by Soviet naval aircraft. The Soviets raised the boat on 22 October 1944 and towed her to Nikolaev. At some point she was added to the Soviet naval list and given the name *TS-16*. There were plans to refit the boat and make her operational again, but after the war, there was no further need for an old, small U-boat and *TS-16* was stricken on 12 December 1946 and broken up.

Lüth went on to become one of only two U-boat men to receive Nazi Germany's highest military decoration, the Knight's Cross with Oakleaves, Swords and Diamonds (*Ritterkreuz mit Eichenlaub, Schwertern und Brillanten*).[20] He commanded three other boats after leaving *U-9* in June 1940, *U-138* (a Type IID) for two patrols, *U-43* (a Type IXA) for five patrols and *U-181* (a Type IXD2, the longest-range U-boat type) for two patrols, one of which lasted 205 days, the second-longest patrol of the war. He was considered to be an expert on crew psychology and, after his second patrol in *U-181*, was given command of the 22nd Flotilla, a training unit, at Gotenhafen in January 1944. In July 1944 he was put in charge of the *Marineschule* at Flensburg, where all *Kriegsmarine* officers were trained. Later that year, he was promoted to the rank of *Kapitän zur See*. He survived the war by only four days. One night as he entered the grounds of the school he still commanded, he apparently failed to answer a sentry's challenge and was shot and died instantly. He had been the second most successful U-boat commander of the Second World War, trailing only Otto Kretschmer, accounting for forty-six merchant ships totalling over 225,000 GRT and one warship – *Doris*. An ardent Nazi to the day of his death, he was given what was is believed to have been the last state funeral of the Third Reich, being carried to his grave by six Knight's Cross holders and eulogised by Dönitz himself. Dönitz stated after the war that he had intended to promote Lüth to command of the German U-boat force had the war continued into 1946.

The wreck of *Doris* was located by two Dutch divers in 2003. A formal wreath-laying was held above the wreck site aboard the French patrol boat *Pluvier* on 16 July 2004, attended by French, British and Dutch officers, including the son of *Capitaine de corvette* Jean Favreul, the retired *Capitaine de vaisseau* Jacques Favreul.

CHAPTER 11

What did ORP *Wilk* Hit?

THEIR HOMELANDS HAVING BEEN overrun by the seemingly unstoppable German *Wehrmacht*, the remnants of the navies of several nations fought on from Britain under the aegis of the Royal Navy. French, Dutch and Polish boats all operated in the North Sea after the fall of their native lands.[1] The bravery of these men, who fought on in a war they had already lost, a war they had every excuse to sit out, is exceptional by any standard.

The Dutch navy had been designing and building its own submarines since the early 1920s, perhaps the smallest country to develop an indigenous design capability.[2] By the time O 13 was laid down in 1928, Dutch submarine designs compared favourably with the best that any other nation was building and incorporated advanced features, such as welding of the pressure hull and, for the time, a strong anti-aircraft battery. They were building two basic types of submarine: big boats intended for service in the East Indies and smaller boats for coastal defence and operations in the North Sea. The former were designated with the letter 'K' (for *Koloniën* – Colonies) and a Roman numeral; the latter were designated with the letter 'O' (for *Onderzeeboot* – Underwaterboat) and an Arabic numeral.[3] O 13 was designed for North Sea operations. She was a 500-ton boat with range adequate for multiple weeks of patrolling in the narrow waters. She had spent the last years of peacetime training and making the occasional port call. During this time, she was twice involved in collisions with surface vessels. When war came to the Netherlands in May 1940, O 13 was on patrol off the Dutch coast. After only two days of combat and repeated air attacks, she put into Portsmouth. Two days later, the Dutch army surrendered and O 13 put herself under British orders. After one brief patrol in the English Channel in late May, O 13 transferred to the submarine base at Dundee, home of the Royal Navy's 2nd Flotilla, arriving there on 7 June. On 12 June 1940, she departed Dundee on her second combat patrol under British orders. Her assigned sector was in the North Sea due west of the entrance to the Skagerrak.

Unlike the Dutch, who had a centuries-long tradition of shipbuilding, the Poles had a much more limited naval history. Not only did the Poles not possess an indigenous submarine design capability in the 1920s, they did not really have any yards with the necessary experience and facilities to build submarines. Given the chaotic history of the nation, that is certainly easy to understand. When Poland was reconstituted by the Versailles Treaty, it again had access to the Baltic and the need to rapidly build up a naval force capable of at least minimal coastal defence. One of the first steps taken was ordering three large submarines from France in 1926. These were to be minelayers, enlarged versions of the *Saphir* class the French were building for their own navy. One of the three, *Wilk*, escaped from the Baltic when war broke out in 1939 and arrived at Rosyth on 20 September. There she was placed under British orders. *Wilk* underwent refit for two months and then transferred to Dundee and began making combat patrols, mainly to the Norwegian coast.[4] On 19 June 1940, she left Dundee, heading across the North Sea towards a patrol zone in the northern approaches to the Skagerrak.

Shortly after midnight on 21 June, at a point approximately two-thirds of the way to her assigned sector, *Wilk* hit something.[5] That is virtually the only thing that is certain about the events that occurred that night. The collision staggered the boat and lifted her stern out of the water. She immediately started back towards England and the dockyards at Rosyth. Able to make no more than 3 knots, it took *Wilk* four days to cover the approximately 250nm. Once at Rosyth, the ship was immediately docked, where examination showed that the damage to the boat was in fact not terribly extensive. The external plating at her bow was crumpled and bent in, but not enough to endanger the pressure hull. Both propellers had been damaged; the port propeller had only one blade remaining. Other than that, the damage was minor. She was repaired in just a few days and departed for her next patrol on 10 July.

The question as to exactly what *Wilk* hit has never been satisfactorily answered. According to the First Officer, Commander Boleslaw Romanowski, who had taken over the bridge at midnight, the sea was calm and the night clear and the boat was making 3 knots in order to leave no visible wake.[6] Less than 20 minutes into the new watch, the signalman, who was watching the forward starboard quadrant, called out that he had sighted a ship at 10° off the bow. Romanowski, who had the best binoculars, quickly found the silhouette of a small ship in the dark. He estimated the range to be approximately 300m. Aware that he was too close to fire a torpedo, he decided to ram the target. He rang up full speed on both diesels and turned the boat towards the target. Only then did the lookout shout out that he now identified the target as a U-boat. Romanowski looked again and confirmed this identification. The U-boat began to dive even as *Wilk* headed for her at increasing speed. The collision occurred just a few seconds later. *Wilk* hit the U-boat forward of her deck gun as the deck of the U-boat was just submerging, sending a shock through the boat. She rode up and over the foredeck of the target and then a second jolt was felt as her screws hit the U-boat's conning tower, lifting *Wilk*'s stern out of the water. A mass of white foam remained at the point of impact. Other than that, nothing remained on the surface to mark the site.

On the strength of this account, *Wilk*'s crew was feted on return to port. The sinking of a U-boat by a Polish submarine was certainly worth celebrating. The official report of the incident filed at the time basically supported Romanowski's claim. It reported that the crew of *Wilk* at first concluded that they had encountered a mine because some on board had heard what sounded like a wire scraping along the hull before the second shock which damaged her screws. This was supported by the fact that this was in a part of the North Sea that was regularly mined. Just a few weeks earlier, the Polish submarine *Orzel* had been lost in a German minefield laid just northwest of *Wilk*'s reported position.[7] The idea that *Wilk* had hit a mine was later discounted because there had been no flash or plume of water seen, as would normally accompany the explosion of a mine, and also because the damage to *Wilk*'s stern was limited to her propellers, which is hardly consistent with the damage a mine would have caused even if the detonation were at some distance or of a low order. Further, there is no way that a mine explosion could also explain the damage to *Wilk*'s bow. The report concluded that, while it was possible that *Wilk* had struck a mine, it was more likely that she had run into something solid, like a U-boat.

Nevertheless there were sceptics who had doubts about the whole affair. First they questioned Romanowski's decision to ram the other boat even before it had been identified. Submarines are fragile surface craft. Anything that interferes with their ability to submerge exposes their weaknesses. Ramming was considered to be a tactic of last resort. *Wilk* had two deck guns: a 100mm cannon and a 40mm anti-aircraft gun. These could have been rapidly brought to bear and one good hit would have been sufficient to render a U-boat incapable of diving. Obviously, it is impossible to know when *Wilk* was sighted by the U-boat. Even the largest U-boats then in service could dive in only 40 seconds, so she might have been able to submerge before any rounds could be fired, assuming she saw *Wilk* at the same time she was sighted.[8] Nevertheless, the common wisdom around Dundee at the time was that it would have been better to let the U-boat escape than to run the risk of being disabled and unable to submerge with a U-boat, even a damaged U-boat, in the vicinity. Most agreed that if Romanowski and his boat had been British, he would have been cashiered for the rashness of his decision.

Rumours persisted that a secret report was written that concluded that *Wilk* had hit a shallow rock or a wreck, but that this was never made public in order not to damage the morale of the Free Polish forces fighting alongside the British. Indeed, many years later, a veteran of *Wilk*'s crew published an account which claimed that the crew believed they had hit a rock.[9] The area where the collision occurred is known as the Great Fisher Bank, a large region of relatively shallow water now extensively explored for oil. While this region is shallow for an area of open ocean, its mean depth is still between 40 and 60m and there are no known areas so shallow that a submarine on the surface could scrape the bottom nor were there known wrecks close enough to the surface.

The possibility existed that *Wilk* had struck some floating object other than a U-boat, such as a small boat or a large piece of debris. The likelihood that there would have been a small boat with no lights in those waters must be considered remote. Also any boat or floating object large enough to have caused the damage seen on *Wilk* would almost certainly have left some debris on the water when in fact none was seen.

One other possibility was mooted at the time. *O 13* was supposed to have ended her patrol and to be returning to port by 21 June. She had been radioed on 19 June, ordering her back to base, which should have put her back in Dundee two days later. She never acknowledged receipt of that order, which in itself was not that unusual, but she also never showed up at Dundee and, on 25 June, she was reported overdue and presumed lost. Depending on when she left her patrol sector to head back to base, she might well have been in close proximity to *Wilk*'s position on the night of 20/21 June. Some at the time, and since, believe firmly that the submarine *Wilk* hit, if *Wilk* indeed hit a submarine, was *O 13*.

There are no strong reasons to believe this is true and at least one reason not to. Romanowski's account specifically mentions hitting the submarine just forward of her deck gun. This would seem to eliminate *O 13* as a possible victim because *O 13* had no deck gun. This class of submarines had retractable twin anti-aircraft guns, located in one mount each in platforms extending from the fore and after ends of the conning tower. Nothing on the deck. The Royal Navy never considered it likely that *Wilk* was the cause of *O 13*'s loss. Post-war investigation by the Dutch navy agrees. The official reason for the loss of *O 13* given by the Dutch is that she most likely strayed into one of the minefields in that region of the Great Fisher Bank, probably the German '16B' field on 13 June.

It was also suggested at the time that Romanowski might have made up the entire U-boat incident. That it never happened. This thesis states that *Wilk* had struck some object and that the lookouts had simply failed to see it, and further that, in the few moments before the captain, Commander Boguslaw Krawczyk, rushed to the bridge, the watch had agreed among themselves on a fictional account of ramming a U-boat rather than admit to gross negligence. This sounds almost plausible except for a few details. Romanowski must have seen something prior to the impact, otherwise how could the order to increase speed and change course be explained? Those could not have been invented after the fact.

But, if *Wilk* had not hit *O 13* and the possibility that she had struck a mine or an underwater obstruction was vanishingly small, then what did she strike? Could Romanowski's story in fact be true? According to German records, there were only two boats which might possibly have been in the vicinity of *Wilk* on the night of 20/21 June.[10] One was *U-99*, under the legendary Otto Kretschmer, which was starting out on her first patrol. She was known to be in the North Sea but not particularly close to *Wilk*'s position because she radioed back to base on the 20th requesting permission to put into a Norwegian port to drop off a sick crewman.[11] The next day, she reported having been attacked by an aircraft and damaged to the extent that she was returning to Wilhelmshaven, where she arrived on the 24th.[12] The only other candidate U-boat was *U-122*. Little is known with certainty of that boat's movements after she left Kiel on 13 June. She stopped in at Helgoland the next day to top off her fuel tanks.[13] Her assigned patrol area was off Cape Finisterre at the northwest corner of Spain. Her route to get there would have been up the North Sea, around the north of Scotland and down to the west of Ireland. There is some speculation that *U-122*, a new boat also on her first combat patrol, might have suffered a mechanical problem while outbound through the North Sea and was returning to Germany through the area where *Wilk* was passing.[14] However, what little evidence exists of her movements all points away from an encounter with *Wilk*. A large British steamer, SS *Empire Conveyor* (5,911 GRT), was lost in the approaches to the North Channel to unknown causes on 20 June. *U-122* is credited by most sources with this sinking because she broadcast a weather report at 2300 on 20 June from a position not far from that sinking.[15] The best research indicates that *U-122* was either lost in a collision with a steamer on 22 June or in a depth-charge attack by the corvette HMS *Arabis* on 23 June, both incidents occurring south of Ireland. Neither incident left conclusive evidence of a sinking, so *U-122*'s loss is officially recorded as unknown in location and cause.[16] No other U-boat was lost in June 1940.

That would seem to leave no strong candidate for the object that *Wilk* hit, but the fact that *Wilk* hit something is the only certainty in this whole tale. Looking at all the objects *Wilk* could have struck, there remains the task of deciding which of this set of unlikely possibilities is the least implausible. In this author's opinion, the least unlikely of these choices is O 13. If she had not been mined on 13 June, she would have proceeded to her patrol zone and would have operated there until being recalled on the 19th. She then might well have been passing through the same waters as *Wilk* the next night.

The argument has been made that O 13 wouldn't have attempted to dive in front of an unknown submarine as close as *Wilk*, since she would have taken almost a minute to submerge.[17] But that argument assumed that O 13's captain, Ltz. I E H Vorster, would have correctly surmised that *Wilk* intended to ram. At *Wilk*'s original speed of 3 knots, it would have taken her more than three minutes to cover the 300m separating the two boats. Even with Romanowski's order to go to full power, *Wilk* must have taken at least a minute-and-a-half to reach the object. Had Vorster decided to submerge upon sighting *Wilk*, and assuming he saw the Polish boat at the same time or soon after being sighted, his decision would have made more sense, and he might not have realised until too late, if ever, that diving might have left his boat fatally vulnerable to the bow of the oncoming *Wilk*. The inconvenient detail that O 13 did not have a deck gun cannot really be explained except to recall that eyewitness accounts of sudden traumatic events often later prove to be wrong in major details.

This is, of course, all surmise, since it cannot be determined with any certainty, given all that is currently known, whether *O 13* was even there. Groups in both Poland and the Netherlands have announced plans to look for the wreck of *O 13*. If it is found, the issue may then be resolved, as the damage caused by a collision would look very different from that caused by mining. Until then, *O 13* and her crew of thirty-four, including three British seamen, rest on the floor of the North Sea.

Wilk returned to combat immediately and continued making regular combat patrols in the North Sea until being taken out of service in April 1942. During at least nine combat patrols, she seems to have had no successes, except perhaps that submarine in June 1940. On 19 July 1941, Commander Krawczyk committed suicide and was replaced as captain by Commander Brunon Jablonski. After the war, the Poles officially turned the boat over to the Royal Navy and she remained in British hands, though not in active service, until she was returned to Poland in October 1952, towed to Gdynia and shortly after that was sold for scrap.[18]

CHAPTER 12

One Busy Week

29 July to 3 August 1940

As far as Karl Dönitz was concerned, the war changed dramatically on 7 July 1940. On that day, *U-30*, at the end of a month-long patrol, put into the recently captured French port of Lorient and officially freed Germany's U-boat force from the strategic stranglehold of the British Isles. Throughout the First World War and the first 10 months of the Second, Great Britain sat like an impenetrable barrier across the exit routes from Germany to the open ocean, forcing U-boats to risk passing through the dense minefields and patrols in the Channel or make the long journey around Scotland and face the hardly less formidable defences across the northern passages.

The fall of Norway began to give the Germans more strategic options, but it was June before the last Allied troops had been driven out and the Germans could begin exploiting the ports along Norway's long coast. But it was the capture of the French Atlantic coast, and the ports of Brest, Lorient, La Rochelle, St-Nazaire and Bordeaux, that really opened wide the door to the Atlantic for Germany's U-boats. After this, the North Sea would become a transit route rather than a battleground for the Germans, something to be survived as the increasing number of new U-boats left German yards and headed for deployment with the new flotillas created at the French ports. But for the British the importance of the North Sea, if anything, increased, because these narrow waters represented the best hope for stemming this flow before it dispersed into the open Atlantic and overwhelmed the fragile convoy system. Add to this British concern about a possible invasion and it is understandable that the Royal Navy would want to maintain a steady presence of Allied submarines along the Norwegian coast, particularly outside harbours such as Trondheim and Bergen, which served as emergency repair yards and replenishment depots for U-boats as well as potential invasion ports.

U-boats were ordered to keep close to the Norwegian coast as they made their transit through the North Sea. They were to follow one of two parallel routes, codenamed 'Blue' and 'Green'. These were considered safer than other routes because they were as far as possible from Great Britain, which reduced the effectiveness of British air patrols and brought Royal Navy anti-submarine vessels within range of German aircraft and smaller naval units operating from Norwegian bases. This German air and surface activity was a mixed blessing, however, as there were numerous instances of U-boats being attacked by friendly forces. Heading up the North Sea away from the coast was seen as a less safe option because the middle of that sea was being filled with minefields laid by one side or the other. Commenting on 21 July 1940 on the presence of a German anti-submarine group sweeping across the mouth of the Skagerrak south from Stavanger, Dönitz said:

> *U-43* is in the same area on her way home and *U-5* on her way out. The position of the new minefields northwest of our own mined area forces the U-boats to take the route along the coast of Norway on the way in and out. Here they are exposed to danger from enemy submarines and our own aircraft in close escort of formations. The commander-in-chief of the *Luftwaffe* has been requested to instruct all aircraft again that, in areas that are not declared open for anti-submarine hunting, only such submarines may be attacked as are unmistakably identified as enemy.[1]

This all explains, in part, the upsurge in submarine encounters along the Norwegian coast at the end of July 1940. Some must be credited to luck, good or bad, that put one submarine in the way of another with such frequency. It was doubtlessly good fortune that allowed so many of the encounters to end with no harm done. Only one of seven encounters in the span of six days actually resulted in the sinking of a submarine.

The sequence started with a chance encounter on 29 July between a small Type IIC U-boat on her way home from her last combat patrol and a veteran workhorse from the 3rd Flotilla at Harwich. The U-boat was *U-62*. She was a very new boat, having been commissioned only 10 days before the start of 1940. Since being declared ready for combat in February, she had completed five patrols, putting into Bergen on 27 July after a 17-day mission that took her around Scotland and as far as the northwest tip of Ireland, where she sank a large freighter.[2] That was supposed to be the end of her combat career. All the new U-boats that would finally start arriving later in 1940 would need trained crews so it was time to pull at least some of the small Type II boats out of combat and put them to the training duties for which they were originally intended. When she left Bergen early on the 29th, she was on her way to an overhaul at Kiel and then assignment to *21. U-Flottille* at Pillau. Nevertheless, these waters were dangerous, and her captain, *Kapitänleutnant* Hans-Bernhard Michalowski, kept her submerged all day as she made her way south along the coast, finally surfacing that night near Egersund to recharge her batteries.

Not that it was ever really dark at night in late July at that latitude. Even at midnight, the sky remained bright enough to detect a boat at a considerable distance, even through a periscope. It was by this light that HMS/M *Triton*, on her last North Sea patrol, had seen *U-62* coming out of Bergen at 0330 that morning. Unable to line up a shot before the U-boat, which apparently saw *Triton*'s periscope, moved off to the west at high speed, she had reported the U-boat's course and all British boats to the south had been alerted. HMS/M *Sealion* was patrolling submerged near Egersund and spotted the U-boat soon after she surfaced at 2033 that evening. *Sealion* had been commissioned exactly five years before *U-62* and was a bigger and far better-armed boat. Against the U-boat's three torpedo tubes, *Sealion* had six; against *U-62*'s 20mm gun, *Sealion* had a 76mm mount. But generally, when one submarine encountered another, it was not the strength of armament that prevailed. Rather, it was a question of which one spotted the other first and could get off the first shot. It rarely took more than that to decide the matter, unless that shot missed.

That, unfortunately, was exactly what happened. Lieutenant Commander Ben Bryant lined up his shot at *U-62* and fired a salvo of three torpedoes at 2049. These apparently missed, because *Sealion* then fired her remaining three ready torpedoes at 2054. The U-boat's lookouts by now had seen *Sealion*'s periscope and then sighted the wakes of the approaching torpedoes. Turning to avoid the torpedoes, which passed barely 100m on either side, Michalowski was stunned to see the British submarine surface 2,500m away and crewmen come out on deck to man her gun. Despite the fact that *U-62* had been on the surface for just 27 minutes and had only started recharging batteries, he ordered a crash dive. Taking on the bigger submarine in a gun duel was not an option in Michalowski's opinion. *Sealion* got off several shots as *U-62* was diving and then found herself in the uncomfortable position of being on the surface with crewmen on deck while an enemy submarine was known to be submerged nearby. Bryant had no choice but to order an immediate dive. Once submerged, *Sealion* was unable to pick up any trace of *U-62*. The U-boat obviously just wanted to get away and was moving at silent speed.[3] The two boats lost contact with each other. The first encounter of this extraordinary week had ended with no damage or loss of life.

More than two days passed before the next encounter. During that time, Dönitz looked hard at the danger his boats were facing on the coastal passage up the North Sea and decided to try another route. On 1 August, referring to a list of U-boats on outward passage, he wrote:

> They have been ordered to use route '1', for the following reasons:[4]
> 1) In the area north of route 'Blue' and off the Norwegian coast, English ships have repeatedly appeared, attacked our forces (*Luchs*, *U-62*, transports) and have been attacked by our own patrol forces and aircraft.[5] At least *U-1* was definitely torpedoed in this area.[6]
> 2) The danger in this area is the greater because for some time the U-boats have entered and left on this route only.
> 3) In view of these <u>known</u> dangers on the northerly route, route '1' appears to be the safer. It has not been used for some time. At the time when a change was contemplated, a chart captured from *Seal* showed two circles entered in this route, which led Flag Officer North Sea Defences to suspect that there were enemy minefields within these circles.[7]

In fact those circles were not minefields; they were patrol sectors for submarines. Late in July, Admiral Horton assigned two submarines to cover those sectors. He reasoned they were uniquely suited to cover these particular sectors, which had seen no enemy activity in recent months. These were new submarines not yet fully worked up to the rigours of combat, the Dutch submarines *O 21* and *O 22*. Both boats had been launched in the months preceding the German invasion of Holland, but neither was complete nor had they undergone normal acceptance trials when the Dutch found themselves at war. Both were hurriedly manned and commissioned on 10 May 1940 and two days later they sailed for Portsmouth rather than surrender to the Germans. Neither carried any armament or had ever submerged. They were hurriedly completed at Rosyth and carried out their first diving trials in June. They then began an abbreviated cycle of training and reported ready for duty at the end of July. Horton thought he was giving them relatively quiet sectors for their first combat patrols. *O 21*'s sector was east and slightly south of Rosyth, almost exactly midway between Scotland and Denmark; *O 22*'s was to the north and a little east of her sister's. Each was a circle, 20nm in diameter.[8]

Heading their way was the first U-boat to be redirected up route '1' rather than route 'Blue'. This was *U-60*, a Type IIC, under the command of an energetic and popular young captain, *Oberleutnant zur See* Adalbert Schnee.[9] He would go on to great success as a commander and on Dönitz's staff; but that was in the future. When he took *U-60* out of Kiel on 30 July 1940, this was only his second patrol in command of a U-boat and he had not yet attacked an enemy ship. He was eager to meet the enemy, but he had no idea he would encounter them so soon. The route he had been assigned, route '1', ran directly through both *O 21*'s and *O 22*'s patrol sectors.

Both Dutch submarines sighted *U-60*. *O 21*, having the more southerly sector, saw Schnee's boat first. At 1602 on 1 August 1940, the Dutch boat, which was submerged, sighted *U-60* on the surface. For 13 minutes, Ltz. I J F van Dulm, commanding *O 21*, tracked the U-boat as it made a steady 12 knots. At 1615, he launched two torpedoes at a range of 2,000m. Both torpedoes ran true; both missed. Schnee was unaware that he had been attacked. Van Dulm watched in frustration as the U-boat continued out of sight, varying neither speed nor course. Schnee continued to the north, directly into the sector patrolled by *O 22*. Ltz. I Johan Willem Ort, commanding *O 22*, picked up the sound of distant screws at 1800. Coming to periscope depth, Ort spotted a conning tower low on the horizon, certainly that of *U-60*. The range this time was too great for an attack and the U-boat once again continued unmolested.

This busy day was not yet over. *U-34* was nearing the end of her last war patrol of the Second World War. This was the same boat that sank the Spanish *C-3* in December 1936, and she had been fully employed ever since.[10] The same need for training boats that led Dönitz to order *U-62* back home caused him to decide that *U-34*, one of the few remaining Type VIIAs still in combat, should also head for the Baltic and duty as a school boat. This last patrol had been a long one. She had left Wilhelmshaven on 22 June for a patrol in the Western Approaches and the Bay of Biscay, under the command of *Kapitänleutnant* Wilhelm Rollmann, who took over the boat in October 1938 and led her on all six of her war patrols.[11] In less than a year of war, *U-34* had accounted for twenty-one merchant ships totalling 97,699 GRT and two warships, a record that earned Rollmann the Knight's Cross. Twelve of those victims had been sunk on this last patrol. *U-34* had only one more torpedo onboard as she rounded the Orkneys and started down the North Sea to Germany and home.

HMS/M *Spearfish* had been just as active in her 11 months of war. She claimed to have been attacked on the first day of the war and to have survived a long, tense stand-off with a U-boat before the war was 24 hours old.[12] While that story is open to doubt, there is no question that what happened later that month was all too real. On 22 September 1939, *Spearfish* found herself in a trap. On patrol in the Skagerrak, Lieutenant Eaden had perhaps chosen to stay on the surface too long after first light and *Spearfish* had been sighted by German patrol boats. Eaden then made his second mistake, more serious than the first; he chose to take his boat down and let her settle on the bottom. What followed was 12 or more hours of intense depth charging by the Germans. At one point, the explosions were coming about one every two minutes. The boat was taking a beating, but the crew held up remarkably under the strain. Every time a leak would appear, men would be there to staunch the flow, then lie back down wherever there was room in an attempt to preserve as much air as possible.

When the clock told Eaden it was dark above, he passed word through the boat that they were going to try to make a run for it. The only good news was that there had been no more explosions for several hours, so there was some hope that the Germans had given up, but, except for this, the outlook was bleak. The engineer declared that both diesels were out of action, as was one of the two electric motors. The radio seemed to be done for. Even worse, he had no confidence that their ballast tanks would hold air when they tried emptying them. And then, even if they got to the surface, the Germans might still be waiting. But, given the alternative, they had to give it a try. The gun crew was gathered around the conning-tower hatch, ready to man the deck gun as soon as they broke water. Scuttling charges were set up and fused, and, just in case, the code books and secret orders were burned.[13]

The tanks miraculously held air and the boat rose to the surface. Even more miraculously, the horizon was clear; there were no Germans in sight and they had slightly over six hours of darkness to try to get clear of the coast. With no radio, no diesels and only one motor, they would not get very far, and when dawn broke, they would not be able to dive – not at least, not if they wished to surface again. But the men worked like their lives depended on it and, during the night they managed to get both diesels working, albeit at nowhere near full power. Right about dawn, they got the radio operating too, so they were able to inform Horton of their plight. The Royal Navy's reaction was to send major units out into the North Sea, which had the effect of drawing the attention of the *Luftwaffe* away from *Spearfish*, which was able to limp back to Rosyth. There she was docked and the damage assessed. She would be out of action until April. When *Spearfish* again went to war, it would be under the command of a new captain, Lieutenant Commander J H Forbes.

Under Forbes, *Spearfish* went out again on 5 April 1940. Five days later, she was off the Skaw when she was detected by German anti-submarine forces and again subjected to a day-long attack, but she kept moving and was eventually able to surface just after midnight on the 11th.[14] There she was greeted by the sight of a large warship moving across her bow at high speed. Forbes decided to take a chance on a quick shot with all six ready torpedoes. Fired with minimal set-up at a range of 2,500m, the torpedoes had little chance of hitting, but luck was with *Spearfish* that night and five minutes later Forbes was greeted by the sound of an explosion. Satisfied they had done what they could, *Spearfish* headed away westward at best speed. The torpedo had hit the German 'pocket battleship' *Lützow*, collapsing her fantail and putting her out of the war until January 1941.

Spearfish conducted patrols again in May, June and July and, on the first day of August 1940 was outbound from Rosyth, headed on a northeasterly course towards the Norwegian coast. *U-34*, now well clear of Scotland, was turning southward. Their paths would cross that evening. According to Rollmann's log, the first thing they saw was *Spearfish*'s periscope shears:[15]

1.8.	Qu. 2784 AN, SWxW 2,
1200	cloudy, good visibility

Northern North Sea	1817 – 2° off the starboard bow, a small vertical object like a periscope or mast is clearly visible on the horizon.
	1819 – dived. Soon it is obvious that this is an approaching submarine straight ahead. The small vertical object we saw can now be seen to be two tall telescope supports standing well above the horizon.
1848	Gradually the tower of the boat comes into view. Enemy course 30°. The type of the boat is hard to identify.
	Begin to set up the attack. Recognise the submarine as *Sterlet* class.[16] Bearing and speed are hard to identify and calculate.

Rollmann increased speed to close the distance between the boats more rapidly.

| 1904 | Qu. 4281 AN | Fire towards the bow, after making an approach at high speed and AK because the range was too great. Depth 2m, target speed 9kt, bearing 100°, aiming point 20 m from bow, running time 1:46 given a range of 1,610m. |
| | | Very powerful explosion that shakes the boat noticeably, in spite of the great distance. Assume the boat's torpedoes detonated. Boat sank in 2–3 seconds. Large pieces of debris flew through the air. |

Without hesitation he surfaced and inspected the site of the sinking.

1905 – surfaced, immediately proceeded to sinking site. There was one man swimming, who was brought aboard at 1910. At 1908, large air bubbles come to the surface. Almost no oil is visible. Only wooden debris can be seen floating nearby. The sunken boat was '*Spearfish*'.

From interrogation of the prisoner: Able Seaman (Torpedo Tester) Victor Williams. Nothing else worth mentioning was found at the site of the sinking. Reported sinking by radio.

According to British sources, the sole survivor was indeed an Able Seaman; his name was William Pester and he had joined *Spearfish* barely minutes before she had left Rosyth the night before, and thus was able to tell the Germans little more the boat's name. Another source gives yet another name for the survivor, Able Seaman W Victor.[17]

Whether Williams or Pester or Victor, he was now confined to a bunk on *U-34*, headed south towards Germany and a POW camp. He was very lucky to be alive. Lucky that his assignment on his new boat included lookout duties, lucky that the watch had been his when *Spearfish* surfaced that night and lucky that he alone among the lookouts had managed to pop up to the surface to be rescued by Rollmann. His luck would hold just a bit longer. The next day, 2 August, at 0750, O 22 spotted a U-boat, this time heading south. She was *U-34*, still on the surface, headed down route '1'.

The morning was foggy, but Ort had no trouble getting a bearing on the U-boat. Unfortunately, the target was well out of range and Ort chose to let it pass undisturbed. Pester lived to witness *U-34*'s arrival at Wilhelmshaven a day later and the awarding of the Knight's Cross to Rollmann by Dönitz.

Later on the 2nd, around 1600, *O 22* sighted yet another U-boat, this one heading north on the surface, much larger than *U-60* and larger even than *U-34*. Determined not to let this chance slip, Ort fired two torpedoes at very long range, 3,600m. Not surprisingly, both missed. The U-boat continued on, again unaware of being attacked. This boat was either *U-37* or *U-38*. Both boats had left Wilhelmshaven on the 1st and would have been in the vicinity of *O 22* at that time. An RAF Hudson reported attacking two U-boats in close proximity to each other about two hours before in the area between *O 21*'s and *O 22*'s patrol zones. Both Dutch boats reported hearing two heavy explosions at the time. Neither *U-37* or *U-38* thought the incident important enough to report back to Dönitz. *U-60* put into Bergen the next day to replenish fuel and supplies and then immediately headed out into the Atlantic.

That same day, 3 August 1940, the last and perhaps strangest of the encounters occurred in this strange week. *U-46*, a Type VIIB boat under the command of *Kapitänleutnant* Engelbert Endrass, had departed Kiel two days earlier outbound to the Atlantic, via Bergen, on route '1'. Endrass was only on his second patrol as a captain, but he was well experienced, having served as Günther Prien's IWO on *U-47* from December 1938 until May 1940, including the famous October 1939 raid on Scapa Flow. At 2200 on 3 August, Endrass had his boat on the surface, heading north at moderate speed, recharging batteries.

HMS/M *Triad*, under Lieutenant Commander George Salt, was another of the large 'T' class submarines, like *Triton* and *Thistle*. *Triad* was relatively new, having been commissioned two weeks after the war began. On her second patrol, in late November 1939, she became disabled while in a gale off the Skaw when her after hydroplane shaft failed. The damage was such that she was unable to manoeuvre and she began drifting towards the Norwegian coast. Two destroyers and a tug were sent out to try to get *Triad* under tow, but the weather refused to co-operate and eventually all four vessels ended up taking shelter in Mastrafjorden, near Stavanger. This was in Norwegian waters and, at the time, Norway was still neutral in the war, so a local patrol boat showed up shortly and informed them that they would have to leave. The British commander countered that he was aiding a disabled vessel, which allowed him to freely enter territorial waters and that the submarine was incapable of navigation and would need to be docked before she could attempt to cross the North Sea. After some negotiation, it was decided that, once the storm abated, the submarine could be towed into Stavanger and there she would have 48 hours to be repaired.[18] Arrangements were made with the Rosenberg Verft at Stavanger to dock *Triad* the next day and, with temporary repairs made, she left Stavanger on 2 December and was towed across the North Sea, not without

Above: Heino von Heimburg commanded *UB-15* (the Austrian *U-11*) and then *UB-14*, both *UB-I* class boats. The truly small dimensions of these boats can be seen from the relative size of the crewmen on deck. More than half of the boat's complement of fourteen officers and men are up top, including the pair of officers standing on the roof of the conning tower in the open bridge. (NHC)

Below: Two French submarines at Mudros in the Aegean Sea, the submarine base for Allied operations in support of the Gallipoli campaign, 1915. The one on the right is a large boat, possibly the steam-powered *Archiméde*. On the left is an *Émeraude* class boat, possibly *Turquoise*.

Above: *Turquoise* in Turkish hands. She was renamed *Müstecip Onbasi* and given a Turkish crew, but she was never recommissioned. She was simply too old and her petrol engine was considered too dangerous. She remained dockside at Constantinople for the rest of the war and was used to charge the batteries of German boats operating there.

Above: E.20 seen in 1915, probably while still working up. She was lost in the Sea of Marmara in November of that same year. (NHC)

Left: Georg Trapp, not yet knighted and years away from world fame as the father of his singing family, commanded the Austrian submarine SM *U-5* in the Adriatic in 1915. This was a Holland-designed boat of very small size. Note the simple canvas hung on the railing around the exposed conning position, which provided only minimal protection against the elements when the boat was surfaced.

Above: The Italian *Nereide* was sunk by Trapp's *U-5* on 5 August 1915 off the island of Pelagosa in the Adriatic. Note the dorsal rudder and the long, low superstructure that was common on many early submarines. (NHC)

Below: The Spanish *C-3* was a somewhat enlarged version of the American post-war 'S' class boats. Note the built-up tower structure with its multiple horizontal flanges intended to deflect wind and spray. Experience during the war had shown that submarines operated in all weather conditions and crewmen needed some protection against the elements if they were to remain effective in less than calm conditions. (NHC)

Above: *U-34* was a Type VIIA U-boat. One distinguishing characteristic of the type was the single, external torpedo tube visible at her stern. She is seen sometime after her encounter with *C-3*. This can be determined from the paint scheme, medium gray with a large white numeral, which was adopted by U-boats not long before the start of the Second World War. At the time of her meeting with *C-3*, she was painted light gray and had a large black numeral on her tower that was painted out for Operation 'Ursula'. (via Ken Macpherson)

Right: ORP *Sep* is seen completing at the RDM yard, Rotterdam, in 1938. When the Dutch tried to hold onto the boat as war approached, she was literally stolen by her Polish crew and sailed to Gdynia. Damaged by a torpedo fired by *U-14* in the Gulf of Danzig on the first day of the war, she was interned in Sweden and not returned to the Poles until 1945. (NHC)

Below: HMS/M *Oxley* was old by the time the Second World War began, but she was still an effective fighting boat. She is seen in the 1930s, probably in the Mediterranean, where she served until 1938. Note the main gun carried high in the forward superstructure, a feature common of larger Royal Navy submarines through the war years. Note also the distinctive bow shape that *Triton* might have been able to identify, had either boat been luckier.

Above: A ceremonial raising of the national ensign at the anchorage of the *U-Bootschulflottille*, probably in 1935 at the standing-up of the flotilla. *U-1*, *U-4* and *U-2* can be identified by the large black numbers on their towers. *U-4* went on to claim the first sinking of an enemy submarine by a U-boat in the Second World War. (NHC)

Below: *Doris* is seen, probably in 1937, in the markings of the Neutrality Patrol that supposedly was preventing foreign intervention in the Spanish Civil War. Vessels participating in this sham were marked in stripes of the nation's colours. *Doris* has broad vertical stripes of blue, white and red (from the bow) painted on her tower. Note the external torpedo tubes near the bow, in the rotating mount aft of her island and at the stern. (Jacques Favreul)

Above: The last known photograph of *Doris*, showing her as she appeared while working up off the coast of North Africa in 1940. (Jacques Favreul)

Below left: One of the several German U-boats involved in the remarkable series of encounters in late July–early August 1940 in the North Sea, *U-62* was a brand new Type IIC at the time. In the foreground in this view, probably from 1941, she has retired from combat and is performing training duties as part of the 21st Flotilla based at Pillau. Note the tactical sign, a downward-pointing arrow, on the tower's side. (John Albrecht)

Below right: Most U-boats carried an emblem of some type painted on the tower. These emblems were most often chosen by the captain, though a wise commander picked one approved by the crew. *U-67*'s was a mountain goat over a five-pointed star, seen here painted on the tower side. The artistry of the rendering is quite exceptional. It is impossible to be certain of the colours. The goat is probably white and gray (or tan), with a black outline. It is possible that the hooves are brown. The colour of the star is even more problematic. If this was shot with panchromatic film, it is probably yellow; if shot with orthochromatic film, it is almost certainly blue.

Right: Looking every bit the bold seafarer, *Kapitänleutnant* Günther Müller-Stöckheim poses after a patrol by his boat, *U-67*. His uniform is highly non-standard. His jacket is a variant of British battledress, large quantities of which were captured by the Germans in June 1940, and which was prized by U-boat crews because it was relatively warm and dry in bad weather. It was no doubt also considered rather stylish, being cut shorter and tighter than the German uniform jacket, and Müller certainly appears to be style-conscious, with his scarf tied like an ascot. (This jacket is probably not of British manufacture in that it is zippered rather than buttoned; it was likely custom-tailored for Müller.) Note the metal badge on his cap which reproduces the boat's insignia. Note also the marked absence of insignia of any kind on his jacket, except for the epaulets.

Left: Merten's *U-68* arriving at Lorient on Christmas Day 1941, at the end of the long patrol that included the encounter with *Clyde* in September and the rescue of over 400 survivors from *Schiff 16* and *Python*. She flies five victory pennants from her periscope, the long, thin commissioning pennant from the commander's flagpole and the national ensign from the aft end of the *Wintergarten*. The boat in the background is *U-A*, which participated with *U-68* in the rescue operation.

Right: *U-95* arriving at Lorient after the completion of her sixth patrol, on 20 September 1941. The off-duty crew is drawn up on the afterdeck; lines and fenders are on deck, ready to secure the boat. Schreiber and the rest of the officers are on the bridge; he is the one in the white cap with his back to the proceedings. (It was traditional for the IWO to bring a boat into harbour at the end of a patrol.) The boat's only distinguishing mark is the 'snorting bull' insignia of the 7th Flotilla.

Below: There were a dozen survivors of the sinking of *U-95* by *O 21* on 28 November 1941. They were picked up by the Dutch boat and landed at Gibraltar. Schreiber is the balding, somewhat portly gentleman leading his surviving crew across the brow, under the watchful eyes of *O 21*'s crew. (NHC)

Above: *O 21* as she appeared in May 1944 on her way to the US Navy's Philadelphia Navy Yard and a long-overdue major refit. The dark area in her side-plating forward of her tower is the location of her trainable external torpedo tubes. (USN)

Below: HMS/M *Unbeaten* tied up at the Lazaretto, just north of Valletta, Malta. The area was regularly bombed by the *Luftwaffe*, making for short and less-than-restful stops between patrols. (via Ken Macpherson)

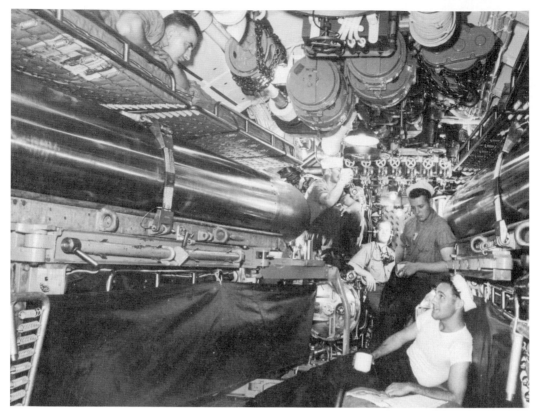

Above: The forward torpedo compartment of USS *Corvina*, in August 1943.
Off-duty crewmen relax on top of and under a pair of torpedo reloads.
The talker with his headset and the junction box on his chest is the only man
on duty in this view. The rear door of the middle of the three portside
torpedo tubes can be seen under his right elbow. At this time,
Corvina was still working up on the US east coast,
so the crew could afford to relax and the boat
could be kept neat and clean. (NARA)

Left: Compare the shot of *Corvina*'s forward torpedo room (*above*) with this view of the same compartment in an unidentified Type VII U-boat on patrol. Off-duty crew are trying to grab some sleep. The most junior of the 'Lords' slept on the deck. This may looked cramped and messy compared to the spacious compartment on *Corvina*, but this actually shows the U-boat at its most comfortable. Only after the first two reload torpedoes, which were stored above the deck, were loaded into the tubes could the lower row of bunks be let down and the relative comfort seen here be achieved. (via Ken Macpherson)

Above: HMS/M *Telemachus* riding high. The crew is drawn up on deck, meaning this is some important occasion, perhaps her commissioning in late 1943. Two of her five external torpedo tubes can be seen, one at her bow and one facing aft behind her tower.

Below: This photograph and the next give another chance to compare the interiors of the most and the least spacious of the submarines produced in large numbers during the Second World War. This time the difference is much harder to see. (Both shots were posed during similar training exercises.) The two planesmen on USS *Batfish* maintain the boat's attitude underwater under the watchful eye of an officer, who stands between the periscope well and the chart table. These men controlled the forward and aft diving planes by means of the large wheels. The indicators in front of them indicated the angle of the planes and other dials showed the boat's pitch angle and depth. (NARA)

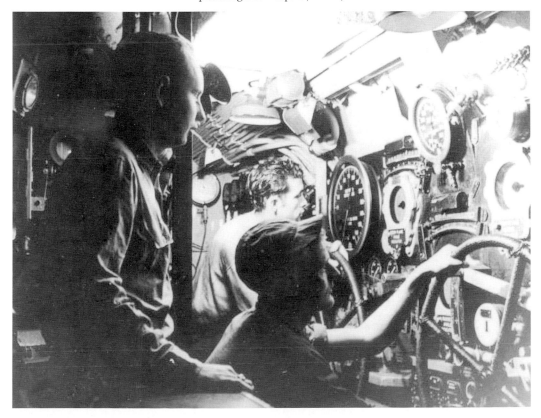

Right: Two crewmen man the planes in the control room of an unidentified Type VII U-boat. Like their American counterparts in the previous photograph, they have wheels to control the planes and very similar read-outs that tell them the state of the boat. Their hands are not actually on the wheels, but rather are on a pair of levers that moved the planes electrically. The wheels were there only in case the servo-motors failed. (*Gato* class submarines had hydraulic assist for the planes, so the planesmen on *Batfish* did not work any harder than the Germans.) It may not appear so from these photographs, but the control room of a Type VII was significantly smaller than *Batfish*'s.

Left: *Batfish* on her return to Pearl Harbor on 3 March 1945. She flies victory pennants like German boats and a war flag like Royal Navy submarines. Antennas for her two main radars can be seen. The old SD air-search radar antenna is on top of the aft-most mast. It looks like a cross-bar with two short aft-pointing whips. This radar was being replaced on all boats as they came in for refit with the much improved SV microwave radar. The oval antenna just forward of the SD is for the SJ surface-search set, also in the microwave band. The short stub antenna pointing forward at the level of the cigarette-smoking crewman in the shears was for the APR-1 radar intercept receiver. (NARA)

Above: USS *Batfish* as she looks today in a sea of grass, Muskogee, OK. Her outer torpedo-tube doors have unfortunately been removed as part of the process of 'safing' the boat for public display. (USN)

Below: While trying to reach a patrol zone off Perth, Australia, *U-537* was sunk by USS *Flounder* in the Bali Sea on 9 November 1944. This view earlier in the war shows the boat with the rather primitive German FuMO 29 fixed-array radar antenna attached to the front of the tower and covered in canvas. Below that is the boat's insignia, the five interlocking Olympic rings. That symbol was adopted by the naval academy crew of 1936, and therefore often became the insignia of boats captained by members of that crew. Peter Schrewe adopted that symbol for his boats not because he was a member of that crew – he was of the Crew of '34 – rather because he was on the sailing team that competed in the 1936 games. (John Albrecht)

Above: The boat that sank *U-183*, the last U-boat sunk by another submarine in the war, was USS *Besugo*, seen here off Mare Island, CA, on 24 July 1945. She has just completed a major refit and is in perfect late-war condition with the 5in/25cal gun on her after deck, a pair of 40mm Bofors AA guns on her cigarette decks and the late war SJ/SV radars. (NARA)

Below: After the war, most surviving Second World War vintage submarines in the US Navy were modernised under the GUPPY programme. The two submarines seen here at Monaco after an ASW exercise in February 1956 are USS *Irex* (inboard) and USS *Grenadier*. They had somewhat similar conversions to streamline their towers, but *Grenadier* has also received a bow form quite similar to the German Type XXI's, while *Irex* retained her original pointed stem. Three years later, *Grenadier* would achieve fame within the US Navy for 'holding down' a Soviet 'Zulu V' diesel ballistic missile submarine until she was forced to surface off Iceland. (USN)

Above: A 'Zulu V' diesel-powered ballistic missile submarine, the type of boat 'held down' by *Grenadier* is seen in November 1970. The two 'Scud-A' missiles she carried fired from tubes that extended up through the aft end of her large sail. The submarine had to surface and extend the missile partway out of the tube in order to launch. (USN)

Below left: The notorious 'Hotel' class SSBN *K-19* earned the nickname 'Hiroshima' for a string of accidents, one involving a coolant leak from one of her nuclear reactors. This photograph was taken from a US Navy reconnaissance aircraft after one of those accidents, this one involving a fire caused by leaking hydraulic fluid, which ultimately killed twenty-eight crewmembers, on 29 February 1972. (USN)

Below right: USS *Swordfish* was one of the early nuclear submarines, the second in the *Skate* class, essentially *Tang* class boats with nuclear propulsion. As such she did not have the more rounded hull form of later US submarines. She may have had a hand in the sinking of the *K-129* – or maybe not. (USN)

Right: One of the more notorious Cold War 'incidents' occurred between USS *Tautog*, a *Sturgeon* class nuclear attack submarine, and *K-108*, also known as 'Black Lila', an *Echo II*-class SSGN. NATO was very interested in the *Echos* because they fired a supersonic anti-ship cruise missile that threatened American aircraft carriers, on which NATO's sea power was based. *Tautog*, seen here in this undated photograph, was assigned the task of shadowing *Black Lila* to learn as much as possible about the characteristics of the Soviet submarine. *Tautog* perhaps followed too closely, as the two boats collided in June 1970. Comparing *Tautog* to *Swordfish* seen in the previous view shows the so-called 'teardrop' hull form of later US attack submarines, which had no flat deck for surfaced operations. (USN)

Left: This US Navy photograph shows an unidentified 'Echo II' class submarine on the surface. There were twenty-nine of this class built, so it is unlikely that this is in fact *Black Lila*, but this gives an idea of her appearance. The four notches along each side of her hull indicate the aft end of a missile canister that would be tilted up to fire one of the 'Shaddock' missiles. The notches were to vent the exhaust of the missile's rocket booster. (USN)

Right: A view from astern of an 'Oscar II' class nuclear cruise missile submarine, as seen 1 June 1994. *K-141 Kursk*, which sank in a controversial incident on 13 August 2000, looked like this unidentified boat. Note the extreme breadth of this boat – the 'Oscar II' boats are second only to the 'Typhoon' class boomers as the largest submarines ever built. Her twenty-four cruise missiles are carried twelve to a side in forward-slanting tubes, two under each of six square hatches on either side of her tower. (USN)

attracting the attention of the *Luftwaffe*, arriving at Rosyth on the 4th.

Soon after 2200 on 3 August 1940, *Triad* was heading to the southwest, on her way back to Rosyth, after a brief patrol in the coastal waters north of Bergen. She was still submerged, though Salt had alerted the watch that, as it was finally getting dark, they would soon surface for the evening. While making his final periscope checks before giving the order, Salt was surprised to see a U-boat silhouetted against the rapidly fading western horizon. He realised immediately that he had no chance to line up a shot with torpedoes; the U-boat was too far away and moving much faster than his submerged boat. He had two choices: accept his bad luck and let the German slip away in the darkness, or surface his boat and give chase. The former was the 'correct' thing to do. Apparently, that night, Salt was not particularly concerned with the correctness of his actions. He wanted that U-boat.

At 2225, Salt passed word through the boat to prepare for surface action. The gun crew assembled in the control room, ready to head up the ladder right after the captain and the watch, and the off-duty seamen assigned to 'hump' the 4in rounds from the ammunition lockers up to the deck gathered behind them. One final glance through the periscope and Salt gave the order. A minute later, the boat was on the surface, the diesels were fired up and the gun crew was bringing the gun to bear on the barely visible outline of *U-46*.

The first shot rang out at 2230. The Germans were taken completely by surprise. Approaching from the east, *Triad* had been invisible to *U-46*'s lookouts until the muzzle flash and the whine of a shell passing overhead alerted them to her presence. No more than Michalowski had five days earlier, Endrass had no intention of fighting a gun duel on the surface, especially not with an enemy he could not see. He ordered a crash dive, which took his boat below the surface in about 25 seconds. *Triad* had gotten off three shots. None had hit.

From Salt's point of view, the situation had just gotten dramatically worse. Now he was on the surface and the enemy below, potentially hunting him. He had no choice but to take his boat down as well. Now both boats were equally blind. As there was no need for concealment, Salt ordered his soundman to try to find *U-46* with active sonar.[19] Liking this situation even less, Endrass decided that the best option was to exit the area as rapidly as possible, so he ordered *U-46* back to the surface and pointed his boat to the east at the best speed she could muster. On *Triad*, Salt heard this manoeuvre and realised that this time they had no chance of catching the German in the dark. He brought *Triad* back to the surface and put her back on course for Rosyth. *U-46* continued eastward and, the next day, put into Bergen for supplies and repairs to a defective radio transmitter.

We will not encounter Endrass again in these pages. Even though he went on to become one of Germany's best-known and most successful U-boat commanders, his success was in the open Atlantic where the chances of meeting an enemy submarine were minimal. Salt and *Triad* will appear again in this book, in another encounter even stranger, if that is possible, than the one just described.[20]

The high rate of encounters, as well as the inability to contact *U-25*, which had also been instructed to use route '1', left Dönitz in a quandary.[21] Now none of his routes through the North Sea were safe. He wanted minesweepers to escort his U-boats but there were too few available for this. He ordered his boats back to the coastal routes and instructed that they be escorted up the Danish coast whenever possible.[22] Beyond that, they were on their own.

Only one submarine was lost to another during this bloody week, but few of those that survived this week would survive the war. The rate of attrition on the boats and men who fought in the first year of this war was horrendous. Often, the only ones to survive were those, like *U-62* and *U-34*, that were reassigned to training duty.

CHAPTER 13

Fratricide III (and more)

R.SMG *Gemma* and R.SMG *Tricheco*; HMS/M *Upholder* and
R.SMG *Ammiraglio Saint Bon*

AS A THEATRE OF OPERATIONS, the Mediterranean could hardly have been
more different from the North Sea or, even more so, the North Atlantic.
Where those seas are cold and unpredictable, given to storms even in
summer and absolutely brutal in winter, the Mediterranean tends to be
relatively placid for most of the year. Violent weather is rare and the sea is
in some places as warm as bath water. Not that this made it an easy place
to fight a war in submarines. In many parts of the sea, the water is shallow
and so clear that a submarine can be tracked from the air while submerged.
Being so narrow, there was no part of the sea that could not be covered by
air surveillance, even from the earliest days of the war.[1]

Despite the inherent problems of fighting a submarine war in the
Mediterranean, its strategic importance made it a battleground from the
first day of the war. The British, with important bases at either end
(Gibraltar and Alexandria) and in the middle (Malta), and their ally France,
with a major base at Toulon, had no intention of ceding control of the sea
to the Italians, who had the advantage of an excellent central strategic
position. There was too much at stake, particularly after the fall of France
left Great Britain alone to contest Italian access to North Africa. Neutral
merchant traffic rapidly disappeared from the Mediterranean at the start of
the war, but fierce battles for control of the sea lanes and the air above them
continued as the British, from Malta, tried to stem the flow of troops and
supplies to Africa, and the Axis tried to starve and bomb the island into
submission. If Malta fell or was simply neutralised, the Axis forces in North
Africa could be rapidly built up to the point that they could easily conquer
Egypt and disrupt the global strategic picture.

At times, it must have seemed as if there were as many submarines in the
Mediterranean as there were targets.[2] The Royal Navy had flotillas at
Alexandria, Gibraltar and formed a flotilla at Malta in January 1941.[3] In
late 1941, the Germans established bases at Salamis and La Spezia, from
which as many as twenty-three U-boats operated at any one time.[4] The
Italians maintained submarine units at La Spezia, Taranto, Naples and
Messina, and also based boats at Leros in the Aegean and at numerous other
smaller ports in Italy, Libya and Tunisia. When they entered the war in June

1940, the Italians had 115 submarines, but, of these, fewer than sixty were fully operational and eight of those were based in the Red Sea or the Indian Ocean. During the war, the Italians attempted to participate in the Battle of the Atlantic, maintaining a contingent of ocean-going submarines based at Bordeaux, known as '*Betasom*', starting in September 1940. As many as twenty-seven boats operated from Bordeaux at any one time. Still, the majority of Italian submarines operated in the Mediterranean.

With this many submarines plying these narrow waters in search of a limited number of targets, it is not terribly surprising that it was a killing ground for submarines. As many as sixty U-boats were lost in the Mediterranean.[5] Approximately forty-five British submarines were sunk there. The Italians lost approximately seventy-six submarines in the Mediterranean. The Greeks lost four. Thus it would appear that at least 185 submarines were sunk in the Mediterranean during the Second World War. Of that total, twenty-one were lost in encounters with other submarines.[6] One of that total was lost in an encounter with a submarine of her own navy.

The submarine *Gemma* was one of the third group of boats known to the Italians as the *Bernardis* 600-type. This referred to the designed surface displacement of 600 tons. As such they were boats of similar size to the very successful German Type VII boats and the British 'U' class, and were designed to fulfill the same requirements, namely to provide good offensive capability over short-to-medium ranges in a boat that could be built faster, cheaper and in larger numbers than bigger ocean-going boats. Like their German and British counterparts, the 600-type boats were generally successful. Testing done on *Gemma* when she was serving in the south showed that the 600-type boats had a tendency to pitch badly at periscope depth in rough weather and to leak toxic coolant from their air-conditioning systems.[7] Eventually, these problems were either solved or the crews learned to cope, and the boats became popular for their manoeuvrability and relatively powerful armament.

Before the war, *Gemma* had served in the Red Sea and Indian Ocean based at Massaua and had served as part of Italy's submarine blockade of Republican Spain during that country's civil war.[8] When Italy entered the war in June 1940, *Gemma* was under the command of *Tenente di Vascello* (Lieutenant) Guido Cordero di Montezemolo and operated out of Leros. She conducted three brief patrols in the Aegean or south to the Egyptian coast, all without success. On 30 September 1940, *Gemma* left Leros on her fourth patrol, one of three submarines assigned patrol sectors between 1 and 8 October in the narrow straits between the islands of Kasos and Karpathos, one of the primary sea lanes between Alexandria and Athens. *Gemma* was assigned the northernmost of the three sectors. The other two submarines, which had the central and southern parts of the passage, were *Ametista* and *Tricheco*.

Tricheco was a bigger boat than *Gemma*. She was an earlier generation of the *Bernardis* design and suffered from a variety of problems that had been ironed out by the time *Gemma* was built. These included, most seriously, a tendency to roll in any kind of seaway, even when submerged. The boats were retrofitted with saddle tanks, which seems to have largely solved that problem. They also suffered from excessive pitching on the surface, which was resolved by changing the shape of the external bow structure to incorporate more freeboard and a larger flotation tank. As modified, they became useful boats and were employed extensively in the Mediterranean and later in the Atlantic. Under the command of *Capitano di Corvetta* (Lieutenant Commander) Alberto Avogadro di Cerrione, *Tricheco* formed the southern end of the patrol line east of Crete.

Each submarine had a discrete sector to patrol. As long as every boat stayed in her own sector and never crossed another's sector without adequate warning, there should have been no problems. The system depended on good communications. If communications became sloppy problems could arise, which is exactly what happened. It started on the third day of patrolling, 3 October 1940. No shipping had been sighted by any of the three boats and *Gemma* was ordered to a new sector. The other two boats were not moved, nor were they informed of *Gemma*'s move. *Gemma*'s new sector was one island further east, in the waters between Karpathos and Rhodes.

This should have caused no problems, as all three boats were supposed to cease patrolling on the 8th and head back to base. However, on the night of the 7th, with the full knowledge of Leros, *Tricheco* left her sector. She had an injured crewman who needed immediate medical care and she was ordered to return to base along the eastern coast of Karpathos. As far as anyone on *Tricheco* knew, this course should have been clear of any friendly submarines, but in fact it passed through the western end of *Gemma*'s new sector. *Tricheco* was not informed of this fact and should not have needed to be, because orders had been generated two days earlier ordering *Gemma* home immediately. She should have started home on the 5th. Unfortunately, due to a clerical error those orders were never sent, so *Gemma* was still patrolling her sector as midnight passed and it became 8 October. Not only was she still on patrol, but, by pure bad luck, she was at the western limit of her sector, within sight of Karpathos. Thus it was that at 0115, close to the fishing village of Kira Panagia, about midway up the east coast of Karpathos, Avogadro di Cerrione sighted the silhouette of a submarine on the surface where none should have been. He reasoned she could only have been British or French and, fearing that the other boat might fire first, Avogadro di Cerrione ordered two torpedoes fired at the unknown boat. Both hit, the target disintegrated and disappeared instantly beneath the waves. There were no survivors. Only after *Tricheco* came up to the site where the other boat had been and examined the debris did it become clear who the victim had been.

That could have ended the story, a tragic case of miscommunication and bad luck, but instead it takes an ironic twist. A form of justice would be served upon *Tricheco* in the unlikely form of Lieutenant Commander

Malcolm Wanklyn and his boat, HMS/M *Upholder*, perhaps the most famous submarine commander and submarine in the history of the Royal Navy.[9]

Wanklyn and *Upholder* were famous long before they crossed paths with *Tricheco*. He had already been awarded the Victoria Cross, the first such award to be given to a Royal Navy submariner in the Second World War.[10] The action for which he was awarded that honor involved an attack on a strongly defended Italian convoy. He took *Upholder* through the ring of escorts and attacked the four large troopships inside the ring with his last two torpedoes, sinking *Conte Rosso* and causing the other three to turn around and head for harbour. Over 1,300 Italian soldiers lost their lives.[11] It was the equivalent of fighting and winning a major land battle, but not a single British life was lost in the process.

That incident took place in late May 1941. After commanding a pair of old submarines on missions in the North Sea in the opening months of the war, Wanklyn was put in command of the new 'U' class boat *Upholder* and took her to the Mediterranean in December 1940, where they joined the 10th Flotilla being formed at Malta. The boats of the 10th Flotilla spent minimal time in port because constant air attacks on Malta made time spent on patrol seem more peaceful. The number of patrols mounted rapidly. The sinking of *Conte Rosso* occurred on what was already *Upholder*'s seventh patrol. In September, *Upholder* sank two more large troop transports and deprived the *Afrika Korps* of yet more soldiers.[12]

By the end of 1941, Wanklyn had accounted for nearly 100,000 GRT of shipping, as well as two destroyers, making him easily the most successful British submarine commander. He and his fellow captains of the 10th Flotilla had become so good at stopping the flow of men and supplies to Africa that the Italians were driven to desperate measures.[13] These included employing warships as high-speed transports. Of particular note was the decision to use four of the newest, largest submarines the Italians possessed for this duty, the '*Ammiragli*' (Admirals) class, which came into service in late 1941. These had been designed for extremely long-range, extremely long-duration missions.[14] To achieve this, they were large and fast, displacing over 1,650 tonnes on the surface, making them very nearly the same size as the large 'fleet' boats with which the Americans fought in the Pacific. With their size and large fuel bunkers, the '*Ammiragli*' class seemed ideally suited to transport desperately needed supplies to North Africa.

So it was that *Ammiraglio Saint Bon*, when she became operational in October 1941 under the command of *Capitano di Corvetta* Gustavo Miniero, was fitted to hold multiple small fuel containers and loaded with 153 tons of petrol. She left Taranto on 10 October headed for Bardia.[15] She completed this mission successfully, but not without excitement, being attacked from the air several times. This pattern was repeated with further missions in November and December carrying supplies to Bardia, Derna and Benghazi.[16] On 3 January 1942, she left Taranto once again loaded with petrol and munitions. The delivery this time was to be made at Tripoli, further west than her previous destinations, so it was decided that, rather than take a straight-line course across the Mediterranean, which would bring her too close to Malta, she would follow an evasive route, heading down the Calabrian coast as far as Reggio, turning north through the Straits of Messina, following the northern coast of Sicily west and then turning south to Tunisia and following that coast to Tripoli.[17] A clever plan, but ultimately vain because chance put another submarine near the northern exit of the Straits of Messina early in the morning of 5 January.

Given the intense pace of operations from Malta and the inability to relax between patrols, the Royal Navy had decreed that 10th Flotilla captains need not make more than fifteen patrols before being relieved. Yet Wanklyn asked to stay on and he seemed so relaxed to Captain G W 'Shrimp' Simpson, the flotilla's commander, that Simpson had no hesitation allowing him to take *Upholder* out again, for her and his twentieth patrol, on the last day of 1941.[18] Knowing that Auchinleck's offensive had pushed Rommel back, *Upholder* was sent to the western tip of Sicily to hunt for enemy traffic to Tunisia. There she expended seven of her load of eight torpedoes on a large tanker without being able to sink her, and was heading back to base along the northern coast of the island. Having surfaced after dark on 4 January, she ran eastward through the night, hoping to find a suitable target for the one torpedo left in her tubes.

According to Wanklyn's post-action report, *Upholder*'s lookouts sighted a submarine about a mile off in the very first pre-dawn light, about an hour before sunrise, approaching at high speed from the west. This makes no sense. *Saint Bon* should have been headed away from *Upholder*. Regardless, the other boat was making more speed than *Upholder* and would soon overtake her. Wanklyn had only one option and he took it. He ordered a crash dive, while swinging the boat through a 180° turn to bring his torpedo tubes and his remaining torpedo to bear.[19] When the pursuing boat saw this manoeuvre, she apparently started to turn and presumably began to dive, but she was still very much on the surface and was now broadside on when *Upholder* settled at periscope depth and Wanklyn was able to line up a snap shot at the other boat.[20] At 0542, *Upholder*'s last torpedo was fired. With the range down to less than half a mile, it took well under a minute for the torpedo to cover the distance to the target. The resulting explosion was described as being nothing short of spectacular, as 155 tons of petrol and munitions were detonated by the torpedo's warhead. Fifty-seven members of *Saint Bon*'s crew died instantly.

Amazingly, there were three survivors. *Upholder* picked up a watch officer, along with two petty officers. The story they told explains some, but not all, of the mysteries of *Saint Bon*'s behaviour that night.[21] They explained that they were part of the gun crews that had been manning *Saint Bon*'s two 100mm guns and were preparing to open fire when *Upholder* had dived. *Saint Bon* had clearly sighted *Upholder* well before she was seen, which makes sense as *Upholder* would have been silhouetted against the brighter eastern horizon while *Saint Bon* was still invisible against the darker western sky. The survivors could not explain the biggest mystery, which is why Miniero had chosen to chase after *Upholder* and initiate a gun battle when he could have slipped away to the west unseen. Clearly, being loaded with a highly explosive cargo and with a simple mission to deliver that cargo safely and return his boat to base, avoiding an engagement with an enemy submarine would have made sense. To choose to do the opposite seems either impulsive or insane, unless Miniero believed he had no other choice.

Under what circumstances might Miniero have concluded that to engage *Upholder* in a gun battle was the least dangerous course he could choose? When Miniero sighted *Upholder*, he was faced with a difficult decision. Even though the other boat showed no sign of having seen him, could he simply continue towards the west? Could he entrust the safety of his boat to the assumption that he hadn't been seen, when the other captain could be playing a elaborate ruse? A prudent commander might well choose to make no such assumption and act as if he had been sighted.

Then what could Miniero do if his boat had been seen? He might have attacked with torpedoes from long range, while the other boat continued on a steady course. After all, his boat was equipped with no less than fourteen torpedo tubes; but that assumes he had torpedoes with which to attack and there is some reason to believe he might not have. Then he might simply have submerged and hoped that he could escape underwater, but that option, especially if he was without torpedoes, left him entirely at the mercy of the skill and daring of his enemy. Not a pleasant prospect. That left only one other choice, a surface gun attack.

Regardless of the reasoning, Miniero committed *Saint Bon* to make such an attack. Apparently his plan was to approach bow-on at his best speed, swing his boat broadside at the last moment and hope that rapid fire from his two guns might disable *Upholder*. It would appear his plan worked right up to the last moment. He brought *Saint Bon* almost close enough and was just about to open fire, according to the survivors, when *Upholder* started to turn and dive. Assuming he ordered a crash dive at the moment *Upholder*'s manoeuvre was noticed in the dim light, how much time would it take to get two gun crews and the regular watch below deck, three hatches closed and secured and his big boat submerged? Enough time for Wanklyn to line up and fire his snap shot? That would appear to be the case. Regardless of the reason for *Saint Bon*'s actions, the end result was a spectacular explosion and another success for the Royal Navy's most successful commander.

When he got back to Malta, Wanklyn was ordered to take a break. *Upholder*'s twenty-first patrol was under the command of his first lieutenant, but Wanklyn eagerly resumed command upon her return. He seemed to thrive on the tension that caused many other brave men to fray at the edges. After three more patrols in January and February, he was informed by Simpson that orders had come from above, that he would be allowed just two more and after that, he would return to England for rest and reassignment. He took *Upholder* out from Malta on 14 March 1942 on his twenty-fourth patrol in command of the boat, headed for Brindisi in the southern Adriatic at the northern exit from the Straits of Otranto, a place where he had had good success in the past.

Four days later, the boat was at periscope depth in the middle of the day, watching the swept channel into the harbour when he sighted a small coastal freighter. He decided that this was too small a target for any of his limited number of torpedoes and chose to wait and see what came next. He was rewarded for his patience. A large submarine was sighted riding high in the water. The shallowness of the target would make this an iffy shot, so Wanklyn took his time and manoeuvred to within 600m before he fired a spread of four torpedoes. The first two hit, one amidships and one aft; that was enough to finish off the target. He learned later that his victim had been *Tricheco*, under a different commander, but otherwise the same boat that had sunk *Gemma* 18 months before. In the meanwhile, *Tricheco* had conducted multiple war patrols, uniformly without success. *Gemma* had been her only 'victory'.

The sinking of a second enemy submarine put Wanklyn in an elite group of commanders who had sunk more than one enemy boat. He was not to have the enjoyment of this success for long. On his next patrol, which was to have been *Upholder*'s last before returning to England, the boat and her entire crew were lost. Much is unclear concerning the details of her sinking. Wanklyn wanted to return to Brindisi one more time, but Simpson insisted he patrol off Tripoli, which was considered a quieter, safer sector. Anyway, there were a couple of secret agents to be landed in Libya. These men were put ashore and then *Upholder* met up with another 'U' class boat, *Unbeaten*, to transfer the agents' handler, since *Unbeaten* was heading to Gibraltar and then home rather than returning to Malta. This was the last time Wanklyn was seen alive. Sometime in the next few days, *Upholder* was sunk, probably on 14 April 1942, probably by depth charges dropped by the Italian torpedo boat *Pegaso*.[22] In his career, Wanklyn had sunk more enemy shipping and warships than any other Royal Navy submariner.[23] None was perhaps more fitting than his last sinking, the submarine *Tricheco*.

CHAPTER 14

The Gunfighters

HMS/M *Triad* & R.SMG *Enrico Toti*

AFTER HER ABORTIVE GUN DUEL with *U-46* on 3 August 1940, HMS/M *Triad* returned to Rosyth, there to undergo a brief refit prior to reassignment to the 1st Flotilla based at Alexandria.[1] *Triad* was a big boat, probably not best suited to operations in the Mediterranean, except that her longer range would come in handy on her transit to her new base. Anyway, in the fall of 1940, there were too few of the more appropriate 'U' class boats to go around.

So Lieutenant Commander George Salt took her out from Dundee on 29 August, taking the long route around Ireland and arrived at Gibraltar on 6 September. The stay there was brief. *Triad* left port on 11 September and patrolled in the northern Tyrrhenian Sea for nearly a month, until she put into Malta on 2 October. Very little is certain about her movements after that. It is known she left Malta on 9 October 1940 and that she was supposed to arrive at Alexandria and officially join the 1st Flotilla on the 20th. Some reports say that her assigned patrol sector was off the coast of Libya and that while in that sector she struck a mine and was lost with all hands. Other reports, which have gained credibility over the years as more evidence has been uncovered, say that *Triad*'s patrol sector was in the Ionian Sea, off the coast of Calabria. In this version, her loss was not due to a mine.[2]

The cause of *Triad*'s loss was most likely the Italian submarine *Enrico Toti*. At the end of the First World War, Italy, like the other Allied nations, picked out a few of Germany's surrendered U-boats for further study. One of the boats chosen by the Italians was *U-120*, a boat of a size and capability far exceeding anything they had built to date. Having in mind the defense of their established colonies in the Horn of Africa, and their ambitions in Abyssinia, the Italians looked at the range and the armament of *U-120* and decided they needed boats of similar capabilities.[3] Except for replacing the mine tubes with a pair of aft torpedo tubes, and increasing the length and displacement to add an auxiliary cruising diesel, the Italian boats were virtual repeats of the German design. Four boats were built as part of the *Balilla* class in 1927 and 1928, including *Enrico Toti*. Along with other Italian boats of the time, they suffered from lateral instability, tending to roll excessively. This was resolved in part by reducing the size of the superstructure somewhat and moving the 120mm gun, which had been housed in a shielded mount in the tower structure, down to the deck in an unshielded mount. *Toti* and her sisters were employed actively during the 1930s, but, by the time war broke again, they were getting old and they were rather too large for Mediterranean operations. Nevertheless, they were put to use. Based at Taranto, *Toti* did not have far to go to reach her assigned patrol sector when she left port on 14 October 1940. Under the command of *Capitano di Corvetta* Bandino Bandini, *Toti* was headed for the Ionian Sea near the Calabrian coast, the same waters that *Triad* was patrolling.

In the early morning of 15 October, the sky was overcast, but the cloud layer was thin and the moon, just short of full, provided some illumination. Bandini had the watch. At 0100, he sighted a shadow off the port bow. As he watched, it slowly resolved into the form of a large submarine approaching at a range of less than a mile. Bandini opted to turn *Toti* towards the other boat.[4] He was under no illusions as to the nationality of the other boat. He knew the boat had to be British because she was in his patrol sector and because the boat had her main gun mounted well up the front of her conning tower, a practice the Italians had abandoned long before.[5] As to why Bandini made the decision to stay on the surface, it is possible to speculate. It is most likely that he concluded that there was already insufficient time to dive, both because by the time his boat could submerge, the enemy would be too close to attack, and because during the time his boat was diving, *Toti* would be an easy target for the enemy's gun while being unable to return fire or manoeuvre. Whatever the reason, he did not hesitate. Bandini immediately ordered gun crews to the deck, manning the 120mm deck gun and the four 13.2mm machine guns mounted on the bridge.[6] He undoubtedly chose a gun engagement because there simply was no time to ready torpedoes for even a snap shot.[7] He ordered the boat trimmed down to present a smaller target and to make diving faster should that become necessary. He turned *Toti* to port so that the two boats were now bow on, approaching at perhaps a combined 15 knots or more, so that it would take only a couple of minutes for the boats to meet.

If we know little about Bandini's thinking on *Toti*, we know even less about what transpired in *Triad*. We do not know if Salt was on the bridge at the time *Toti* was sighted or if he came rushing up, perhaps woken from a sound sleep. Regardless, we do know that *Toti* was sighted, most likely even before *Triad* was seen, and that a conscious decision was made to remain on the surface, to maintain course towards the enemy and to man the main gun, a 4in Mk XII in the semi-shielded mount halfway up the front of the conning tower. We know this because *Triad* opened fire before *Toti* was ready to fire her first shot.

The range indeed must have been closing faster than *Triad* expected because the first shots were well over. As soon as she could, *Toti* responded with fire from her two pairs of machine guns. It would take longer to bring the big gun into action. On *Triad*, after her first wild shots, the gun crew found the range as the boats rapidly approached each other and the next few shots fell much closer to *Toti*. After that, though, *Toti*'s machine guns began to have effect and the fire from *Triad*'s gun slowed and then stopped. Whether her gun crew was killed, wounded or just forced to duck behind the shielding, will never be known. *Triad* also fired a torpedo, but the wake was seen in time and *Toti* turned briefly away and the torpedo missed. Just as quickly, she swung back on course towards *Triad*.

With *Triad* no longer firing and the two boats now within a few dozen metres of each other, the guns on *Toti* also fell silent and in the momentary lull, the two boats passed each other on opposite courses, close enough that Bandini could clearly see Salt, dressed in white overalls, shouting orders. Suddenly *Triad* turned towards *Toti*, obviously intending to ram the Italian boat. She missed *Toti*'s stern by only a few metres and, now once again pulling away, opened fire again. *Toti* was hit twice, once in the bow and once in the conning tower. Fortunately, neither shot damaged her pressure hull. The hit in her bow just ripped up some sheet metal and the hit on her tower ricocheted off the side and exploded harmlessly.

As the two boats turned around each other, the distance between them slowly increasing, *Toti* finally opened fire with her main gun, and the first shots appeared to hit but not explode.[8] The sense of frustration at this turn of events was so acute that, according to the popular account, one of the seamen on *Toti*'s deck, Nicola Stagi, took off his boot and threw it at *Triad*. At one point, *Toti* was bow-on to *Triad*, and Bandini, torpedoes now ready, ordered a snap shot. The torpedo appeared to hit, but it too failed to detonate; the range was too close and the torpedo must have failed to arm.

Finally, at about 0145, several things happened at the same time. Apparently Salt decided to dive, probably concluding that this action could not end to his advantage and that *Toti* seemed as incapable of delivering a decisive blow as he was. At the same time, just as *Triad* was beginning to submerge, *Toti* fired two rounds from her main gun that exploded properly. One appeared to hit at or near the base of *Triad*'s conning tower and the other one further up the tower structure. The second hit set off a spectacular display. Apparently, the shell hit the locker on the bridge where signal rockets were stored, as there was an immediate burst of black smoke punctuated by streaks of light in what looked like all the colours of the rainbow.

As pretty as the sight may have been, it could not obscure the deadly effect of those two hits. For a few more moments, *Triad* continued to dive on an even keel, but then she seemed to stagger and plunge bow first. Her crew, aware too late of the situation, must have blown her tanks, because her dive slowed and then reversed and she rose nearly vertically out of the water and then plunged again, straight down. There were no survivors.

Triad was to be Bandini's and *Toti*'s only success. Soon after this patrol, *Toti* was reassigned to training duties and later served as a transport, a role she performed admirably until April 1943. With the last Axis troops squeezed into a shrinking toehold in Tunisia, it was obvious that there was no further need to transport supplies to North Africa. Too big and too old to fight in the increasing hostile Mediterranean, *Toti* was laid up. After the war, she was stricken and sold for scrap. Bandino Bandini served in the Italian Navy until his retirement in 1949.

CHAPTER 15

Trouble in Paradise

HMS/M *Clyde*, *U-67*, *U-68* and *U-111*

IF AN ENCOUNTER BETWEEN two submarines is a complicated, deadly ballet in four dimensions, imagine one between four submarines. As improbable as that might seem, that is exactly what happened off the Cape Verde Islands on 28 September 1941. The islands lie at 16° North latitude and 350nm west of Dakar. Today, they are an independent republic and a popular tourist destination; in 1941, they belonged to Portugal and lay just west of the important convoy route from Freetown, Sierra Leone to Gibraltar and points north. All cargo to or from South Africa and the Indian Ocean passed this way. Portugal was neutral in the Second World War like Spain, but, unlike Spain, they tried to stay neutral in practice as well as in theory. They were quite content to treat both sides the same and profit from the traffic in people and information that passed through their territory. As such, they could not afford to overlook even minor infractions of this neutrality. So, when *U-68* showed up in Tarrafal Bay, on the western side of Santo Antão Island shortly after noon on 27 September, followed just a few minutes later by *U-111*, it generated considerable interest on shore.[1] The local police, who kept a careful watch on goings-on in the bay, might have been even more interested if they had know that a British submarine, HMS/M *Clyde*, was only a few dozen miles offshore, on her way specifically to intercept these German boats and another one, *U-67*, shortly to arrive.

These were some of the finest boats Germany had ever built, commanded by experienced and successful captains. *U-67* and *U-68* were close sisters, both long-range Type IXC boats, built at the same yard and launched within weeks of each other in October and November 1940. *U-111*, despite her higher hull number, was built to the older Type IXB standard at the same yard, AG Weser at Bremen. She was launched earlier than the other two by a month.[2]

U-111 was the first one ready, leaving Wilhelmshaven for the North Atlantic on 5 May 1941 under the command of *Kapitänleutnant* Wilhelm Kleinschmidt. *U-111* had good success on this patrol, sinking three ships totalling more than 15,000 GRT in three separate attacks east of Greenland. She put into Lorient on 7 July. Kleinschmidt may have had success, but he was not a popular commander. He had joined the *Kriegsmarine* in 1932 after seven years as a merchant marine officer, but had only transferred to U-boat duty in late 1940 and was considered by his crew to be neither very brave nor particularly intelligent.[3]

His next assignment was in warmer waters. *U-111* joined two other long-range boats in mid-August for a sweep south from the vicinity of Azores as far as St Paul Rocks.[4] She accounted for two more large ships before being ordered to head back to base towards the end of September. Since she still had torpedoes onboard, but insufficient fuel to continue patrolling, she was ordered to meet up with a pair of southbound boats to transfer provisions.[5]

The two boats she was to meet were *U-67* and *U-68*. The second of these, under *Korvettenkapitän* Karl-Friedrich Merten, prepared for combat in a conventional manner and left Kiel for her first patrol on 30 June 1941. She took part in two convoy operations west of Ireland with no success, putting into Lorient on 1 August. She left again, this time southbound, on 11 September, headed for the rich hunting grounds off Freetown. Three other boats left Lorient at about the same time, and on 18 September they joined forces to form a sweep line heading south. One of those boats was *U-67*. She had come to this point by a somewhat less direct route. She had been commissioned in January 1941 under *Kapitänleutnant* Heinrich Bleichrodt, who already received the Knight's Cross for his success in command of *U-48*. While under his command, *U-67* was a testbed for the application of a rubberised coating designed to make a U-boat harder to detect with sonar.[6] Bleichrodt left the boat in May to take over *U-109*, which had just completed her first combat patrol. *U-67* continued working up under her former IWO for a month and then was taken over by *Kapitänleutnant* Günther Müller-Stöckheim in July. He took *U-67* out to sea on 1 August 1941, but did not arrive at Lorient until the 29th. The trip included a two-week stopover at Bergen, apparently due to problems with the anti-sonar coating. When she left Lorient on her first combat patrol, she joined *U-68* in the group forming up north of the Canaries.

This group had immediate success. They found the northbound Convoy SL.87 southwest of the Canary Islands and attacked it over the course of four nights. The escort group was inexperienced and out of eleven ships in the convoy, seven were sunk during these attacks. *U-67* accounted for one of those and *U-68* for another. They then were to continue to the south, though now without full loads of torpedoes. *U-68*, in particular, had been profligate in her use of torpedoes, firing off ten in attacks on three targets, only one of which was sunk.[7] Therefore, Merten was in particularly dire need of more torpedoes if he wanted to have a successful patrol. He thought he had a solution to that problem.

> *U-67* and *U-68* are assigned the operational area around St. Helena at a depth of 400 sea miles. At the suggestion of *U-68*, the acoustic torpedoes onboard the homeward bound *U-111*, are to be transferred to the former. Assembly point should be Grid EJ 1696 on 27.9.[8]

That is all well and good. One U-boat had extra torpedoes, another needed them, why not arrange for a transfer in a secluded bay off a neutral shore, far from any possible interference. What could go wrong? In the two years since the war began, a systematic process for the transfer of supplies between boats out on the open ocean had been developed. Mainly fuel oil, but also other provisions, even crewmen, were shifted between boats as needed. (The transfer of torpedoes was rarely done because it was a slow and difficult process.) It had become common practice for U-boats to extend their range far beyond design parameters by a complex process of sharing provisions between boats.[9] This process was not just arranged between boats on the open seas but rather carefully coordinated from Dönitz's headquarters in France.[10] All of which required significant radio traffic between individual boats and headquarters. That was the weakness in the system and explains what happened next.

> *U-67*, which is on the way to an assembly point for the purpose of transferring a sick man to *U-111*, reported hearing two explosions in EJ 1695, close to the ordered meeting place in the Tarafal Bay, at 0630 [on 28.9.][11]

This simple entry in Dönitz's log glosses over one of the most bizarre incidents in the history of submarine warfare involving several days of intense and intricate planning in two countries, countless radio messages passing between boats at sea and commanders ashore and the frenzied decryption of some of those messages by the ULTRA network, all of which brought four submarines together on 28 September 1941.

It all started simply enough with Merten's request for resupply and Dönitz's response two days earlier, as found in *U-68*'s log.[12]

25.9.	Atlantic, west of West Africa	
0130		W/T 2131/24/297 from BdU: Order for meeting with *U-111* for torpedo transfer at Tarrafal (San Antonio) Cape Verde.

It got more complicated when Müller, who obviously had been reading the traffic between *U-68*, *U-111* and *BdU* decided that Dönitz could solve a problem on his boat that was rapidly becoming an emergency.[13]

25.9.		
1820	Qu. 7728 DH	W/T to BdU: Qu.7782 DH. Crewman with suspected advanced gonorrhoea. Request rendezvous with *U-111* for transfer.
2244		From BdU to *U-67*: Rendezvous for transfer of sick crewman in Qu. EJ 1696. Send short signal when in contact.

The only problem with all this intricate planning was that every radio message that passed between the three U-boats and Kernéval had been heard by the British as well. Every morning, messages sent in that day's new code settings would be attacked by the 'bombes' at Bletchley Park; in September 1941, solutions were generally available by noon and the day's intercepts decrypted before new code settings began the process all over again at midnight. The British, in fact, had become so proficient at reading the traffic between Dönitz and his U-boats that the only question was how often and how well could they act on this information without arousing German suspicions. Some opportunities were therefore allowed to slip away out of caution, but some were simply too good to pass up. One of those was the chance to drop in on this quiet meeting of three U-boats. The boat chosen to crash this particular party was HMS/M *Clyde*.

Clyde was one of the biggest, fastest, longest-ranged submarines the British had ever built.[14] She had operated in the North Sea at the beginning of the war, putting a torpedo into the *Gneisenau* in June 1940. Then, as the centre of Royal Navy activity moved away from the North Sea, *Clyde* was transferred to the 8th Flotilla at Gibraltar. When the decision was made to send a submarine to Tarrafal Bay, the choice of *Clyde* was easy, given that she was already lurking near Santa Cruz de Tenerife in the Canary Islands on another ULTRA-derived mission.[15] Given her speed and range, and the experience of her captain, Lieutenant Commander David Ingram, she was really the only choice. She was ordered to drop everything and head for Santo Antão at high speed.

Ingram had hoped to reach Tarrafal Bay before the U-boats, but *Clyde* was still well out to sea when *U-68* and *U-111* made contact. Merten reported in his log:

27.9.	Atlantic, Cape Verde Is.	
0000	ES 2154, NE 2–3 Sea 3, mild swell	Course 180°, economical speed.
0705		San Antonio Is. in sight.
1240		Course 50°, starboard motor, slow speed. At the specified meeting place, will wait until *U-111* is sighted.
1248		*U-111* in sight, bearing 245°.

Whatever else Kleinschmidt may have been, at least he was punctual. The two boats manoeuvred cautiously while they waited for the sun to go down.

1920		55°, 9kt, while there is still too much light and danger we lay off the island and reconnoitred.
2000	ES 1693	77° from intended anchoring place. The bay appears to be in sight straight ahead of us, from the few

landmarks we can make out. There appears to be a broad swell in the bay. In order to lay alongside, we must actually get very close to the coast, despite the danger from the land.

2020

Anchored with 90m of chain in 30m of water, 180m from land.

2035

U-111 is made fast alongside to port.

They immediately began the dirty and difficult task of transferring torpedoes. *U-111*'s crewmen later reported:

A derrick was erected on the forward deck of each U-boat. It was added that the erection and subsequent removal of these derricks took a long time, and great care had to be exercised as the least damage to the gear would result in difficulty in stowing after use, due to its accurate fit into the stowage space; this accurate fitting was designed to avoid any noise while under way.

To remove a torpedo from the container the after end of the container was raised by means of a worm-gear, and the torpedo was drawn out; it was then transferred by means of the derricks in both U-boats.

The transfer of each torpedo was said to take one hour.

The transfer of torpedoes from the interior of the U-boat proved too difficult, and, in any case, Kleinschmidt wished to retain some torpedoes for any victims he might meet on his homeward cruise.

While this was going on, the local authorities decided to investigate. Merten continued:

On the land, we noticed a large number of people gathered at the wharf, acting like they were soldiers. Maybe 30 men. A disturbance began.

2050

A boat from the wharf comes out near us. The boat attempted to ask us our nationality. Our crews were ordered not to speak with anyone on the boat. Receiving no reply, the boat turned towards the shore. We heard from the boat remarks that they believed we were American. The two U-boats were lying well side-by-side. The swell was barely noticeable. The transfer continued.

2230

When the boat from shore came

> alongside again, I spoke briefly
> with the captain . . . after which
> it returned to the shore. There
> were only locals in the boat.

The belief on the part of the local authorities that the submarines anchored in their bay were American is curious, but actually not surprising in context. While technically not yet in the war, the Americans were acting more and more like belligerents. They had occupied Iceland on 7 July 1941 in order to relieve British troops there, and had earlier in September started escorting convoys in the western Atlantic. It is therefore not very surprising the Portuguese authorities might have feared American action given the strategic importance of the Cape Verde Islands.

Crewmen from *U-111* added a few details:

> According to . . . a boatswain's mate, 2nd Class, who might have been on duty on the bridge, a very dark-skinned man rowed out in a boat and asked if they were Americans; on receiving a denial the man rowed ashore but returned with a sealed envelope; he was then sent away again.[16]

Merten apparently refused to accept the envelope, which certainly was a demand that the U-boats depart. Since the torpedo transfer was almost complete, he must have felt that if he simply ignored the problem, the issue would shortly resolve itself.

<u>28.9.</u>	Tarrafal Bay, San Antonio Is., Cape Verde Is.	At anchor.
0000	ES 1693, Quiet Sea 0, thin mist, moderate visibility, moonlight	
0025		Torpedo transfer completed. 4 G7as, three to the bow, one aft. *U-111* cast off. The boat was clear to dive.

The two boats intended to leave the bay together, as they were planning to return after sundown the next day to meet with *U-67* and complete their business. After that, *U-111* would head north and the other two boats would continue south in company. But all did not go as planned.

0030	The anchor is raised, but the brand-new steel anchor cable comes up tangled with six to eight short loops. The anchor is jammed.

0030- 0050	We send a man over the side to clear it. A flashlight is needed. 'The anchor is clear' 260°, proceed at 7kt.
0105	Course 260°, 9 kt. *U-111* is barely visible at 300°.

Kleinschmidt had waited briefly for *U-68* and then decided to head slowly out to sea and let Merten catch up later. He watched *U-68* get underway. When he saw she was coming out of the bay at a higher speed and well to the south of him, he turned his boat to the southwest on a course that would bring the two boats together in deeper water. What happened next, however, was probably the last thing in the world he expected.

> As *U-68* did not join her within a short time, *U-111* proceeded; Kleinschmidt, Rösing and the boatswain's mate, 2nd class, mentioned above, were on the bridge.[17] According to the latter they saw a shadow which they thought might be a Portuguese destroyer, and then made out a large British submarine estimated at 1,800 tons, the submarine then glimmered white, and was in fact described by prisoner as showing up 'snow-white' and very clearly indeed.[18]

Clyde had indeed shown up, too late to break up the rendezvous of *U-68* and *U-111*, but in time to make their exit from the bay a lot more interesting.[19] *Clyde*, in fact, had arrived in a position 20 miles west of the island only about two hours after the Germans caught sight of each other. Ingram, still thinking he might be early, planned on coming in close to shore submerged and surfacing only long enough for his Engineering Officer, a strong swimmer, to exit the tower hatch and swim to land. There the engineer would then have a look around and swim back. Whether or not that was a good plan, one look through the periscope revealed sharks in the vicinity and the scheme was quickly dropped. Ingram's next idea was to remain submerged until dark, surface well out to sea and approach the bay from the west. The inshore mist and moonlight noted by Merten made that plan a bad idea as well. When he surfaced, Ingram could see nothing inside the bay, but *Clyde* would have been easy to see against the western horizon. The only choice left was to patrol submerged across the mouth of the bay until the moon set at 0124.[20] *Clyde* surfaced again at 0130 and, with the mist still obscuring visibility to the east, took up a position perhaps three miles from shore, facing into the bay, listening for the sounds of the U-boats. Within a minute, her hydrophones picked up screws at relatively high revolutions, approaching on her starboard bow. Ingram surmised correctly that this was most likely one of the U-boats he was hunting and turned his boat to starboard to give him a bow-on shot. Less than a minute later, he sighted *U-68*, just clearing the southern edge of the bay and heading just south of west. The boat he did not hear, because she was going too slowly, and did not see until it was almost too late, was *U-111*, much closer than *U-68*, bearing down from her port beam.

Clyde being in an extremely vulnerable position both to torpedo fire and ramming, was compelled to break off her attack on *U-68* to attend to *U-111*. It was assumed by *Clyde*'s captain that the latter U-boat would be in doubt as to whether *Clyde* was a hostile or a friendly craft: *Clyde*'s wheel was put hard to port and she went full speed ahead to ram, and ordered gun action.

A few seconds later, however, . . . *U-111* altered course away and her main vents were seen and heard to be opened.[21]

Diving at this point was, at least in the opinion of some of *U-111*'s surviving crewmen, a very dangerous action, yet it may have been the only manoeuvre that could have saved *U-111* to fight another day, as she was about to be rammed by a much larger submarine:

U-111 was stated to have been heading straight towards the submarine, and Kleinschmidt appeared not to have known what to do, to have lost his head and ordered his U-boat to crash-dive; the boatswain's mate thought this course particularly dangerous as the opening of the vents inevitably cause so much noise.[22]

U-111 was seen to dive at a speed that astonished the captain of *Clyde*. As the bow of the British submarine passed over *U-111*, the wash of the U-boat's conning tower was seen on one side and the wash of her propellers on the other. It was estimated by *Clyde*'s captain that the keel of his submarine missed the U-boat by a matter of inches.

The survivors of *U-111* while appreciating they had had a very close shave, did not realise how very nearly they were rammed or that *Clyde* passed immediately over their U-boat.[23]

Merten on *U-68* had seen none of this. He kept his boat moving west at 9 knots to the point where he was now to the west of *Clyde*.[24] It would appear that at this point Merten turned his boat to starboard, most likely because he had lost sight of Kleinschmidt and wanted to re-establish contact.

Clyde then turned back to follow *U-68* of which she had lost sight, and sighted her to the westward steering northwest.

The U-boat seemed to be trying to make a signal but her light was very dim and unreadable. *Clyde* steadied on a firing course and at 0037-1/2 fired a bow salvo of six torpedoes on 130 track at a range of about 1,400 yards. As the second torpedo went, *U-68* was observed altering course away, so *Clyde* altered slightly to port and fired the remainder fanwise, the last torpedo being straight at the U-boat.

Clyde's wheel was then put hard to port to bring the stern tubes to bear.

U-68 turned at least 180° after which she disappeared completely and was presumed to have dived.[25]

At 0048 *Clyde* dived to reload torpedoes and tried in vain to establish contact; neither were submerged signals between the U-boats nor any H.E. heard.[26]

U-68 did not dive, but obviously was lost to sight, probably due to gradually diminishing visibility now that the moon had set. Merten remained blithely unaware of the close brush *U-111* had just had or of *Clyde*'s presence on the scene even after two torpedoes detonated in the vicinity. His log states:

0150	Loud explosion, so loud that I believe it is only 500m from the boat.
0151	Another more distant ringing explosion. I take it that *U-111* has fired at a target.

He was clearly unaware that he had been the target of six torpedoes, two of which he now heard explode at the end of their runs.

> Eighteen and twenty-one minutes respectively after *Clyde* fired her first torpedo, two moderately distant explosions were heard.

> It would appear that the suggestion made by the captain of *Clyde* is correct, namely, that the explosion may have been his torpedoes exploding on the bottom, having sunk in about 800 fathoms.[27]

The two German boats were now clearing the area – *U-111* submerged and heading west, *U-68* on the surface and heading south. That left *Clyde* alone outside Tarrafal Bay, or so Ingram thought. However, there was now yet another boat approaching – Müller's *U-67*:[28]

0215	Bright moonlight, good visibility	San Antao in sight.
0400	Qu. 1692 EJ, NE 3–4, Sea 3, moon setting, good visibility	Two, for a time three, small lights visible in Tarrafal bay. Assume this is *U-68* and *U-111*.
0349 and 0415		At each of these times heard a distant explosion in a southeasterly direction. It appears possible to me that one of the two boats has attacked a steamer going in or out of Porto Grande.[29]
0417– 0504	Qu. 1695 EJ	Dived on hearing, but with no hurry. Slowly descended to maximum depth at 40°.
0505		Because I want to avoid any unfortunate encounters with our own boats, with the port diesel ahead slow we head out to sea at 250°; I decide we will meet *U-111* in the morning. We will – once at a safe

> distance from the island – once
> more listen.

Müller was early for his planned rendezvous with the two other boats. The plan was that they would meet the next night, that Dr Gernot Ziemke on *U-68* would have a look at the sick crewman and, if the doctor ruled that he could not be treated on the spot, the sick man would be transferred to *U-111*.[30] Showing up a day early, perhaps he thought he could meet up with *U-68* and *U-111*, get the business of his sick crewman taken care of and everyone would be on their way that much sooner. Regardless of his thought processes, once he heard the explosions, Müller opted for discretion and headed west away from the island. Even after he surfaced just after 0500, he continued to the west at a leisurely pace. This did not, however, take him away from danger. If anything, it increased the risk to his boat because *Clyde* had resurfaced shortly after *U-67* and was headed in almost the same direction, but at a higher speed. The two boats were literally on a collision course.

> Having reloaded torpedoes and not having established contact, *Clyde* surfaced at 0215.[31]

> At 0315, with two hours of darkness left, a charge was necessary and was started.

> At 0330 *Clyde* was four miles west of the position in which the first encounter took place, steering 280° at 10 knots, charging.

> The sky was overcast and the night had become pitch dark; there was a strong wind blowing and some sea.[32]

From *Clyde*'s point of view, a submarine now appeared rather suddenly out of the darkness.

> A streak of white foam was seen broad on the starboard bow and the wheel was put hard to starboard towards. A few seconds later the conning tower of a U-boat was sighted and her course was estimated to be similar and parallel; it was evident that she had only just surfaced.

U-67 had in fact not just surfaced. This was simply Ingram's way of explaining why *U-67* had not been spotted sooner. Müller was just as surprised to see *Clyde* emerge from the dark and described the encounter in remarkably similar words.

c.0628	Qu. 1695 EJ, NE 3–4, Sea 3, high veil of cirrus, dark horizon	Away to port off the bow, sighted a streak of foam, like a long object awash in the sea. I thought at first it was the track of a torpedo – a surface runner – because the disturbance of the surface looked smooth.
		'Hard starboard rudder, port diesel twice full speed ahead.'

U-67 was to starboard, and perhaps slightly ahead of *Clyde*, and on a converging course. Ingram turned hard to starboard to engage, calling his gun crew to the deck. Müller made the correct call, also turning to starboard, away from what he initially took to be a torpedo. When he realised it was not a torpedo, he quickly countermanded that order.

> The next moment, suddenly something black appears above the white patch of foam, what looks at first to be a small coastal patrol boat, a small, dark, long low shape.
>
> 'Both engines AK astern, hard to port!'

Müller was not the only one to get the initial sighting wrong. Ingram may have correctly identified the other boat as a U-boat, but he clearly got her distance and course wrong.

> As the ship began to swing to starboard it was seen that the U-boat was on a much more converging course than had been first estimated and that she was turning towards *Clyde* and closing very rapidly.[33]

U-67 was slowing and turning to port; *Clyde* was moving faster and turning to starboard into the path of the other boat. Müller was struck with the horrible thought that he might be ramming one of his own boats. With relief, he made the correct identification at the last minute.

> My next thought is that it's one of our own U-boats. Its tower is a little to the port of our bow. Its bow is to the right. Range 100. Steering 330°, moving at very high speed. Estimate 16kt. There's nothing more I can do, just hope we pass clear of the boat's stern; I thus have time to accurately observe the boat. While this was going on, loud shouts were heard from the boat's bridge. It was obviously an English submarine of *Clyde* class. A very long, big boat, long bridge structure with portholes in the front. The forward long gun built into the bridge, no aft gun. Tall, bulky, perforated periscope supports.[34]

Ingram saw a collision was unavoidable and, after a moment's hesitation, made the right decision.

It was immediately obvious to *Clyde*'s captain that he could never get round in time to ram the U-boat and that he would be rammed amidships himself unless he could dive fast enough. The wheel was put amidships, the gun's crew and all hands were ordered below, and the captain was about to press the Klaxons, when he realised that a collision could not be avoided and that his ship would stand a better chance on the surface with the engines kept at full speed.

U-67 struck *Clyde* right aft on No. 7 torpedo tube.[35] Her sloping bow rode up slightly, but she very quickly went ahead again and passed under *Clyde*'s stern. As she did so, her main vents were heard to open and she was soon lost to sight.[36]

In fact, *U-67* did not dive; she simply accelerated to maximum speed and disappeared in the dark.

0629	7.5nm west Cape Verde Is.	At the next moment we rammed the boat. We hit it directly at its main exhaust. From us came no noise. Order: 'Close all hatches!' Reports, the boat is closed tight just as practiced. On the other side, there was a considerable racket to be heard – obviously they were pretty well 'battered' – the two boats lying nearly parallel; then with AK ordered, we pointed our stern at the other boat, but meanwhile it is moving so fast that it quickly disappeared in the dark. Lay a course away from land, leaving us in peace to assess the damage to our boat.

This effectively ended the incident, at least as far as *Clyde* was concerned. Her damage seemed serious at first. When Ingram lost track of *U-67*, he ordered a test dive to see if the boat was watertight and was shocked to hear that two crewmen in the aft compartment had seen water coming in and, without waiting for orders, had abandoned the compartment and slammed the hatch shut behind them.[37] The Engineering Officer remained calm and opened the hatch to personally inspect the damage. He found that the leaks were minor and quickly had them stopped with rubber patches and wooden balks. *Clyde* continued searching for the three U-boats for eight more hours and then was ordered back to Gibraltar to be patched up.

U-67 was more seriously damaged, though never in any danger of sinking.

1345	After full assessment of damage, including during a dive, it was determined: The outer doors of Tubes I & II

	leak, Tube III cannot be opened, the outer door fairing of Tube I is torn away, the after door of Tube II bent, the bow is pushed in and bent over to starboard.
1353	W/T to BdU: Damage seen by day: Snout bent, outer doors Tubes I – III jammed.
1706	Question from BdU, whether tubes can be repaired with onboard resources, replied with short signal: 'No'.

Dönitz had followed the whole affair back in France with considerable bewilderment. He ordered *U-67* to head back to France and the other two boats to report in. Kleinschmidt reported in, as note in *BdU's KTB*:

> A message was received from *U-111* at 1139 as follows: 'English U-boat *Clyde* or *Triton* and a silhouette in the left centre of EJ 1696, after observed handing over of torpedoes. Forced to submerge, two torpedo detonations heard. Request return passage without sick man.'

The boat was instructed to begin the return passage immediately.[38]

After causing considerable anxiety, Merten in *U-68* also reported in. The irritation is obvious in Dönitz's comments:

> *U-68* also reported eventually requested replenishment of supplies from *U-67* and suggested the right edge of grid EK 70, for this. The fear therefore, that one of the German boats had been torpedoed by the English submarine, proved groundless. It is more likely that our cypher material is compromised or that there has been a breach of security. It appears improbable that an English submarine would be in such an isolated area by <u>accident</u>. The Naval War Staff is therefore taking the necessary steps to safeguard cypher material.[39]

Given the seriousness of the possibility that the British were reading his radio traffic, Dönitz's reaction appears remarkably mild. This was to be one of his great mistakes, not realising that the tight tactical control he maintained on his boats' movements was, in fact, putting them in danger. Repeated incidents of the Royal Navy finding his boats and supply ships in the open ocean led simply to repeated spy hunts that again and again found nothing.[40]

U-67 and *U-68* were ordered to meet again on 2 October off a deserted stretch of African shoreline north of Dakar. *U-68* topped up with fuel and torpedoes from the damaged boat which then continued back to Lorient for repairs. She arrived there on 16 October 1941. *U-68*, with a full load of fuel, continued south to the area of St Helena, where she sank the large tanker *Darkdale*, the first sinking by a U-boat south of the Equator in the

Second World War. She then continued south and sank two more large merchantmen off South-West Africa.[41] On 13 November, she replenished again, this time from the raider *Schiff 16* – aka *Atlantis* – near St Helena. Nine days later, *Schiff 16* was surprised and sunk by the cruiser HMS *Devonshire* while refueling *U-126*. In fact, *U-126's* captain, *Kapitänleutnant* Ernst Bauer had been on board *Schiff 16* when the attack occurred. The U-boat resurfaced after *Devonshire* had left the scene and began carrying or towing in lifeboats over 300 survivors. (*Devonshire* cannot be faulted for leaving the scene with so many survivors in the water, including men taken off Allied shipping sunk by *Schiff 16*, as there was a U-boat nearby.) *U-126* headed for the coast of Brazil, but met up with the German supply ship *Python* the next night and was able to transfer all the survivors to her.

U-68 was scheduled to refuel yet again, this time from *Python*, in order to carry out operations even further south near Cape Town. A rendezvous was therefore arranged for the evening of 30 November south of St Helena. A second U-boat, *U-A*, was scheduled to replenish at the same time and then also head south towards Cape Town. Both boats were still taking on fuel when daylight broke on 1 December. They were greeted by the sight of another Royal Navy cruiser, HMS *Dorsetshire*, approaching at high speed. The U-boats both submerged and *U-A* managed to fire torpedoes at the cruiser, but without success. *Dorsetshire* made quick work of the lightly-armed *Python* and then just as quickly departed the scene. Now *U-A* and *U-68* had even more survivors to handle than *U-126* had the week earlier.

> *U-A* reported at 0015 on 2 December from GF 9367 that *Python* was sunk by a heavy British cruiser at the supply point of rendezvous. Therefore, within 10 days two ships of this type have been lost.

> *U-A* also reported that, together with *U-68*, two tow groups have been formed. Course 330°, speed 5 knots. Fuel will be sufficient in the case of both boats to reach Western France.[42]

Both attacks, on *Schiff 16* and on *Python*, had been guided by ULTRA intercepts. The raider and the supply ship employed a rarely used code that the British never read, but the U-boats they were meeting used the standard naval code which was recovered daily at Bletchley Park, something which German experts repeatedly assured Dönitz was impossible.[43]

With over 400 survivors now on board or in tow, the two U-boats represented a real crisis for Dönitz. *U-124* and *U-129* were instructed to meet the two boats and assist in handling the survivors. On 5 December, Dönitz's log reported:

> According to a report of *U-68* all four southern boats have met in FU7486 and are returning each with 104 . . .

> The boats have been ordered to proceed to square EJ 40. It is planned that 260 survivors in all shall be taken over there by Italian U-boats in the period from 15 to 17 December.[44]

The grid square designated for the rendezvous with the Italian boats was west of Dakar, already more than halfway back to France from the location where *Python* was sunk. Merten tried to convince Dönitz that a transfer of survivors was not necessary, but Dönitz was having none of it.

> *U-68* reported transfer of survivors unnecessary, since boats are able to dive and provisions will suffice until they reach base. Since BdU. wishes to ensure the possibility of a longer surface run (Biscay) it has been ordered that the transfer be carried out as planned.[45]

Each German boat was assigned an Italian boat to meet.

The following order was given to the southern boats:

> Point of rendezvous *UA* with *Torelli* on 14 December as from 1400 in EJ 14. The following rendezvous are also planned:
>
> *U-129* with *Finzi* at midday on the 15th in latitude of EJ 14.
> *U-68* with *Tazolli* on the morning of the 16th in latitude of DT 78.
> *U-124* with *Calvi* on the morning of the 16th in latitude of DT 76.
>
> Transfer of survivors: *U-A* 50 men, other boats 70 men each.[46]

Incredibly, after all that misadventure, all four rendezvous took place without a hitch, 260 survivors were transferred to the Italian boats, and the four U-boats and the Italian boats all returned to France without further incident. *U-68* entered St-Nazaire on 24 December, disembarked her guests, and reached Lorient on Christmas Day after a patrol of more than three months.

Of the four boats that had met in Tarrafal Bay, only *U-111* did not eventually make it back to base. On 4 October, west of the Canaries, *U-111* was sighted by lookouts on the trawler HMS *Lady Shirley*. At first the lookouts thought they had seen the funnel of a ship, but on closer investigation, it proved to be a conning tower. The U-boat submerged as *Lady Shirley* approached, but the attack by the trawler was efficient and effective. One pattern of five depth charges was sufficient to force *U-111* to the surface. Fire from the trawler's single 4in gun killed Kleinschmidt, two other officers and five crewmen. The only remaining officer, a 'prospective' commanding officer, *Korvettenkapitän* Heinecke, on board to gain experience, surrendered the boat after assuring that the seacocks had been opened. *U-111* sank quickly; *Lady Shirley* picked up forty-four survivors.[47]

U-67 and *U-68* both went on to considerable success. The former completed eight patrols before being sunk in July 1943 in the Central Atlantic. The latter completed nine patrols before being lost in April 1944. Müller was awarded the *Ritterkreuz* in November 1942. He remained on *U-67* and lost his life in her sinking. Karl-Friedrich Merten was appointed commander of the 26th Flotilla and later the 24th Flotilla in charge of training would-be U-boat captains. He was awarded *Ritterkreuz mit Eichenlaub* (Knight's Cross with Oakleaves) and the *U-Boot-Kriegsabzeichen mit Brillanten* (U-boat War Badge with Diamonds) reserved for exceptional commanders who had already received the *Eichenlaub*. Merten survived the war, dying in 1993.

Clyde survived the war as well, serving in the Mediterranean, where, because of her size, she made multiple 'Magic Carpet' supply runs to Malta. In 1944, she joined the Eastern Fleet but saw little action against the Japanese. She was old and tired by then and there were plenty of newer, more capable boats to carry on the fight. She was sold for scrap less than a year after the war ended.

CHAPTER 16

East of Gibraltar

O 21 and U-95

FOR THE GERMANS, AND FOR Dönitz in particular, the Mediterranean was a sideshow, not to be mistaken for the main theatre of operations. Nevertheless, the inability of the Italians to wrest control of these waters and the land around them from the British repeatedly distracted Hitler and the German High Command from more critical matters. This happened on the ground in the spring of 1941 when in both the Balkans and in North Africa, German forces were diverted to rescue failed Italian offensives, in the process delaying the planned assault on the Soviet Union by five critical weeks.

Once German forces under Rommel were committed to North Africa, the control of the sea lanes in the Mediterranean became a problem for the Germans as well. The Italians had failed to prevent the passage of British convoys to Malta from Gibraltar or Alexandria, and, likewise, had proved unable to counter the effective attacks on Italian convoys carrying vital supplies to the *Afrika Korps*. Despite vigorous protests from Dönitz, on 7 September 1941 Hitler ordered the transfer of an unspecified number of French-based U-boats to the Mediterranean. The first impact of this order was that six boats passed though the Straits of Gibraltar in the second half of the month, assembling at Salamis where they formed the 23rd Flotilla.[1] When this force failed to stem the losses to the Axis convoy traffic, a second wave of six more boats was ordered to the Mediterranean on 4 November. The first four boats of the second wave were immediately ordered south with the other two to follow when available. One of these four, *U-433*, was sunk soon after passing Gibraltar. Dönitz first heard of this loss on 20 November.[2] Reluctantly, two days later he ordered *U-95* to break off her planned operations in the North Atlantic and head towards Salamis.

U-95 was one of the first Type VIICs. This was the type of boat Dönitz had wanted all along. They were big enough to range across the Atlantic and carried enough torpedoes to do serious damage if they found targets.[3] Still, they were small enough to be highly manoeuvrable and could be built in something like the kind of quantities Dönitz wanted. *U-95* was launched in July 1940 and joined the fleet on 31 August under the command of *Kapitänleutnant* Gerd Schreiber. He had commanded *U-3* for two combat patrols in March and April 1940. He had taken over that boat from

Joachim Schepke, who went on to great success in command of *U-19* and *U-100*. While returning from her second patrol under Schreiber, *U-3* had been attacked by HMS/M *Porpoise*, 'Shrimp' Simpson's boat.[4] Neither boat was harmed in that engagement.

Schreiber left *U-3* in June 1940 and proceeded to Kiel where he supervised the completion of *U-95*, his new command. He had moderate success in charge of this boat. He took her out on six patrols, operating out of St-Nazaire and Lorient. On those patrols, he was credited with sinking eight ships totalling over 28,000 GRT and damaging four more. On 19 November 1941, he took *U-95* out of Lorient on her seventh patrol. Three days out, he received orders changing his destination from the North Atlantic to the Mediterranean. *U-95* would replace *U-433* on the strength of the 23rd Flotilla.

The Dutch submarine *O 21* had already had an active career before she too was reassigned to the Mediterranean. Under the command of Ltz. I. Johannes Frans 'Jantje' van Dulm, she had been actively engaged in the North Sea, conducting six patrols there before the centre of activity shifted away from those waters and, in February 1941, she was reassigned to the Royal Navy's 8th Flotilla at Gibraltar. There she was actively engaged in convoy escort duties, protecting several HG and OG convoys between Gibraltar and England. In July, *O 21* resumed combat patrols, this time in the Tyrrhenian Sea. On 31 August 1941, during her second patrol in those waters, van Dulm sighted and attacked an Italian submarine, identified as one of the *Marcello* class boats, but the attack failed. Finally, on 5 September 1941, *O 21* had her first success, the large Italian freighter *Isarco*, which she sank west of Naples. After that the successes came more frequently; three smaller vessels were sunk during patrols in October and November. The last of these was a small sailing vessel, *Unione*, sunk off the east coast of Sardinia on 24 November 1941. Too small to waste a torpedo on, van Dulm tried sinking the *Unione* with gunfire, but when that seemed not to be working, he rammed the target, which finally sank her.

Three days later, *O 21* turned back towards Gibraltar. Just after midnight on the 28th, she was headed westward on the surface south of Cabo Sacratif, midway along the southern coast of Spain between Almería and Málaga. The lights of the Spanish coast were a bright background to the north.

> On the afternoon of November 27th, we were ahead of our sailing schedule and, in order to stay within the territory, we needed to dive at around 3 o'clock. We surfaced again after dark and continued our course, zigzagging at a speed of 15 knots.[5]

Being ahead of schedule and needing to stay within a prescribed area in order to avoid being mistaken for a U-boat by RAF patrols, she needed to proceed slowly. At the same time, van Dulm could not ignore the threat of enemy submarines. Hence the decision to zigzag at high speed. Jan Biesemaat, a seaman, took up his position as lookout soon after the boat resurfaced.

I was on the forward watch. This means that you search a sector of 180 degrees together with the officer from the watch who is also responsible for the two look-outs who keep an eye on the aft side. . . Mr. Kroeze, the Second Officer, had eagle eyes. He always saw everything; it was incredible.[6]

What the watch officer saw was a bow wave some distance astern, barely discernable in the gloom. He had Biesemaat ring for the captain. The time was 0030 on 28 November 1941.

In fact, O 21 had been sighted well before she saw her adversary. *U-95* had cleared Gibraltar the night before, and, having spent the daylight hours of the 27th submerged, was now headed east on the surface when her lookouts spotted a submarine silhouetted against the Spanish coast. Schreiber immediately came to the bridge and ordered a turn to port on the trail of the unidentified target. His problem was simple. He knew that other U-boats had been ordered into the Mediterranean at the same time as *U-95*, but he had no way of knowing exactly where they were.[7] Despite the fact that the boat was headed to the west, he could not be certain the silhouette he saw was not German. If another U-boat had cleared Gibraltar just ahead of him and had then suffered a mechanical failure or had been damaged, she might well have turned back or even be heading for Málaga, which would account for the position and course of the submarine he had sighted. To make matters worse, unlike the British or Italian boats that also operated in these waters, O 21's silhouette looked somewhat similar to a U-boat's.[8] After only a few minutes pursuit, *U-95* was within range and Schreiber ordered the bow tubes readied, but he did not dare fire without being sure he was not shooting at another U-boat. Reluctantly, he ordered the signal lamp brought up to the bridge. He had to be sure.[9]

> Neither lookouts nor officers could make up their minds about the identity of the strange submarine, her angle of inclination as seen from the conning tower of *U-95* making this exceptionally difficult. Schreiber proceeded to stalk his quarry, not caring to risk an attack until he could be convinced that he was not attempting to sink a sister U-boat. Shortly before 0300 three ratings were ordered to man the 2cm gun, and a signalman was instructed to flash a challenge with a pocket torch.[10]

On the bridge of O 21, there was no such hesitation. Any boat encountered in these waters had to be an enemy.[11] Van Dulm's problem was different. He had expended all his forward torpedoes, as well as the two torpedoes in the traversing external mount forward of the tower, and, even worse, all of the rounds for his deck gun. His sole means of engaging the approaching U-boat was the two torpedoes in the pair of after tubes. The only good news was that the enemy was approaching from astern, so he could bring these tubes to bear without too much manoeuvring. Given that he would have just the one salvo to fire at the German, he needed to make that shot as sure as humanly possible. It seemed best to van Dulm that he let the distance between the boats close quickly. Therefore he ordered both engines slowed and stood, along with the watch officer, looking over *O 21*'s stern as the U-boat rapidly drew nearer.

To his amazement, he saw the boat flash a coded signal with a blue lamp. Van Dulm called the English signalman Rees up to the bridge and they watched as the lamp flickered again. Assured by Rees that it was no signal he knew, van Dulm decided that the time had come to take his chance. He ordered both engines reversed to kill *O 21*'s way and them stopped both engines. With his boat now drifting to a stop, van Dulm stood in the centre of the bridge facing directly aft. He stretched out his arm and when he was able to line up his thumb, the boat's stern and the oncoming U-boat, he gave the order to fire one torpedo. At the same time, he ordered engines ahead full, so he'd have some way on in case he needed to manoeuvre.

On *U-95*, Schreiber waited as long as he could for the other boat to respond to his signals and then lined up a straight-on bow shot at the target directly ahead of him. All this was being witnessed by a surprisingly candid observer, the bosun's mate Kurt Günzel.[12] This account shows the confusion and uncertainty typical among the crew as an engagement unfolded:

> The Old Man said I might go on the best watch from 1800 to 2000. He was a queer customer, but he knew a lot about his job, and he and I got along very well together; I used to give him some assistance when he was taking bearings of the stars and so on; I used to write down the figures and help a little with the calculations, and get out the charts, and help him to plot the course, and so on. 'Well,' he said to me, 'that's the end of our keeping watch together. The new Lieutenant is to take the watch.' When we had been at sea ten or 12 days he said: 'The First Lieutenant will go ashore in Italy and then I'll see to it that we get our watch together again.' Then he said: 'The First Lieutenant is going on watch tomorrow morning at 0400, instead of the Chief Quartermaster.'[13] When I came off watch I happened to meet him. I said: 'Shall we have a little celebration this evening?' He replied: 'I'll be along later.' He brought a glass of brandy and we sat down; there were four of us, and we played 'Skat'.[14] When I go on watch at 0400, I usually turn in at ten or half-past – by that time, after the news, I am tired enough to fall asleep at 2300, and wake up at 0400.[15] At 2300 we were just going to stop, after one more hand, when suddenly the order came through the speaking tube, spoken in a rather quiet voice: 'Lower deck, action stations.'[16] We thought it was a joke. Then we heard that someone on deck had seen a shadow, and a rating in the conning tower, returning from his smoke, came in and said: 'There's something happening.'[17] Then they all came along and nobody said a word, the control room was quite quiet. All of a sudden the loud-speaker said: 'Lower deck, action stations.' No. 1 Boatswain's Mate was asleep at that moment; No. 3 was due to go on watch. He came out of his bunk and said: 'What's up?' I put on my leather jacket and quickly put my cigarette case in my pocket, folded back the seat, and went up into the conning tower. Then No. 1 said: 'Take your life-jacket, we're in for something.' At that moment I had no idea where mine was; under my pillow, perhaps. Anyway, I said: 'Time to fetch that later,' and as I went into the conning tower the order came from the control room: 'Port!'[18]

It was at this point that Schreiber swung his boat around in pursuit of *O 21*. Günzel was now in the conning tower, but not outside on the bridge where he could see what was happening. He could, however, hear all that was being said on the bridge and also below him in the control room.

My God, I thought, what's happening now? The men forward opened the torpedo-tube caps; you can imagine how they ran forward to open them.[19] Then the show started. What sort of boat was she? Italian? German? There had been three other boats with us. In the meantime we got the order: 'Close the caps,' then again: 'Open the caps,' and then another order to close them. The men forward were starting to curse. Then, for the third time, they wanted to fire. The order was given again: 'Open the caps.' As we were about to make our fourth approach they spotted us because we came too close. It was a beautiful moonlit night, just three days before full moon. You could see your way about better than by day, when it is often a bit misty down there at that time of year. You could see the coast and the dark mountains better than by day. When we were seen we were in an unfavourable position with the moon behind us. They could see us in the moonlight better than we could see them. When we still held our fire, they drew away and showed their stern; so we challenged them two or three times in Morse. The Captain ordered: 'Guns' crew, clear away'! As a matter of fact we always had the guns ready, and the ammunition lay ready below in the control room; it always lies there. So the first thing was to get the gun loaded and sights on the target. For the time being I was to stay in the conning tower in case we began to fire. I had my recorder with me in the conning tower as messenger. He was there to take notes, because I have to write down the data when we fire.[20] He said we must hoist a few rounds to the upper deck, when the order came to fire.

While they were getting the gun ready, we went ahead at slow speed. Then the Captain said: 'Now try some gunfire,' and we went full speed ahead. At that moment the Dutch fired their torpedoes and we couldn't see them easily on account of the moonlight.[21] Luckily the Junior Officer saw it; he has good eyes trained in flying.[22] He shouted: 'Torpedo track to port!' The Quartermaster, who was standing forward at the port lookout, pushed him out of the way, leapt to the bridge rail, had a look over the side and put the helm hard over to starboard. Suddenly I heard a hissing noise – if that one hit us amidships or forward I shouldn't have been able to get out; it was a very nasty feeling! I heard a bang aft and we supposed that the first torpedo had just grazed along our side.

Van Dulm watched in frustration as the bubble trail of his torpedo reached *U-95*, and then nothing happened. The torpedo appeared to hit but there was no explosion. As it became clear that the U-boat was turning to starboard, it was suddenly obvious both why the torpedo had missed and what he had to do next. Van Dulm ordered a turn to port. Biesemaat noted:

As the U-boat turns away, we turn with it. The commander is still on the casing of the bridge and the chief officer, while looking over his thumb across the stern, cries, 'Fire!' Our second torpedo hits the U-boat precisely behind the tower. In its throes of death the U-boat sticks straight up into the air. And then disappears into the depths.

U-95's bosun's mate saw it from the other end:

The second one came a bit further over to port, so we turned to starboard and turned, so to speak, right into the course of the torpedo. The torpedo must have exploded right on the screw. There was a loud report and I thought my head would split. I looked down and saw a red flame and a fearful cloud of smoke. I pulled myself up and at that moment water began to come in. I was outside. I looked round and there were a few men aft and a few to our right. The Captain shouted: 'Keep together!' Then he began to count us all and call our names to see who was there. He asked me: 'Has anybody else come out?' And I said: 'No, I'm the last.' Then we began swimming.

The bridge watch plus the captain, both watch officers, the bosun and the navigator, the two-man gun crew, a war correspondent who had been on the bridge to take notes on the action and the bosun's mate who had been in the conning tower, all made it into the water, a dozen men in total.[23] Thirty-three men went down with the boat.

After the explosion, *O 21* turned and returned to the site of the sinking, looking for any evidence as to the identity of her victim. The first thing they noticed was the unique smell that lingered after the sinking of a submarine. Biesemaat remembered:

Fuel oil was floating on the water everywhere and there was this awful cordite smell. A truly disgusting stench!

The second thing they noticed was the shouting of the men in the water. Van Dulm did not hesitate hauling the men aboard.

The commander had already fished twenty-two Italians out of the water, so he says, 'We should get them out'. . . So we pull up the Germans. They aren't even on deck and the German commander Gerd Schreiber starts mouthing off! He was a highly experienced submarine commander. He starts yelling at his men who had just been rescued, '*Maul halten, nichts sagen!*'.[24]

This kind of behaviour on the part of captured German crews was fairly typical. German sailors tended to be quite friendly after they were captured, relieved no doubt to be out of the war and still alive. A surprising number of them spoke freely to their captors. Officers, on the other hand, consistently showed good discipline after being taken prisoner, and many tried, like Schreiber, to order their men to keep quiet. It was for this reason, among others, that the British made every attempt to separate officers and men as soon as possible after they were captured. But on *O 21*, crowded already with the survivors of the two small ships she had already sunk on that patrol, there was no possible way to segregate the captives. They were herded into the forward torpedo compartment, the logical place to put them, since they could do little harm there with all the torpedoes fired off and there was only one exit, which could be easily guarded.

The captives were treated entirely correctly, including being given fresh, dry coveralls to wear. Naturally, this required the Germans to remove everything they were wearing, and, as was standard in these cases, the clothing they removed was searched for anything of intelligence value.

Equally naturally, in keeping with longstanding naval tradition, anything of utility or monetary value was liberated at the same time.[25]

> The Germans have all kinds of good equipment on them. Good quality binoculars in watertight cases with chamois cloths for cleaning them. Much better equipment than we had.

They were only a few hours sailing from Gibraltar, but this nevertheless left Schreiber and his officers time to attempt mischief, as Biesemaat relates:

> Because I was one of the youngest sailors I have to fetch coffee for the Germans. I only brought it to the sailors, not the officers. I had no interest in bringing them coffee. When the commander instructs me to do so, I tell him I need to go on watch again. The cook was then told to do it but, because he's from Rotterdam (that had been bombed by the Germans a year earlier), he initially refuses. But the commander insists. Our telegraphist Joop van der Pijl, a big guy, keeps them covered with a gun. But you had to be careful. If one of the German officers goes to the head you need to go with him because they leave the outboard valve open in an attempt to flood the boat. That's what those guys are like, not the sailors, but the officers. They tried that at least once.

Arriving at Gibraltar, O 21 was greeted with full ceremony, it being an auspicious occasion for the Royal Navy to honor the exploits of one of its Allied forces. O 21 served out the war as a front-line combat boat. She was refitted at Rosyth between January and July 1942 and then again at Simonstown, South Africa between October 1942 and January 1943, reflecting the hard service she had already seen. From February 1943, she was based at Colombo and patrolled the waters of the Andaman Sea, the Malacca Strait and further east into the Java Sea and the waters around the Dutch East Indies. There, she had two more successes, sinking a pair of large Japanese freighters. Problems with her diesels forced a return to England for repairs in December. She was again based at Dundee until April 1944, when she made the long voyage to Philadelphia, where she was refitted once more. From May 1945, she was based at Fremantle, Australia until the end of the war, serving mostly on special missions. In April 1946, she was placed in reserve, but was brought back to active duty again in 1950 to serve as a torpedo trials boat. Finally, in 1957, she was decommissioned for the last time and sold for scrap the following year.

Failing in his attempts to sabotage O 21 *en route* to Gibraltar, Schreiber continued trying his best to make life complicated for his captors. Once at Gibraltar, he and *Oberleutnant zur See* Hans Ey, the former commander of *U-433*, made an escape attempt that very nearly succeeded.[26]

J F van Dulm turned O 21 over to F J Kroesen in March 1944. He then served as the senior officer of the Dutch submarine service, first at Dundee and then, after the war, at Rotterdam. He rose through the ranks, eventually retiring as a Commodore in June 1962 after commanding the Naval Intelligence Service for nine years. In terms of tonnage sunk, he was the third most successful Dutch submariner of the Second World War.

CHAPTER 17

In the Narrow Sea

HMS/M *Unbeaten*, U-374 and R.SMG *Guglielmotti*

ABOUT FOUR MONTHS AFTER Malcolm Wanklyn brought *Upholder* to Malta, Lieutenant Commander E A 'Teddy' Woodward was doing the same with his new boat, HMS/M *Unbeaten*.[1] She lagged so far behind *Upholder* because, unlike Wanklyn's boat, which had been sent to the Mediterranean as soon as she was ready for service, *Unbeaten* was kept in home waters to keep a watch out for *Scharnhorst* and *Gneisenau*, not being sent on to Malta until April 1941. Despite this somewhat different start to their careers, there were plenty of similarities between the two boats and their commanders. Both boats were 'U' class submarines, launched within a day of each other at the Vickers-Armstrong yard at Barrow-in-Furness. Time and again, the boats would be involved with each other throughout their brief careers. The commanders, likewise, had careers with similar trajectories, both brave, cool under fire and lucky in the face of the enemy, though their fates would differ greatly in the end.

Like *Upholder*, *Unbeaten* joined the 10th Flotilla at Malta under 'Shrimp' Simpson and was in action continuously until it was time to return to England. On her first patrol, close in to the African shore, *Unbeaten* fired three torpedoes at a large troop transport escorted by a destroyer. Two of the torpedoes lost depth control and apparently headed straight down to the sea floor, where they detonated. The resulting explosion raised *Unbeaten*'s stern out of the water for a few crucial seconds, long enough for the Italian destroyer to pinpoint her location. What followed was a long attack in shallow waters, some of the depth charges falling disturbingly close. The shaking was enough to pop light bulbs, throw heavy items of equipment around like projectiles and spring a few serious leaks. As water accumulated in the bilge, it became necessary to start up the pumps for a few moments to maintain buoyancy, but the sound made by the pumps was enough to alert the lurking destroyer to *Unbeaten*'s location and the depth charging would start again. Finally, the destroyer must have run out of depth charges, because, after several hours the attack slowed and then stopped. At midnight, Woodward decided to take a chance and brought *Unbeaten* to the surface. Mercifully, the horizon was clear and, as Woodward said: 'with a sigh of relief, we cleared the area'.[2] When *Unbeaten* returned to

Malta, a rat was sighted jumping ship as soon as she tied up at the Lazaretto.

That ill omen affected crew morale only briefly, as *Unbeaten* continued making the frequent, short-duration patrols that were typical of the 'U' class boats operating from Malta. In September, she participated, along with *Upholder*, in one of the most successful attacks of the war.[3] The two boats, along with *Upright*, formed an east-west sweep line northeast of Homs, east of Tripoli, designed to intercept a fast convoy of three large Italian troopships.[4] *Ursula* took position south of this line to catch any ships that broke through. At the eastern end of the line, *Unbeaten* spotted the convoy, which was heading west to the north of her position. It was too late to get into attack position. Woodward tried using his sonar to report his sighting to Wanklyn, who was in tactical command, but was unable to make contact.[5] Finally, after reluctantly turning to his wireless, Woodward was able to get through and got word to Wanklyn just in time for him to spot the passing convoy and put four torpedoes in the water. Always a good shot, Wanklyn holed two of the transports, leaving then afloat but dead in the water, one of them slowly sinking, the other still riding high.[6]

Unbeaten meanwhile had turned and set off in pursuit of the convoy, though with a top speed of barely 11 knots, there was little chance she would catch the faster convoy, at least until Wanklyn stopped two of the three transports. While *Unbeaten* approached from the east, Wanklyn took *Upholder* down and frantically set his crew to reloading his four tubes. He figured he would take advantage of the rising sun, so he manoeuvred *Upholder* around to the east of the two cripples. Thus, as dawn was just breaking, the two submarines, unbeknownst to each other, were both submerged and on parallel courses within a few hundred metres of each other, both approaching the more stricken of the two ships. They were both lining up shots when that ship abruptly rolled over and slipped beneath the waves. That left the less damaged of the two. Wanklyn's first shot had blown off that ship's propellers, leaving her unable to move but otherwise basically intact. Seeing that this ship was well protected by escorts, the two captains chose different strategies. Woodward manoeuvred on the eastern side of target, trying to find an opening in the screen. Wanklyn took his boat deep, ran at his best speed under the escorts and the target and brought *Upholder* up on the other side, inside the ring of escorts. Woodward had just lined up his shot and was seconds away from firing when this target erupted in smoke and flames and quickly sank beneath the waves, a scene Woodward must have watched with very mixed feelings. This would not be the last time the two boats crossed paths.

Another boat that would cross paths with *Unbeaten* was U-374. She was as typical a U-boat as could ever be found. Although she was ordered less than a month after the war began, it was 21 months later, on 21 June 1941, that she was commissioned into the *Kriegsmarine*. She had taken that long to complete because she was built at Howaldtswerke, Kiel, one of the many yards that had received orders for U-boats at the beginning of the war that had no prior experience building modern submarines.[7] But, the cumulative effect of all the orders placed early in the war was that by mid-1941, U-boats were beginning to join the fleet at a sharply increasing rate. *U-374* was one of eighteen U-boats to be commissioned that month. Unlike the boats which had fought the first year-and-a-half of the war, *U-374* was truly just one of many. Making her even more typical, she was a Type VIIC, of which more than 570 would be built.[8]

Her captain was equally typical. All these new boats required captains and, of necessity, they would be men with limited experience, not at all like the heroes of the early days of the war, who had put in years of service in the pre-war training flotillas. *Oberleutnant zur See* Unno von Fischel was one of these men. Twenty-five years old when he took command of *U-374* at her commissioning, the sum total of his experience in U-boats had been three patrols as watch officer under *Kapitänleutnant* Udo Heilmann on *U-97*. Based on that, he was given his own boat in May 1941.[9] He arrived in Kiel after *U-374* had already been launched, in time to oversee her completion and acceptance trials. Limited experience for someone taking a new boat to war.[10]

Nevertheless, von Fischel seems to have been a competent commander. He took *U-374* to sea on 29 September 1941 on her first combat patrol. After replenishing in Norway, she ranged as far as Newfoundland in search of convoys, most of which were being routed around the German sweep lines.[11] She managed to sink a large British motor vessel sailing independently east of St John's on 31 October. She located an eastbound convoy the next day and trailed it for most of a day. After other boats had joined the hunt, she tried attacking, but was unable to penetrate the screen and was forced to endure a long depth charging by a Canadian corvette.[12] After a patrol that had lasted 44 days, *U-374* put into Brest on 11 November.[13]

U-374 set out again on 6 December 1941, this time with a different destination. Dönitz had decided that four more boats were needed in the Mediterranean, as losses there had already been as high as he had expected.[14] Since the first boats had been sent to Salamis in September, even getting through the Straits of Gibraltar had become much more difficult, as the Royal Navy had significantly reinforced patrols there.

> *U-374* requested immediate aircraft aid, as she was being chased in CH 7441 by four destroyers. *U-374* later sank two escorts in the Ceuta area. (Aircraft aid was not possible in CH.)[15]

This terse entry in Dönitz's log for 11 December speaks volumes. Von Fischel was most likely trying to get through the Straits by hugging the African coast, but he had clearly been detected and was being hounded by no less than four ships.[16] He again showed his skill at evasion by slipping away from these hunters, and, later that morning, he found and torpedoed two small subchasers off Ceuta, a Spanish-occupied city on the Moroccan coast.[17] His request for air support is interesting. This kind of aid was something U-boat captains could expect if they were under attack near a friendly shore. Von Fischel clearly thought Spain was a friendly country, given the smiling photographs of Hitler and Franco shaking hands so often seen in Germany. The reality was that, as much as the Germans would have liked to base aircraft in Spain, Franco was far too cautious to allow it. Despite the fact that at the end of 1941 it still looked like the Germans were winning the war, Franco demanded commitments by Hitler to immediate financial and military aid and promises of territorial concessions after the war at the expense of the British and French empires that the Germans were unwilling to make.

Despite the lack of assistance by friendly aircraft, von Fischel managed to get *U-374* through the Straits and into the relative safety of the Western Mediterranean. The boat arrived safely at La Spezia on 14 December 1941. Only four days were allotted for provisioning before von Fischel put out again. *U-374*'s destination was the coast of Egypt and Cyrenaica. Four weeks patrolling those waters yielded no sinkings. The only excitement came when, on 8 January 1942, a British coastal convoy was sighted heading for Mersa Matruh from Benghazi during daylight.[18] Von Fischel opted to move ahead of the convoy, submerge and wait for it to pass in front of his bows. He was, however, apparently betrayed by the notorious clarity of the Mediterranean, as *U-374* was sighted from the air and was, at 1600, attacked by two destroyers, which dropped forty-three depth charges over a period of three hours off the Egyptian coast north of Sidi Barrani. *U-374* sustained some damage in this attack, none of it critical: her radios and depth gauges were put out of action, there was damage to both fore and aft torpedo tubes such that she could no longer launch torpedoes and water was leaking in around both propeller shafts. With this damage and fuel running low, *U-374* headed towards Messina where she could get patched up.

Unbeaten had spent a quiet New Year's at Malta, the *Luftwaffe* providing the only fireworks, and then had put to sea again, along with the Polish *Sokol* and HMS/M *Thrasher*, on 4 January on Woodward's fourteenth patrol in the Mediterranean.[19] They were assigned patrol sectors stretching across the base of the Gulf of Taranto. When weather and a lack of targets (as predicted by ULTRA) made that an unproductive sector, *Unbeaten* was ordered to move west, to patrol the shore off the very 'toe' of the Italian 'boot', between Cape Spartivento and the entrance to the Straits of Messina. Shortly after 1000 on 12 January, submerged near the eastern end of his sector, within sight of Cape Spartivento, Woodward picked up the unmistakable noises of a boat on the surface close by.

As Woodward described the brief encounter in his log, the whole affair took 11 minutes from sighting to sinking, perhaps a record for the efficient destruction of an enemy submarine.[20] *Unbeaten* was at periscope depth, headed just west of north in deep water a bit more than four miles offshore. At 1013, the sound room reported picking up 'hydrophone effect' bearing 065°. Two minutes later, a quick look through the periscope showed a U-boat, making 11 knots on the surface bearing 080° at barely 1,800m.

Woodward increased speed to full and looped around to bring his bow on to the target. It took all of eight minutes to manoeuvre into position, ready his tubes and launch a full salvo of four Mk VIII torpedoes at 1023. The range was 1,300m. The four torpedoes were individually aimed – an 'A' salvo. After a run of just over a minute, two of the torpedoes hit; *U-374* disintegrated.

> Ploch said that he had just come off watch and had come up on to the bridge where he was standing in front of von Fischel.[21] Suddenly there was a huge explosion on their starboard side and he was flung into the water. His first impression was that his boat had struck a mine and it was not until he was swimming in the water that he noticed the conning tower of a submarine and realised that his boat had been torpedoed. *U-374*, he added, sank almost at once, and the only trace of her was oil and wooden slats from the upper deck.[22]

Forty-three men went down with *U-374*. *Unbeaten* circled for almost ten minutes after the sinking and, convinced that no other ships were within the area, only then did Woodward surface. He found *Matrosenobergefreiter* (Seaman 1st Class/Able Seaman) Ploch, nearing exhaustion amid the flotsam and oil bubbling up from the wreck.

> At 1037, *Unbeaten* surfaced and picked up Ploch. Although the sea was 43 and wind W., Force 5, it only took four minutes to get the man on board over the fore-planes and to dive again.

> As this action took place only four miles from the Italian coast, *Unbeaten* immediately proceeded southwards to clear the area.[23]

Pulled from the water, cleaned up and plied with hot tea, the survivor proved to be a simple seaman who boasted of the great successes of Germany's U-boats and provided a good deal of information, much of which later proved to be completely fictitious.[24] Woodward was awarded a bar to his DSO for this sinking.

Upon return to Malta after this patrol, Woodward went on sick leave. His first officer, Lieutenant J D Martin took the boat out for two patrols, after which Woodward took command again for *Unbeaten*'s last patrol from Malta, starting on 12 March 1942. Once again ULTRA came into play. *Unbeaten* was directed to the same place where she had sunk *U-374*, just off Cape Spartivento.

The target the cryptanalysts had found for *Unbeaten* was the Italian submarine *Guglielmotti*. When they entered the war in June 1940, the Italians had eight submarines based at Massaua on the Red Sea. Completely surrounded on land by British or French colonies and cut off by sea by British control of the Suez Canal, the Red Sea flotilla fought a desperate war with diminishing supplies and increasingly worn-out equipment.[25] Four of the eight submarines (*Galilei*, *Galvani*, *Torricelli* and *Macallé*) were lost in the first month of combat.[26] The other four soldiered on until February 1941, some boats completing as many as eight patrols in the Red Sea and

Indian Ocean, though the only recorded success in this time was the sinking of the tanker *Atlas* by *Guglielmotti* south of the Farasan Islands in the Red Sea on 6 September 1940. Finally, with British forces pushing into Eritrea from Sudan, the decision was made to evacuate the four remaining submarines the only possible way, around Africa to the Italian Atlantic squadron base at Bordeaux, a cruise of more than 12,700nm. The smallest and slowest of the four, *Perla*, left first on 1 March 1941. She replenished twice along the way, once from *Schiff 16* near Madagascar and once from *Nordmark* in the South Atlantic. The other three boats, *Guglielmotti*, *Ferraris* and *Archimede*, were bigger, faster and had greater range than *Perla*. They left a few days later and were able to make the journey with a single replenishment. *Guglielmotti* met *Nordmark* in the South Atlantic, took on 150 tons of fuel and a ton-and-a-half of food and water, arriving at *Betasom* in Bordeaux after 64 days at sea. *Perla* was the last to arrive, taking 81 days to complete the journey, but all four boats made France safely. After that, their luck was not nearly as good. *Ferraris* was sunk east of the Azores on 25 October 1941. *Perla* was transferred to the Mediterranean, where she was captured by the corvette HMS *Hyacinth* near Beirut on 9 July 1942. She was put into Royal Navy service briefly as *P.712* and then, in 1943, became the Greek *Matrozos*, serving until 1947. *Archimede* had the most success of the four, sinking over 25,000 GRT of shipping, before being sunk by US Navy aircraft approximately 500nm off the coast of Brazil on 15 April 1943. About twenty crewmen were seen in the water after the sinking and the aircraft dropped three inflatable life rafts and then headed back to their base at Pernambuco. Twenty-seven days later, one of the rafts was found by Brazilian fishermen with one survivor, barely alive. After recovering, he sat out the rest of the war in a US POW camp.

The fourth of the boats, *Guglielmotti*, was also transferred to the Mediterranean, though not until the late summer of 1941. She had no further successes in the Atlantic or Mediterranean. It was, in fact, when she was returning from another unsuccessful patrol that ULTRA intercepts put *Unbeaten* precisely in her path just before dawn on 17 March 1942. Woodward made almost as quick work of *Guglielmotti* as he had *U-374*. Sighting the Italian boat at dawn, Woodward fired a full spread of four torpedoes. Sixty-two men lost their lives. There were no survivors.

Woodward and *Unbeaten* were now both in desperate need of refit. Unlike Wanklyn, Woodward did not resist the order to take himself and his boat back to England. After putting into Malta one last time to refuel and replenish supplies, *Unbeaten* headed for Gibraltar and home, with just one stop on the way. On 11 April, *Unbeaten* rendezvoused with Wanklyn and *Upholder* off the coast of Tunisia. The latter had just dropped off a pair of agents on the African coast and their 'handler', a Captain Wilson, was needed back in England as soon as possible. *Unbeaten* took Captain Wilson and some mail from *Upholder* and headed west. They were the last to see Wanklyn and his crew alive.

Unbeaten arrived back in England without incident and was immediately docked. Woodward was detached for a much-needed rest and reassignment. He then took command of the new submarine HMS/M *Tactician*, which he took back to the Mediterranean and then on to the Indian Ocean. He ended the war as 'Teacher' in charge of the Commanding Officer Qualifying Course ('Perisher') at Gosport. *Unbeaten* was taken out again under a new captain, Lieutenant D E O Watson. She left Holy Loch on 23 October 1942, with the mission to land an agent near Vigo on the Atlantic coast of Spain near the Portuguese border. Having reported that task accomplished on 1 November, she was ordered to conduct a patrol in the Bay of Biscay, looking particularly for a pair of blockade runners expected to be leaving France. This was a dangerous hunting ground, frequented as it was by U-boats on their way to or from patrol and the RAF Coastal Command aircraft which hunted them constantly. When the patrol was over, *Unbeaten* was to have met an escort on 12 November near Bishop's Rock at the tip of Cornwall. She never kept that rendezvous. The day before, RAF aircraft reported attacking a U-boat in the area where *Unbeaten* would have been had she been on course to the rendezvous. Despite the fact that the 'U-boat' was northbound in the Bay of Biscay where U-boats normally went east or west and that the boat was within a restricted 'no attack' corridor, the aircraft bombed and reported sinking the submarine. Post-war analysis showed that the Germans recorded no sinkings in that area at that day and time. The assumption must be made that *Unbeaten* and her entire crew were lost to 'friendly fire'.

CHAPTER 18

Fratricide IV

U-254 and *U-221*

WOLFPACK TACTICS WERE BASIC to Dönitz's attack on Britain's lifelines. Central to the idea was the belief that a concentration of U-boats could overwhelm the escorts protecting a convoy. So successful were these tactics in practice that the US Navy and Royal Navy both adopted similar, though not identical, tactics as the war progressed. The great fear was that multiple submarines operating in close proximity to each other would interfere with or, even worse, damage or sink each other. What would happen to torpedoes that missed? Would they hit friendly submarines attacking from the other side of the convoy? What could prevent submarines manoeuvring to attack the same target from colliding with each other? After all, *Upholder* and *Unbeaten* had got uncomfortably close while attacking the Italian convoy in September 1941.[1]

The US Navy generally limited the size of their packs to four boats and always had a local tactical commander directing the action.[2] The Royal Navy adopted a similar approach. The Germans used larger packs and left each boat free to seek whatever tactical advantage could be gained. There were actually good reasons for this difference in approach. In the Pacific and the Mediterranean, convoys were almost always rather small, at the most a dozen merchant ships. This made the target rather compact and increased the likelihood of interference if multiple boats attacked simultaneously. On the other hand, the Atlantic convoys that were the primary target of the German *Rudeltaktik* (Pack Tactics) were comparatively huge. A typical mid-war Atlantic convoy would contain between forty and fifty merchantmen, arrayed in parallel columns of four to six ships.[3] This made for a wide, but relatively short formation, the idea being to minimise the broadside exposed to U-boat attack. Attack from ahead or astern of a convoy was less likely to be successful; in particular it reduced the chance that a torpedo that missed its intended target would hit a ship in another column. Thus a convoy could easily stretch two or more miles deep and four or more miles across. A convoy of this size, Dönitz concluded, could be freely attacked by a dozen or more U-boats without undue risk of interference. With only one exception, that judgment proved to be correct.[4]

Convoy HX.217 was a fairly typical mid-war convoy. As the designator indicated, this was an eastbound convoy out of New York, the 217th of the type.[5] It was a fast convoy composed of thirty-three merchant ships, protected by Escort Group B6, which included two destroyers, four corvettes and a designated rescue ship. The convoy was somewhat smaller than typical; the escort group was standard for late 1942. B6 was composed of escort ships crewed by members of three different navies (two British, three Norwegian and one Polish), but was nevertheless quite experienced, this being their fourth convoy together.[6] Most of the ships in HX.217 cleared New York harbour on 27 November 1942 and the convoy formed up off the Ambrose Lightship. The weather was already deteriorating, and, after passing close to Halifax and St John's, Newfoundland, HX.217 headed into the open ocean in a full-scale North Atlantic winter gale.

This weather was seen as a blessing by the merchantmen. As unpleasant as the heavy seas were to the crews of the freighters and their escorts, they were that much worse for the lookouts out on the bridge of any of the twenty-one U-boats that comprised the two groups converging on HX.217. It would be one of the biggest concentrations yet against a single convoy. The 'Panzer' group had originally been formed to scout for a westbound convoy.[7] It was initially a group of seven boats formed 800nm west of Ireland on 29 November.[8] Its original intent was to sweep westward in search of a slow outbound convoy, ONS.151. The group swept to the southwest in a front over 100nm wide without sighting anything until it reached 45°W, approximately 500nm east of Newfoundland, on 4 December. Another group was formed in the meanwhile. The 'Draufgänger' (Daredevil) group was formed from ten boats on 30 November southeast of the 'Panzer' group to intercept another slow westbound convoy.[9] This convoy was sighted briefly by U-603, which was part of neither group, but the visibility was so limited in the area due to sea fog that no further contact was made and the 'Draufgänger' boats were ordered to the north to back up the 'Panzer' boats.

U-524, one of the 'Panzer' group boats, was fitted with an experimental VHF radio receiver and carried a team of radio operators from the B-Dienst, the German radio intelligence service, in an attempt to intercept the short-range TBS traffic used between ships in convoys.[10]

> U-524, a member of the Group 'Panzer' covered coded English R/T from 1800–2000 in AJ 8766. There were ten participants. No visual or hydrophone bearing. As, according to dead reckoning the expected convoy must be somewhere in this region, Group 'Panzer' received instructions to proceed on a course of 50° at high speed and to patrol from AJ 8321 - 9762 on 5.12. at 1100 in the patrol channels.[11]

This order, on 4 December, sent the 'Panzer' boats back towards the northeast at their best speed. Dönitz believed the U-boats were ahead of the convoy; he wanted the boats to stay ahead of it through the night and then wait for it to catch up during the next day.[12] In fact it was not until the day after, 6 December, that U-524 sighted HX.217 for the first time. Poor visibility and rough weather prevented an attack that first night, but by dawn five U-boats had gathered around the convoy and more were coming. That day, Dönitz ordered the '*Draufgänger*' boats to join the attack, which meant that by the next morning, 8 December 1942, as many as seventeen boats would be dedicated to attacking HX.217.

U-524 drew first blood. After missing with a full spread of four torpedoes just before dawn on the 7th, *U-524* attacked again that night and hit a large tanker.[13] Coming back to the site just before dawn on the 8th, she found the ship abandoned but still afloat and dispatched her with another torpedo. Surely, with so many U-boats swarming around the convoy, that night would bring more successes.

That, however, was not to be. What it brought, was perhaps Dönitz's worst nightmare.

> *U-221* reported ramming *U-254* at 2225 in AK 2551 and having taken survivors on board. It continued the search and intended to begin the return voyage after daylight. No more survivors were found. *U-221* began her homeward voyage after dawn.[14]

He had to wait until *U-221* arrived home before he got more details. Not that there was much to say, but *Kapitänleutnant* Hans Trojer's log had a few more things to say about what happened.

		Proceeded in pursuit of convoy at high speed.
2134	Night dark, Sea 5, Squalls of rain.	German U-boat sighted through rain squall on starboard bow. Turned away with full rudder, but could not avoid sharp blow on after pressure hull. Collision hardly noticeable to us.
		The other boat remained afloat, but started to settle in the water. Observed a few pocket torches and about thirty men in lifejackets and escape gear. Switched on searchlights and warned men to keep calm. Constant shouts for help. Used Sander pistol and heaving lines in attempts to help, but all attempts frustrated by heavy seas.
		Some of my own men, attached to lifelines, went overboard, but could do nothing. Only one petty officer and three men succeeded in grabbing lines and were hauled aboard, in spite of heavy seas which were breaking over the bridge. It is *U-254*. After we

> persisted in our efforts for two
> hours, during which searchlight was
> in constant use, two star shells
> were fired to the east of us and a
> vessel switched on two lights.

U-221 then cleared the area, reported in to Dönitz and, as noted, after one more fruitless look around at dawn, started for home with a damaged bow and the four survivors from *U-254*. No-one, it appears, saw *U-254* sink. Perhaps she went down with men still clinging to her. We will never know. It is known that no additional survivors were picked up. For some time after the war, it was claimed that she was sunk by depth charges dropped by a Liberator of 120 Squadron RAF, but research now shows that this was not the case.[15] It must be assumed that she sank that same night from damage sustained in the collision. She was not seen again after *U-221* departed the scene. Forty-one members of her crew, including all her officers, died that night.

The fact that more than three years of war had passed before this happened made it no less easy to accept. Dönitz pondered the event that night and concluded the log entry for 8 December with the following rumination:

> For the first time during a convoy operation a ramming has taken place between two U-boats, and thereby caused the loss of one of them. As far as can be seen here, this accident took place on a dark night and in a rough sea, so that the ramming boat cannot be blamed. The presence of so many U-boats on convoy operations has for a long time made this kind of damage a possibility. Reflection on this matter shows that generally speaking, it is not practicable to have more than thirteen to fifteen boats on to one convoy. Any tactical limitations in connection with the number of attacking boats, the time of the attack, the disposition for attack, by which such collisions could be avoided will be refused, as it is wrong with the difficulties of convoy warfare to apply even the smallest conditions. With the difficulties of convoy warfare every chance of attack must be exploited to the utmost and the maxim impressed again and again on the boats, 'on to the target as quickly as possible, attack as often as possible, utilise every chance of attack at once', may not be repudiated on the grounds of security.[16]

Four more boats came up during the day on the 9th, bringing the ultimate total of attackers to twenty-one boats.[17] The results for all that effort, were disappointing. Only one more ship, the motor freighter *Charles L.D.*, was sunk. One more U-boat was also lost.[18] As per Dönitz's decision of the night before, this was the last time so many boats would be concentrated in such a small area. It was not the last time that the effort of so many U-boats would lead to disappointment. The defences in the Atlantic were stiffening as the number and skill of the escorts were increasing and more long-range aircraft were closing the 'air gap' in the middle of the ocean. It would only be another few months until May 1943 and the sudden, complete failure of the U-boat offensive against the convoys.

CHAPTER 19

The Only American Loss

uss *Corvina* and *I-176*

THERE ARE A NUMBER OF major myths regarding American involvement in the Second World War, many of them believed by many Americans. One was that before the Japanese attack on Pearl Harbor, the Americans were inward-looking, content to tend their cornfields and watch their baseball games and let the Europeans bash each other to bits. That may, in fact, have been true for a great many Americans, but not for the one that mattered most, President Franklin Delano Roosevelt, known universally as FDR. He knew the stakes were high in the European war. He knew that a German victory would be very bad for the United States. More importantly, he was willing to take steps that would almost certainly have eventually brought the US into that war without any help from the Japanese.

These included escorting convoys in the western Atlantic and basing US Navy warships in Iceland starting in July 1941. The *Greer* incident in September pushed the US even closer to war. At that time, FDR declared: 'From now on, if German or Italian vessels of war enter the waters the protection of which is necessary for American defense, they do so at their own risk.'[1] Not that far short of a declaration of war. Furthermore, the US was at the same time taking a very tough stand in negotiations with the Japanese.[2] It is clear that most Americans expected war to start in the Atlantic before the Pacific, but it is unlikely anyone was terribly surprised that America was in the war before the beginning of 1942. There is, however, no question that the attack on Pearl Harbor was a bigger, and just as unpleasant, surprise for Hitler than for FDR.

The second major myth was that the Japanese attacked Pearl Harbor on 7 December 1941 and on 8 December 1941, the Americans began building the massive military machine that would dominate the second half of the twentieth century, including the largest navy the world has ever seen. In fact, this military, and in particular this navy, had been in the works for some time before Pearl Harbor. Every battleship and many of the aircraft carriers, cruisers and destroyers that dominated the Pacific were laid down before the Japanese attack. The *Gato* class fleet submarines, with which America fought and won the Pacific war, were likewise conceived and the first boats launched before the Pearl Harbor attack.[3]

In a manner not terribly different from the way Dönitz decided that the

Type VII boat best met his needs, the US Navy settled on the *Gato* class as best fitting their requirements. As the perceived requirements were different, so too were the boats. The Type VII was designed originally to fight in the waters of the Atlantic around the British Isles. That it later proved capable of operating as far afield as the coast of North America was an added bonus. Dönitz needed a boat with great manoeuvrability and small enough in size that a large number could be produced from Germany's limited resources. It was a boat designed to operate in packs. The *Gato* class was designed first and foremost to operate alone over the vastly greater expanse of the Pacific. As such, it was bigger, faster, longer-ranged and better-armed, in some aspects by a factor of two or more when compared to the Type VII. But the fact that the Americans built as many *Gatos* as they did was a testament to the far greater industrial capability of the US, rather than any plan to design a submarine best suited for production in large numbers.

There was nothing unusual about uss *Corvina*, except that she alone among the 185 *Gatos* to see war service achieved a unique and sad distinction.[4] She was the only US Navy submarine to be sunk by an enemy submarine in the Second World War. *Corvina* was built by the Electric Boat Co., the primary private builder of US Navy submarines. She was laid down in September 1942, launched in May 1943 and commissioned in August of that year. In common with nearly all US Navy submarines, she was built on the east coast and worked up in the waters around New London, Connecticut. Her captain was Commander Roderick Rooney, who graduated from Annapolis in 1929, making him older and more senior than the typical US Navy submarine commander. *Corvina* left New London on 18 September 1943, using the long cruise down the eastern seaboard, across the Caribbean, through the Panama Canal and on to Hawaii to further train the crew in the routines of submarine operations. She arrived at Pearl Harbor on 14 October and, after a brief refit and provisioning, left on her first patrol on 4 November. Two days later, she stopped in at Johnston Island, maintained as a refueling stop 700nm southwest of Hawaii. There she topped up her fuel bunkers. That was the last time she was seen by friendly forces.

Her assignment was a tough one for a first combat patrol. The US Navy was about to start its 'island hopping' campaign across the Central Pacific. The first stop would be the Gilbert Islands, specifically the islands of Tarawa, Makin and Apamama.[5] *Corvina* was one of ten submarines reporting to the Commander, Submarine Force, US Pacific Fleet (COMSUBPAC) assigned to support the landings. Her specific assignment was to patrol off the southern exits from the Truk Atoll, looking for Japanese fleet movements that might interfere with the planned landings.[6] On 14 December, she was to transfer officially to the control of the Commander, Submarines, US Southwest Pacific Fleet (COMSUBSWPAC), based at Fremantle.[7]

I-176 was a submarine of Type KD7. Like other navies, submarine development in the Imperial Japanese Navy (IJN) followed several separate paths. One of those paths closely resembled that taken by the Americans that eventually led to the *Gato* class – the development of large, fast submarines intended to support fleet operations across the Pacific.[8] Influenced by German *U-Kreuzer* designs and the Royal Navy's 'J' class boats of 1915–17, the Japanese designed their first true ocean-going submarine, the *Kaidai* Type 1 (or KD1) boat, No. 44 in 1920.[9] The series was refined through intermediate steps, culminating in the ten Type KD7 boats, which were laid down in 1940–1.

I-76 was the first KD7 boat; she was launched in 1941 at the Kure Naval Yard and completed on 4 August 1942. In May 1942, in a general re-organisation of the submarine service, the IJN renumbered *I-76* as *I-176*. Her commander was *Sho-sa* (Lieutenant Commander) Tanabe Yahachi. Tanabe had previously commanded *I-168*, a KD6A boat (formerly *I-68*).[10] In that position, he established himself as one of Japan's most successful commanders. At the Battle of Midway, *I-168* provided the only real successes for Japanese forces. On 6 June 1942, two days after the main carrier air battle, *I-168* sighted the damaged aircraft carrier USS *Yorktown* escorted by six destroyers. The initial sighting was made at 0410 at a range of 12 miles. Approaching slowly, Tanabe had closed to within a mile of the carrier by 0600 when he sighted the escort and submerged. Over the next six-and-a-half hours, Tanabe maneuvered at periscope depth to put *I-168* in position to fire at *Yorktown*. He was on the carrier's starboard side, where the destroyer *Hammann* was tied alongside providing power and water to fight the fires still burning on the carrier. At 1331, at a range of 1,300m, he fired two salvos of two torpedoes each. The first hit *Hammann*, Tanabe watching her break in two. The next two struck under *Yorktown*'s bridge in her starboard side and the fourth passed astern. *I-168* was immediately detected and attacked by three destroyers. The attack continued intermittently for the next six hours and included more than sixty depth charges. With air and battery power failing three hours into the siege, *I-168* had surfaced and the crew prepared for a gun duel, but the destroyers reacted slowly and gave Tanabe enough time on the surface to get fresh air into the boat and partially recharge the batteries before he was forced to submerge again. Finally, at 2000, having squeezed the last volt out of his exhausted batteries, he surfaced to find the destroyers departed and the horizon clear. He triumphantly, and prematurely, reported the sinkings to the flagship. *Hammann* had indeed sunk in less than four minutes, but *Yorktown* was still afloat. In fact, she appeared to be healthier than before Tanabe's attack. The damage done by the air attack on the 4th had included two torpedoes in her port side, and, when *I-168* found her, she was listing 26° to port. The two torpedoes Tanabe put in her starboard side evened out the flooding to the extent that her list decreased to 17°. But the damage was such that the Americans prudently pulled the salvage crews off as darkness approached, planning on resuming the fight to save the carrier the next morning. At first light, the carrier was still afloat but the list was visibly increasing and, at 0701 she rolled over and disappeared beneath the waves. Tanabe had achieved perhaps the greatest single victory for a Japanese submarine in the Pacific war.

Not long after taking *I-168* back to Japan, Tanabe was promoted to the rank of *Chu-sa* (Commander) and ordered to take over the brand-new *I-176*. She was commissioned under his command at Kure on 4 August 1942. Despite Tanabe's success in sinking *Yorktown*, the war had turned disastrously against Japan at Midway; nothing demonstrated that better than the successful American landings on Guadalcanal and Tulagi just three days after *I-176* was commissioned. *I-176* hurried through her working-up and departed Kure for Truk on 10 September, arriving six days later.[11] The forward base for US Navy forces supporting the landings was at Espiritu Santo in the New Hebrides.[12] Tanabe was sent, along with two other submarines, to intercept US Navy traffic between Espiritu Santo and the waters off Guadalcanal.

I-176 left Truk for the Coral Sea on 18 September 1942. Specifically, her assigned area was the stretch of water in the eastern Coral Sea bordered by the New Hebrides in the south, the Santa Cruz Islands on the east and San Cristobal, the southernmost of the Solomon Islands, on the northwest. The Americans dubbed these waters 'Torpedo Junction' for the frequency with which they encountered Japanese submarines. There, at 2040 on 20 October, Tanabe sighted a group of three cruisers and four destroyers from Rear Admiral Willis Lee's TF 64 heading roughly southward, zigzagging at 19 knots. In the moonlight, Tanabe misidentified his targets as two battleships, two cruisers and several destroyers. He lined up a shot at a '*Texas* class battleship' and fired a full salvo of six 'Long Lance' torpedoes at 2115.[13] The ship Tanabe was actually aiming at was USS *Chester*, a heavy cruiser of the *Northampton* class.[144] One torpedo hit *Chester* on her starboard side amidships below her armour belt; fortunately, the other five missed. Eleven sailors were killed and a further twelve were wounded. *Chester* remained afloat, but lost power and ended up dead in the water for an hour-and-a-half, after which she was again able to raise steam and make her way back to Espiritu Santo under her own power. She eventually sailed across the Pacific and up the Atlantic coast to Norfolk, where she was repaired and refitted for nearly 10 months. *I-176* was chased for three hours by escorting destroyers, but was eventually able to surface and arrived back at Truk on 29 October. Tanabe correctly surmised that he had not sunk the 'battleship' he had fired at, only damaging her.

Over the next year, *I-176* operated out of Rabaul, employed mainly in running supplies to the beleaguered Japanese troops on New Guinea and Guadalcanal.[15] These were risky missions for which submarines were ill-suited. For example, on 19 March 1943 she was unloading supplies in Lae harbour when three B-25 Mitchell bombers attacked.[16] One bomb hit, but exploded on rice drums stacked on the afterdeck. The rice absorbed the blast so that *I-176* suffered only minor damage, but there were three casualties among the crew on the bridge. Two helmsmen were killed outright and *Chu-sa* Tanabe was seriously wounded. The submarine put out to sea, but a test dive quickly revealed numerous leaks. Rather than risk the passage back to Rabaul on the surface, Tanabe ordered *I-176* grounded just outside Lae harbour, where army lighters were able to complete the offloading of the supplies. The crew then patched enough of the leaks that they were able to float off at the next high tide and successfully submerge the boat for the passage back to base. At Rabaul, *Sho-sa* Itakura Mitsuyoshi took over temporary command.

I-176 returned to Japan for more permanent repairs, returning to Rabaul in July 1943. While in Japan, *Sho-sa* Yamaguchi Kosaburo, formerly commander of *I-154*, took over the boat. From Rabaul, the boat made no less than ten supply runs to Japanese bases on New Guinea between mid-July and the beginning of November. While returning on 2 November to Rabaul from Sio, an outpost on the north shore of New Guinea's Huon Peninsula, *I-176* was diverted to look for survivors of the light cruiser *Sendai*, sunk by carrier aircraft after the Battle of Empress Augusta Bay. While on the surface approaching the site of the sinking, *I-176* was spotted by a US Navy seaplane and attacked with depth charges. One exploded close to her port side, causing damage sufficient to persuade Yamaguchi to call off his mission and return to Rabaul. Emergency repairs were made at Rabaul, but it was clear that the boat needed more extensive work, possible only at Truk. On 13 November 1943, *I-176* left Rabaul.

The radio traffic that informed the repair base at Truk of the damage to *I-176* and of the timing of her planned transit from Rabaul was encrypted using a code called Baker-9.[17] By the end of 1943, US Navy cryptanalysts were reading Baker-9 on a daily basis. These intercepts were codenamed 'MAGIC'.[18] Just as the Royal Navy used ULTRA information to target Axis convoys in the Mediterranean and re-route Allied convoys in the Atlantic, the US Navy was using MAGIC intercepts to guide its submarines to high-value targets. Like the British, the US had to be judicious in its use of MAGIC in order not to tip off the enemy that its mail was being read.[19] The knowledge that *I-176* was on her way to Truk was considered important enough to put three submarines on alert. Two of them were South Pacific boats operating out of Brisbane. *Blackfish* had been operating in the Atlantic since her commissioning; she was north of New Guinea on her first Pacific patrol. *Drum* was an experienced boat on her eighth patrol; her assigned sector was between the Bismarcks and the Caroline Islands, which included Truk. *Corvina* was the third boat notified of *I-176*'s passage. *Blackfish*, in fact, sighted a submarine at sunset on 16 November which must have been *I-176*, but did not fire at her because Commander R W Johnson could not be sure the submarine he sighted was hostile. *Drum* was unable to get in position to intercept *I-176*.

That left *Corvina*. She had not acknowledged receipt of the message informing her of *I-176*'s route, but that was standard procedure.[20] However, it is reasonable to surmise that she received the message since she was in position to intercept the Japanese boat just after midnight local time on 17 November – except it was *I-176* that did the intercepting.[21] Yamaguchi, in his subsequent report, identified the boat he sighted on the surface at 0015 as being a *Perch* class boat. The mistaken identification is understandable, in that very nearly all US Navy submarines built from the mid-1930s up to the end of the Second World War, which included the six *Perch* class boats, were very nearly identical in size and appearance and could be distinguished visually only by minor details. Regardless of the misidentification, he correctly identified the boat as American, so he ordered his boat to dive and began a methodical approach on the target, which was maneuvering at slow speed in what was probably a search pattern. It took over two hours for Yamaguchi to obtain a firing position, but when he did, he did not hesitate. *I-176* fired three torpedoes at 0220. Two of them hit *Corvina*, which disappeared in a massive explosion, taking her entire crew of eighty-two to the bottom. Having failed to appear in Australia as expected, a message was sent to *Corvina* on 30 November ordering her to meet a surface escort off Tulagi. When she failed to make that rendezvous and did not respond to further messages, she was listed as presumed lost on 23 December 1943.

I-176 arrived at Truk later on 17 November and then left for Japan and a four month-long refit. Yamaguchi was given a new submarine, *I-46*. He died when that submarine was sunk by the American destroyers USS *Helm* and *Gridley* on 28 October 1944 while trying to penetrate the screen around Admiral Halsey's fast carrier task force east of Leyte in the Philippines. *I-176* was taken over by *Sho-sa* Okada Hideo, who took the boat back to Truk in March 1944 where she was involved in further supply missions to isolated Japanese garrisons. Returning from one such mission to Buka Island at the northern tip of the Solomon chain, she was spotted by a US Navy patrol plane on 12 May 1944. As Rabaul was now no longer a usable naval base as a result of Allied air attacks, *I-176* proceeded up the eastern side of New Ireland Island on her way back to Truk. There she was located by a force of four American destroyers on the 16th. In an attack that lasted over 20 hours, *I-176* was finally destroyed the next day, with her entire crew of 103 officers and men. Tanabe Yahachi, who was hospitalised when he returned to Japan with *I-176* in April 1943, made a full recovery and survived the war.

CHAPTER 20

Sister Act

K XVI, K XVIII, I-66 (I-166),
HMS/M *Telemachus* and HMS/M *Taciturn*

THE DUTCH WERE ABOUT to go to war . . . again. Technically, they had been at war since May 1940, but in the East Indies the European conflict seemed far away. Since the rapid fall of the Dutch homeland, forces in the Far East had been making routine patrols and little else for a year-and-a-half. But now, the Japanese were making aggressive moves. They had occupied the northern part of French Indo-China in September 1940, directly threatening the Dutch position in Indonesia. Now, as 1941 was drawing to a close, that lull was clearly coming to an end. Tensions between the Americans and the Japanese were rapidly rising. On 25 July, it was announced that Vichy France had agreed to a Japanese protectorate over all of Indo-China, allowing Japanese troops to occupy the whole country. The next day, President Roosevelt had ordered Japanese assets in the US frozen, which was effectively an embargo on oil exports to Japan.[1]

Approximately 80 per cent of the oil used by Japan was imported from the US, so any restriction of oil exports from there had a potentially devastating effect. The Japanese had seen something like this coming and had tried to negotiate long-term oil contracts with the Dutch in Indonesia in late 1940. The talks failed both because the Dutch, who depended on the US and Great Britain for any hope of regaining their homeland, had every reason to put off the Japanese, and because the Japanese approached the talks with incredible arrogance, demanding concessions similar to those granted by the French in Indo-China. It soon became obvious that the only way to assure a supply of oil not controlled directly or indirectly by the United States would be to take the Dutch East Indies.

Thus, the Japanese knew they had either to capitulate to US pressure, which would mean withdrawal from most of their conquests on the Asian continent, or seize the resources denied them by the US embargo, which would mean war. They had oil stockpiles sufficient to last almost two years at current levels of consumption. It would last a much shorter time if war broke out with the United States. Add to that the knowledge that it would take some time to restore any conquered oil fields to peacetime production levels. The implication was clear. If the Japanese waited too long, they would have insufficient fuel to wage war. Not only were they facing a choice between capitulation and war, but the choice would have to be made soon. They had only a few months to make up their mind.

As summer turned into autumn in 1941, it became increasingly clear that Japan had no intention of withdrawing from China or Indo-China. The resignation of Prince Konoye as Prime Minister and his replacement by General Tojo Hideki on 18 October was correctly interpreted outside Japan as a sign that any chance of major Japanese concessions had passed. After that the only thing that could have prevented war was for the US to reverse course. Given FDR's determination to bring America into the European war, it simply was not an option for the US to make those kinds of concessions to an Axis partner.[2] From this point on, the progress to war in the Pacific was inexorable.

It is an interesting mental exercise to ponder which of the American-British-Dutch-Australian (ABDA) forces was least prepared for the war when it came on 8 December 1941.[3] Everyone knew the Japanese were coming and correctly expected the blow to fall primarily to the south from the Japanese bases on Formosa, Hainan and Indo-China.[4] As early as 30 November, at least some of the twelve Dutch submarines in the east were put under the operational control of the British Eastern Fleet as a pre-cautionary measure.[5] The three submarines of Division III were forward-based at Tarakan, on the east coast of Borneo, from 22 November. One of those three was *K XVI*, commanded by Ltz. I Louis Jan Jarman. She was a *K XIV* class boat, designed specifically for service in the East Indies, with better range and armament than any previous Dutch boat.[6] She had been commissioned in 1934 and the next year made the long journey to the east, where she served her entire career. News of the fall of 'metropolitan' Holland had little effect on the day-to-day activities of *K XVI* or any of the other Dutch boats in the east. However, two days after learning of the Pearl Harbor attack, the Dutch government in exile declared war on Japan and *K XVI* suddenly found herself in a shooting war.

The next two-and-a-half weeks were hectic as Japanese forces were repeatedly spotted and Jarman was sent off in various directions hunting for sometimes non-existent enemy concentrations. A Japanese convoy, a very real one this time, was sighted off the east coast of the Malay Peninsula on the 8th and *K XVI* was sent to intercept. Before she could reach that location, she was ordered south into the Java Sea, where a Japanese carrier force had been reported on the 11th. Running low on fuel, having now done a high-speed circuit of Borneo, Jarman was ordered into Surabaya to replenish supplies. On the 15th, *K XVI* was again underway, headed again for the South China Sea. Reports of Japanese movements now came in even more frequently. In the next few days, Japanese aircraft carriers were spotted numerous times off the west coast of Borneo. Landings on the north coast of Borneo started on the 16th.

Arriving off the coast of Borneo near Kuching on 23 December, *K XVI* began looking for the Japanese invasion fleet which, that same day, had begun putting troops ashore just up the coast. This time, the wandering

Dutch boats found targets. During the day on the 23rd, *K XIV* spotted the troop convoy and sank two transports and damaged two more. That night Jarman located the covering force of warships – three cruisers and two destroyers – and made his attack. Two torpedoes hit the destroyer *Sagiri*. The resulting fire was fed, in part, by the pure oxygen in the Type 93 torpedoes onboard the destroyer. Eventually, the warheads of those torpedoes ignited and the destroyer disintegrated in a massive explosion. Jarman manoeuvred closer to the landing ships and, later that day, attempted to torpedo the destroyer *Murakumo*, but that attack failed. As darkness fell, Jarman took his boat away from the coast so she could come to the surface to recharge batteries. He planned to resume the attack the next day. After dawn on the 25th, Jarman began working his way back towards the invasion fleet. Unfortunately, his was not the only submarine in the vicinity.

I-66 was a KD5 boat, a design antecedent of *I-168* and *I-176*. Like those later boats, she was large and designed for long-range operations. In late November 1941, under the command of *Chu-sa* (Commander) Yoshitomi Zenji, *I-66* was posted to Samah, a major port at the southern tip of Hainan Island.[7] Situated where the Gulf of Tonkin meets the South China Sea, Hainan was an ideal launching pad for an invasion of the East Indies. On 5 December, *I-66* left Samah for Borneo, where, on 16 December, Yoshitomi conducted a reconnaissance of the port of Kuching through his periscope. Finding no unusual activity, he sent the report that cleared the way for the landings by Japanese marines and specially trained army assault troops.[8] Aware that Dutch submarines were in the vicinity, Yoshitomi stayed to patrol north of the landing site. At 1145 on 25 December, while submerged approximately 60 miles northwest of the port, Yoshitomi was informed by his soundman that there was a contact off his starboard bow. Raising the periscope, he sighted what he described as a 'quite large' submarine on the surface less than 50m away.[9] Far too close to fire from that distance, he turned sharply and put *I-66* on a circular course that would, 13 minutes later, put him in a firing position. This allowed him to fire a single torpedo that hit his target, the Dutch *K XVI*, which sank with all hands, thirty-six officers and men.

While *K XVI* had been kept busy in those first weeks of the war in the Pacific, her sister *K XVIII*, part of Submarine Division I, was doing very little, spending most of the time patrolling near her base at Surabaya. Finally, in January, she was put to work, heading into the Makassar Straits, looking for an anticipated Japanese invasion fleet. Having taken Tarakan further up the eastern coast of Borneo on the 11th, the Japanese did indeed plan on moving down the coast. With word that the invasion fleet was leaving Tarakan on the 21st, *K XVIII* approached Balikpapan, the most likely target for the next landings. The following day, she sank the Dutch lightship *Orion* by gunfire outside the harbour to deny the navigational aid to the Japanese. Along with *K XIV* and six US Navy submarines, she patrolled in the straits.[10] In the afternoon of the 23rd, *K XVIII* sighted the invasion fleet and fired a salvo of torpedoes at what was believed to be one of the escorting destroyers. That night, *K XVIII*'s captain, Ltz. I C A J van Well Groeneveld, reported the destroyer's destruction. Post-war analysis indicates that the ship at which he actually fired was the old light cruiser *Naka*, which he missed. The torpedoes, however, continued on and at least one of them found a target, sinking the troop transport *Tsuruga Maru*.

The next day, 24 January 1942, *K XVIII* made one more attack. In the Makassar Straits off Samarinda, she fired torpedoes at a Japanese warship, at least one of which hit. The ship she attacked was *Patrol Boat No.37*, formerly the destroyer *Hishi*. The target did not sink, but the damage was such that she was never repaired, being stricken shortly thereafter.[11] Later that same day, *K XVIII* was damaged so severely by Japanese depth charges near Balikpapan that she was no longer capable of diving and was forced to head back to Surabaya for repairs. She remained in port, under repair, as the Japanese landed on 28 February, 100 miles up the coast. The Japanese troops advanced rapidly against light resistance. That same day, despite being unable to manoeuvre, *K XVIII* nevertheless used her deck gun to sink the damaged destroyer *Banckert*, which was also in harbour at Surabaya in non-seaworthy condition. Finally, as the Japanese forces approached the city, *K XVIII* was herself scuttled on 2 March 1942.

That would seem to end the story of these ill-fated sisters, but a few twists remained, involving two more sisters. HMS/M *Telemachus* and *Taciturn* were wartime repeats of the basic large 'T' class design that had included *Triton* and *Thistle*. They were big and fast, ideally suited for war in the east and both ended up being assigned to operations in the Indian Ocean and around the Indonesian archipelago. *Telemachus* did not join the fleet until the beginning of 1944 and was making only her second patrol, her first in the Far East, when she entered the narrowest part of the Malacca Straits between Sumatra and the Malay Peninsula on 17 July. There she encountered *I-166*.

The Japanese submarine *I-166* was, in fact, the same boat as the *I-66* which had sunk *K XVI* in 1941. She had since had a long, busy and successful career under several commanding officers. In May 1942, in the general restructuring of Imperial Japanese Navy submarine forces, she was renumbered. Under the command of *Tai-I* (Lieutenant) Suwa Koichiro, she had been operating in the Indian Ocean from Penang since late September 1943.[12] On 16 July 1944, she left Penang for Singapore to take part in anti-submarine exercises with forces located there.[13] She was on the surface, making high speed through the area of the One Fathom Bank, south of Klang, at the northern entrance to the narrows. At that point, the navigable channel is less than a mile wide. Just after 0700, she was sighted by Commander William D A King at the periscope of *Telemachus*. King tracked *I-166* for almost half-an-hour before launching a full spread of six new-type torpedoes at the fast moving Japanese submarine. These torpedoes had heavier warheads than the older model they replaced, for which *Telemachus* had not been properly prepared. As a consequence, the submarine broached after launching the torpedoes, the amount of water let into the forward compensating tank being too small. Fortunately, this made no difference, as one of the six torpedoes hit *I-166* a minute later, sinking the submarine instantly. *Tai-I* Suwa and four others of the bridge watch were thrown clear and were picked up later by Japanese patrol boats. Eighty-nine other crewmen went down with *I-166*. Suwa was given command of the new sea-going boat *RO-55*.[114] He died when that boat was sunk by US forces, most likely on 7 February 1945. *Telemachus* survived the war, was taken over by the Royal Australian Navy and served there until being returned to Britain in 1959 and broken up in 1961.

One more boat becomes involved in this story – HMS/M *Taciturn* – which began operating in the Indian Ocean out of Trincomalee in early 1945 after a brief stint in the Atlantic. As such, she frequented the waters around Java. On one patrol, in June 1945, she sighted and sank a stationary submarine in the Madura Strait east of Surabaya. This was *K XVIII*, salvaged by the Japanese in 1944, made marginally seaworthy, fitted with radar and anchored out in the straits as a radar picket hulk on the lookout for Allied air raids. Her dispatch by a single torpedo from *Taciturn* on 16 June 1945 ended her long and convoluted career.

CHAPTER 21

Battle at Periscope Depth

HMS/M *Venturer*, *U-771* and *U-864*

BY THE AUTUMN OF 1944, the Battle of the Atlantic certainly appeared to be all but over. The defeat of the U-boats in the convoy lanes of the North Atlantic, starting with 'Black May' in 1943, had been decisive, and with the surrender of Axis troops in Tunisia that same month, the submarine campaign in the Mediterranean was also as good as won. Understandably, the attention of the Royal Navy increasingly shifted towards the Indian Ocean and the Pacific, but there remained one area where the U-boat menace stubbornly refused to go away: the waters of the far north. The presence of U-boat bases along the Norwegian coast from Kristiansand in the south to Hammerfest in the north, meant that U-boats could still attack the vital shipping between Britain and the Soviet Union with somewhat less exposure to Allied air superiority than they would have faced in the open Atlantic.

This meant that the North Sea and the Norwegian Sea further north were again, or perhaps still, the frequent operational areas for British submarines. The medium-sized 'S' class and big 'T' class boats coming out of Britain's shipyards were almost all being sent out to the Far East, but many of the smaller 'U' and 'V' class boats were retained in home waters and were venturing out into turbulent waters in search of the old enemy, Dönitz's U-boats.

The most successful of this newer generation of submarines and commanders was HMS/M *Venturer*, fighting under the command of Lieutenant James S 'Jimmy' Launders. She was a close, but not identical, sister to boats such as *Unbeaten* and *Upholder*, which had carried the burden in the Mediterranean. Compared to those boats, *Venturer* was somewhat longer and heavier, both of which tended to make her a bit quieter underwater, though otherwise she was quite similar to her famous sisters. Like the captains of those boats, Woodward and Wanklyn, Launders would also join the elite group of submarine commanders who accounted for more than one enemy submarine.

The first of those was *U-771*. She was a typical late-war Type VIIC boat, meaning she had been launched and commissioned well after the weaknesses of the type had rendered them largely ineffective against constantly improving Allied defences. Commissioned in November 1943 under the command of *Oberleutnant zur See* Helmut Block, the boat trained in the Baltic for six months before departing for Norway. Though nominally assigned to the 9th Flotilla based at Brest, *U-771* sailed from Stavanger for her first operational patrol as part of *Gruppe 'Mitte'*, patrolling off the coast of Norway. They were there to detect any British moves to invade that country.[1] After three-and-a-half weeks of fruitless patrolling, Block put his boat into Bergen to replenish. The only 'success' of this mission was the downing of an RAF Liberator on 26 June, a small measure of revenge for the still frequent air attacks that dogged patrolling U-boats in the Norwegian Sea.

On 2 August, *U-771* departed Stavanger for what was meant to be her second patrol, but while still under escort of a local patrol boat, she was attacked by a pair of RAF Mosquitoes.[2] One of the aircraft was flown by an experienced pilot. He strafed *U-771* with 20mm cannon fire and then dropped a pair of depth charges that straddled the boat. The second aircraft, flown by a newly-minted Sub-Lieutenant, perhaps disturbed by the flak being put up by *U-771*, came in too low and clipping the mast of the patrol boat, crashed into the sea. *U-771*, with major damage from the depth charges, put back into Bergen for repairs. It was nearly two months before she was cleared for operations again; it was early October before the boat, now assigned to the 13th Flotilla and forward-based at Hammerfest, the northernmost U-boat base, sortied against the Murmansk convoys. She participated in an unsuccessful attack on Convoy JW.61 and then in an equally fruitless sweep of the Barents Sea. She was heading back to Narvik on 11 November 1944 when she was sighted by *Venturer*.[3]

Launders had left Dundee on 4 November for Operation 'Hangman', a mission to run supplies to Norwegian coastwatchers in the Narvik region. At 0735 on 11 November, that put *Venturer* submerged near the entrance to Andfjord on the northern approaches to Harstad. Andy Chalmers, the first lieutenant and watch officer, making a sweep through the periscope, sighted the conning tower of a U-boat on the surface, crossing from north to south. Calling Launders to the control room, it took them only a few minutes to line up the target and get a spread of four torpedoes ready to fire. The range had come down to 2,000m by the time the salvo was fired. Approximately 90 seconds later, there was a single loud explosion, after that only breaking-up noises and the small detonations of *U-771*'s batteries were heard. Numerous fishing boats were detected off to the south. Knowing that the Germans often used fishing boats as anti-submarine auxiliaries, Launders decided to head north out of the fjord rather than search for survivors. The whole operation, from sighting to sinking, had taken less than six minutes. The U-boat's entire crew of fifty-one perished; in her brief career, *U-771* had, excluding the downed aircraft, achieved no success.

Less than three months later, *Venturer* was once again off the Norwegian coast, further south this time. Once again, Launders would detect, stalk and sink a U-boat, though the engagement could hardly have been more different. At 0932 on 9 February 1945, Chalmers again had the watch and *Venturer* again was submerged when her soundman picked up faint mechanical sounds to the north. The sounds were soon identified as coming from a submerged U-boat, which proved to be *U-864*, a Type IXD2 boat, one of the largest 'conventional' attack submarines built by Nazi Germany.[4] Earlier Type IXs had been nicknamed '*Seekühe*' (Seacows) by the Germans because they were relatively sluggish, in particular taking almost half again as long to dive compared to the handier Type VIIs. These late-model Type IXs added considerable range and thus became mockingly known as '*Überseekühe*' (Overseas-cows). *U-864* was commissioned in December 1943 by *Korvettenkapitän* Ralf-Reimar Wolfram. He had previously commanded *U-108* for a period of 13 months, during which he took her out on three patrols that lasted a total of 112 days. For all this effort, Wolfram could claim only one sinking and even that claim is unsubstantiated.[5] Despite that signal lack of success, Wolfram was promoted and given command of the *U-864*.

Intended from the beginning as a '*Monsun*' boat, meaning a boat dedicated to operations in the Indian Ocean, she took a long time to work up, not reporting '*frontreife*' – ready for combat – until 1 November 1944, when she was assigned to the 33rd Flotilla, the base unit in Germany for these long-range boats, and even then, it took her another two months to move forward to Bergen, from where she would head out for Japan. There were many reasons why her progress had been so slow, not the least of which was that she had been fitted after her completion with a *Schnorkel* and working up with this new device took time.[6] After she was declared ready for combat, she moved by stages from Flensburg to Horten on the Oslofjord for final *Schnorkel* trials and then on to Farsund and Bergen, arriving there on New Year's Day 1945.[7] Twelve days after arriving at Bergen, *U-864* was damaged in an RAF raid, which further delayed her departure on patrol. Thus it was not until 7 February that Wolfram took his boat out of Bergen *en route* to Japan. His mission was only secondarily about sinking enemy ships; his primary mission was transporting materials and high-value personnel to Germany's ally.[8] Reports vary, but it is known that she was carrying a large quantity of mercury and possibly a disassembled Me 163 *Komet* rocket fighter, plans for the Me 262 jet fighter, radar and torpedo parts, as well as a contingent of *Luftwaffe* engineers, all bound for Japan. The plan was that she would drop these off and pick up a full load of strategic materials of which Germany was desperately short, such as tin, rubber and tungsten.

She never even made it out of the Norwegian Sea. Within a day of leaving port, heading northwest to pass around the Shetlands, she experienced a critical equipment failure and turned around.[9] It is possible that it was a failure of the *Schnorkel*, because these proved tricky to operate for inexperienced boats and because Launders reported not hearing the characteristic 'gefuffle' made by a snorkelling U-boat.[10] Wolfram had his boat on course back to Bergen near Fejeosen when the sound of his submerged passage was detected by the hydrophone operator on *Venturer*.[11] This, in and of itself, was quite unusual, but not unheard of. The detection of one submerged submarine by another submerged submarine requires that they be quite close, so it did not happen terribly frequently. What made this encounter absolutely unique was what followed. Normally, unless one of the submarines surfaced, the encounter led to no result other than the two boats eventually losing contact with each other.[12]

There are two reasons for this. One is the ever-present fear of fratricide. In this case, Launders had every reason to be certain that the boat he had detected was hostile, as he knew he was the only Allied submarine astride this approach to Bergen. But the main reason why these detections had never before developed into a successful attack was the primitive state of the underwater sound equipment of the time. The Germans had advanced the state-of-the-art in passive sonar, developing first the GHG (*Gruppenhorchgerät* – group listening apparatus) before the war and then the far more sophisticated *Balkongerät* (balcony apparatus) in 1943. This device was given this unusual name because it was composed of a short cylinder 2m across – the 'balcony' – around whose perimeter sound receptors were arrayed. As the war progressed, the basic structure of this apparatus remained the same, but the Germans continuously improved the wiring of the receptors so that the version fitted to late-war boats could determine the bearing and speed of contacts with considerable accuracy.[13]

The equivalent device mounted on *Venturer* was a Type 129 hydrophone. This was a far more primitive apparatus. Yet, in the hands of a skilled operator, it could be used to good effect, and *Venturer*'s operator was skilled. Launders' boat was heading north; the source of the sound appeared to be approaching from off her port bow.

> At 0932 faint hydrophone effect was picked up bearing 340°. This soon faded but was again picked up at 1010 bearing 295°.[14]

Making periodic peeks through the periscope in the direction of the sound, Launders was finally rewarded 40 minutes later with the sight of a 'thin mast' at a range of approximately 5,000m.

> *Venturer* closed to the northward to intercept and again sighted the periscope at 1115. A snap attack could then have been carried out, but *Venturer*'s captain decided to shadow his prey so as to get more accurate estimations before firing. At 1122 two periscopes were sighted, one showing about eight feet and the other about three. It appeared that *Venturer* was very broad on the bow and that the target would have to alter course to starboard to make Fejeosen.

It is unlikely that what Launders saw was two periscopes. More likely, it was one of the periscopes and the U-boat's high-frequency radio antenna.[15]

Passing up the opportunity for a quick shot based on very incomplete data, Launders opted to try his luck shadowing the U-boat, so he turned *Venturer* towards the southeast on a course parallel to his target's. (It is not

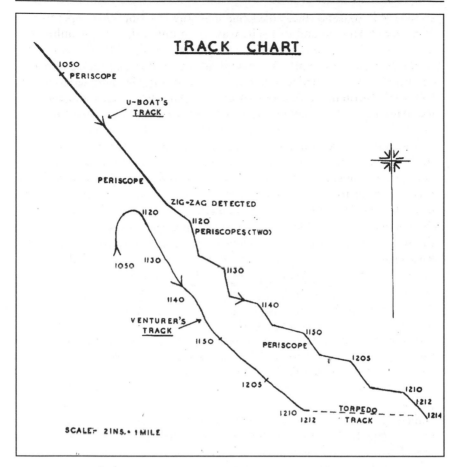

This chart was included with the *Monthly Anti-Submarine Report* for February 1945 along with the account of *Venturer*'s sinking of *U-864*. It shows *Venturer* trailing the U-boat as she zigzagged and finally lining up her salvo of four torpedoes.

known why *U-864* appears not to have detected *Venturer*'s presence at any time during this long engagement, especially since the boat was almost certainly fitted with a *Balkongerät*. Possibly the failure that caused Wolfram to turn around had also affected his sound gear. Or, perhaps, the noise being made by his boat made it impossible for his sound operator to hear outside sounds.)

As regards range, he considered that to transmit on the asdic would be to court detection and he only used it to listen for hydrophone effect; the plot had therefore to depend on his estimate of the range of the periscope and the asdic operator's estimate of the intensity of the hydrophone effect. This latter's task was made more difficult by the way in which the bearing of the hydrophone effect would draw aft steadily and then, at about five-minute intervals, make a sudden change as if the enemy had altered course. It is conceivable that this was due to the enemy zigzagging while proceeding submerged, but this must remain a matter for conjecture.

Launders was correct; *U-864* was almost certainly zigzagging around a base course of 135° at exactly five-minute intervals. He commented that the target was guilty of 'shameful periscope technique'. By this he meant that Wolfram kept his periscope raised for long periods of time, making it easy for him to obtain the sightings that allowed him to confirm what his hydrophone operator was telling him. It is possible, however, that what he took to be a periscope was the radio antenna, and that Wolfram was trying desperately to contact his base to warn them of his unplanned return and prevent an attack by his own anti-submarine forces. In any event, his message never got through. It is possible to speculate that an electrical fault had occurred that disabled all his sensor/communications systems, perhaps a power surge that damaged the delicate vacuum-tube-based electronics of these systems.

> At 1212, 2½ hours after the enemy boat was first detected, four torpedoes were fired in the direction of the sound source, with a spread of 1½ lengths on a target course of 140°, based on a target base course of 135° and 3½kt speed. As it was likely that the enemy would hear the sound of the approaching torpedoes, in order to take into account any evasive manoeuvres on his part, the centre of the salvo was towards the aft; the first torpedo was aimed at the bow of the enemy. The salvo was, because of the enemy's slow speed, fired at longer than normal time intervals.

Launders fired a 'hosepipe' salvo of all four torpedoes.[16] Range was estimated to be just under 2,000m. The accuracy of this estimation was critical as the spread of a salvo increased as a direct function of range. In fact, Launders underestimated the range, but not enough to ruin the shot.

> At 1214½ an explosion was heard, and then breaking-up noises. Three fainter explosions, which occurred at intervals of 16 or 17 seconds about five minutes after the salvo had been fired, were thought to be the torpedoes that had missed striking off Fejeosen and their regularity suggested that either the first or last torpedo had hit. It seems most likely that it was the last torpedo that had found its mark, as its running range was 2,300 yards and wreckage was found at this distance.

There were no survivors. *U-864* had been sunk just two days into her first war patrol. She had achieved no sinkings.

At first, *Venturer* did not approach the site of the sinking. For half an hour the boat maintained position, simply watching and listening. As when Launders had sunk *U-771*, there were again fishing trawlers near the scene. When these showed no sign of interest in the events taking place nearby, Launders approached cautiously, still submerged.

> She entered an extensive oil patch and saw floating in it a long steel cylinder, a little bigger than a torpedo; one end had a door with 'butterfly nuts', the other end being welded.

Launders speculated that this was one of the two storage containers used to house a Focke-Achgelis Fa 330 autogyro kite, such as was often fitted on boats headed for the Far East, although it could just as easily have been one of the watertight canisters from the forward deck casing used to store lifejackets or inflatable rafts. Launders then left the scene. The incident remains the only officially acknowledged instance of one submarine sinking another while both were submerged for the entire engagement. For this success, Launders received a bar to the DSO he had already been awarded for the sinking of *U-771*. Both awards were presented to Launders by King George VI on 27 July 1945. His hydrophone operator received a DSM for the skillful use of his equipment.

CHAPTER 22

One Magnificent Patrol

USS *Batfish* and two (or maybe three) Japanese submarines

IT IS POSSIBLE TO QUESTION whether USS *Batfish* really did sink *RO-115* on 10 February 1945.[1] Evidence exists to support the claim, but some sources say the Japanese boat was sunk ten days earlier approximately 650 miles away from where *Batfish* was that same day.[2] Other sources suggest that the boat *Batfish* sank that day was *I-41* or *RO-55*, or maybe even one of several other Japanese submarines that went missing during this period. Some even suggest that the attack on 10 February sank nothing at all, that the brilliant explosion Lieutenant Commander John K 'Jake' Fyfe saw was a premature detonation by a malfunctioning torpedo. But it is not necessary to credit Fyfe with this sinking to admit him into the elite ranks of those commanders who have sunk more than one enemy submarine. Even without considering *RO-115* or any of the other possible victims of *Batfish* that day, Fyfe joins von Heimburg, Wanklyn, Woodward and Launders, and is the only one of that select few to achieve his multiple victories in one magnificent patrol.

USS *Batfish* was a *Balao* class fleet submarine, meaning she was in the second of the three almost identical series of *Gato* class boats produced by the United States during the war.[3] She was launched on 5 May 1943 and commissioned on 21 August under the command of Lieutenant Commander Wayne Merrill. Merrill was neither particularly lucky nor particularly aggressive and lasted only two patrols in command of the boat. Before her third patrol, Fyfe took over from Merrill. However, *Batfish* had still been under Merrill's command when she had her first encounter with an enemy submarine.[4]

Batfish was still in the Atlantic, on her way through the Caribbean heading towards the Panama Canal, when she sighted a surfaced submarine in late October 1943. Assuming that the boat he had sighted could only be a U-boat, Merrill fired a single torpedo at the target. The torpedo missed and the submarine dived; *Batfish* lost contact and continued on to Coco Solo at the Caribbean end of the canal, docking there on 1 November. It is uncertain what boat *Batfish* fired at. Available records show no U-boats in or even near the Caribbean at the time. The closest boat appears to have been *U-214*, which had been operating in the Caribbean, laying mines off Colon on 8 October. Those mines might have claimed the submarine USS

Dorado.[5] However, *U-214* appears to have cleared the area well before *Batfish* arrived.[6]

Even after Fyfe took over the boat in May 1944, *Batfish*'s record was unspectacular. Over the next three patrols, which took her to Japan, the Carolines and the South China Sea in more than five-and-a-half months of active patrolling, she had accounted for just two small victims: a tramp steamer and a minesweeper.[7] These slim results discouraged neither Fyfe nor his superiors. By the second half of 1944, the war had shifted dramatically in the Pacific. There was no question, at least on the Allied side, who would win. The defeat of Japan was only a matter of time as she was being starved of food and all the resources necessary to wage a war. Her merchant fleet and her navy had either been sunk or forced to lurk in harbours, where they were only marginally safer than on the high seas. Thus Fyfe remained in command as *Batfish* left Pearl Harbor on 30 December 1944 on her sixth patrol. She spent a night at Guam and departed on 10 January 1945 along with *Archerfish* and *Blackfish*. Together, these three boats formed a group named 'Joe's Jugheads' under the command of Commander J F Enright on *Archerfish*.[8] On 16 January, the group passed through the Luzon Strait north of the Philippines and entered the South China Sea. The next day brought the first real excitement of the patrol:

0601 Dove. Fire in the after distribution board. Had to remain submerged all day to effect repairs ... Was without lights, ventilation and several other conveniences all of which made for a very uncomfortable day.[9]

It is easy to understand the concern an electrical fire can cause in a submarine and admire the laconic tone with which Fyfe recorded the event for his superior's consumption. Nor did things immediately improve. By the 18th, *Batfish* was off Hainan and in heavy weather. The weather got better over the next several days, but her luck did not. Finding nothing off the northern tip of Hainan, Fyfe took the boat to the southern end on 29 January and began patrolling off Yulin Bay. For the next four days, *Batfish* played hide-and-seek with a small freighter making a local run between several coastal towns, getting in a three-torpedo spread at one point which apparently ran harmlessly under the target. Fyfe was determined to get this elusive freighter, but received orders on 2 February ordering him and the rest of 'Joe's Jugheads' back to the Luzon Strait. MAGIC intercepts had revealed that the Japanese intended to send in multiple submarines in an attempt to evacuate personnel, and perhaps, more from the northern Philippine port of Aparri.[10] The 'Jugheads', joined by *Plaice* and *Scabbardfish* and later by *Sea Poacher* as well, were assigned to interrupt that operation.[11]

The Imperial Japanese Navy never thought of their submarines in the same way as Dönitz did or the Americans learned to. They thought of their submarines as part of their battle fleet and hoped that they, like their battleships and cruisers, would get a chance to face the US Navy in some climactic Pacific Jutland. They thought that using submarines to sink merchant shipping was almost demeaning to the warrior spirit of their navy. In the early months of the Pacific war, Japanese submarines had some signal successes, sinking *Yorktown* and *Wasp* among other warships, but targets like these were few and well protected, and the excellent, large and fast submarines in the Japanese fleet were, for the most part, underutilised. Inevitably, as the war turned against Japan and island garrisons were isolated by US forces, these boats were used increasingly to run cargo and evacuate isolated personnel. It was just this kind of mission that the 'Jugheads' were being ordered to intercept.

Ordered to patrol the wide pass between Babuyan and Calayan Islands and south into the Babuyan Channel, on a direct line to Aparri, *Batfish* spent five days encountering nothing other than aircraft until late on 9 February, when the action heated up noticeably.

1823	Surfaced.
2210	Radar signal on APR at 158 mgcs, 500 PRF.[12]
2250	SJ contact bearing 240 True, 11,000 yards.[13] Commenced tracking. Target tracked on course 310°, speed 12 knots so went to battle stations and commenced approach, broadcasting dope to other wolves in pack.[14] Saturation signals on APR at 158 mgcs which increased in intensity as range decreased.
2331	Commenced firing tubes 1, 2, 3, and 4 on 130° starboard track gyros practically zero, range 1,850 yards torpedoes set for six feet using a 2° divergent spread. All missed.
2339	(10s–40s) Four end of run explosions. Pulled out to 5,000 yards off target's track and commenced new end around while making reload.[15] The night was very dark, no moon, partially overcast and the target was not seen on first run but was believed to be a Japanese submarine. Decided to close to visual range for next attack and verify type of contact but tentatively set torpedo depths at 4 feet, 2 feet, 2 feet, and 0 feet.

This was a new kind of warfare, one in which attacks could be made without ever seeing the enemy. It added tremendous power and safety for the attacker but led to situations such as that faced by Fyfe. He has tracked a target solely by radar. He assumed that it was enemy because its radar signature as read off the APR was inconsistent with any of the radars carried by American submarines, which should have been the only friendly naval units he might encounter in the area. Anyway, if the target was friendly, it would be 'interrogated' and recognised by his IFF (Identification Friend or Foe) equipment. With this assurance, he attacked, but the attack failed despite a good setup. Fyfe concluded that the failure was due to the torpedoes running under the target; the obvious conclusion was that he was firing at a shallow-draft target, most likely a submarine. (It is interesting to note that Americans were not alone in experimenting with such 'blind' firing techniques. The Germans were using a different technology, sonar rather than radar, but were building boats designed from the outset to find targets and attack them without ever rising to periscope depth, much less the surface. The German Type XXI and XXIII U-boats, being equipped with advanced *Balkongerät* sound equipment and an array of torpedoes designed actively to seek out targets, and possessing high speed and exceptional endurance underwater, were expected to revolutionise the Battle of the Atlantic. Only the collapse of German land forces in early spring 1945 and the ability of Allied air forces to disrupt German industry prevented these exceptional boats from entering combat in meaningful numbers.[16])

A minute after midnight on 10 February, Fyfe returned to the attack:

0001	With range to target 1,020 yards a Japanese I class submarine was clearly visible from bridge. We were in a beautiful position – 90 track zero gyros so at
0002	Commenced firing tubes forward. #1 was a hot run in the tube, #2 hit, and number three passed over spot where submarine sank. The hit was accompanied by a brilliant red explosion that lit up the whole sky and the target sank almost immediately. Radar indications on the APR ceased abruptly. This radar signal was apparently non-directional type, and probably anti-aircraft since we closed to 900 yards without his giving any indication that he was aware of our presence.[17] Target disappeared from visual sight and on radar screen almost immediately, screws stopped and loud breaking up noises were heard on sound gear.
0015	Commenced reload forward, sent results of attack to pack commander and rigged searchlight preparatory to returning to scene and search for survivors.
0120	Very strong oil smell, heavy slick on water. A cut shows we are two miles east of the point of attack. Turned on our searchlight and after a short experiment decided we were advertising ourselves needlessly and accomplishing little except ruining the night vision of the bridge personnel and probably drawing airplanes.
0150	After running through the 'spot' several times decided to wait until daylight and come back to investigate. It was too dark to have been able to see any debris or survivors and while oil slick was indication submarine had sunk, would still like to salvage some Nip submariners and see what makes them tick.[18]

In the event, Fyfe never made it back to check out the site of the sinking. Almost continuous air traffic overhead kept *Batfish* submerged until late in the afternoon on the 10th. His inability to recover any debris or survivors that might have identified his victim helped fuel the uncertainty over what boat, if any, he really sank that night.[19] To start with, it is likely to the point of certainty, that Fyfe sank something that night. (Some sources have speculated that the explosion he saw was a premature

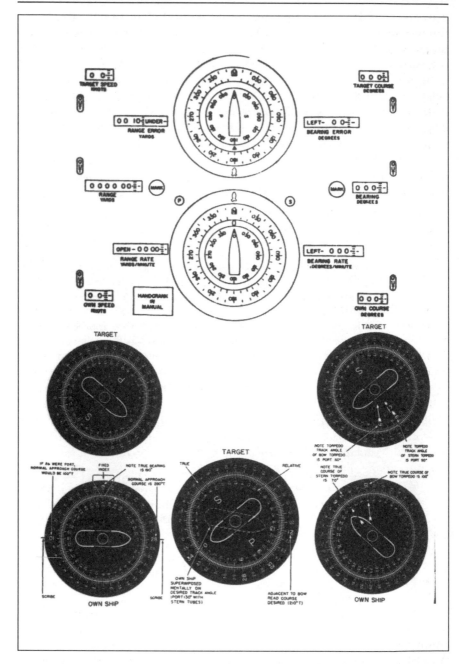

The US Navy's version of the analog attack computer found on British and German submarines in the Second World War was know as the TDC (Torpedo Data Computer). This chart shows the appearance of the face of a 1940 version of the TDC fitted to USS *Tambor* (SS 198). The main difference from the later Mk III version was that own-ship course and speed were manually entered in this version, while the later version received these values automatically from the gyro-compass and pitometer log. By the end of the war, target range and bearing were fed in automatically as well from the SJ radar. (USN)

detonation of the second torpedo, that he hit nothing with this salvo.) But the fact that his radar and his APR both ceased to register the enemy's presence at the same time that the explosion occurred, as well as his description of the site of the sinking matching so closely other descriptions of similar events, both make it highly likely that something was sunk. (The telltale oil slick and smell and the clearly audible breaking-up noises undermine the thesis that the explosion occurred near an enemy submarine which then safely submerged.) So, could the victim have been some vessel other than a submarine? The answer is that it is highly unlikely, given that the vessel was definitely a warship and large enough to carry one of the relatively rare Japanese radars, and that no Japanese surface vessel of any size is recorded as being lost in those waters anywhere near that time.[20]

This leaves the possibility that the victim that night was, in fact, the type of boat Fyfe claims he saw: a Japanese submarine. There are five Japanese submarines that have been suggested as *Batfish*'s possible victim: *I-41*, *RO-45*, *RO-46*, *RO-55* and *RO-115*. They make the list because they were all lost without definite proof sometime during this period. Of these, three are easy to dismiss as candidates. *I-41* and *RO-45* were already presumed lost by the Japanese months before this incident. *RO-46*, on the other hand, was seen at Kure two months after 10 February. That leaves *RO-55*, which is believed to have been attacked and sunk by USS *Thomason* off the west coast of Luzon on 7 February. That incident occurred 260nm from *Batfish*'s attack three days later. If *RO-55* survived *Thomason*'s attack, she could have reached the Babuyan Channel in enough time to cross paths with *Batfish*. *RO-115* is generally considered to have been sunk southwest of Manila on 31 January, but she was ordered on 4 February, along with *RO-46*, *RO-112* and *RO-113*, to rescue pilots stranded near Aparri by the collapse of Japanese forces on Luzon.[21] If she survived the attack on 31 January and if she received the orders to proceed to Aparri, she too could have been within range of *Batfish*'s torpedoes on the 10th. It is impossible to be sure, but, based on available evidence, it seems most likely that Fyfe's log is accurate, that *Batfish* sank a Japanese submarine, most likely *RO-115*, in the early morning of 10 February 1945. It is known that *RO-46* successfully rescued forty-six airmen and transported them to Takao, dropping them off on 12 February.[22] The fate of the other two boats, *RO-112* and *RO-113*, is not in dispute.

Early in the morning of the next day, 11 February, *Batfish* received orders from Enright to move to a new patrol sector west of Calayan Island, approximately 70 miles northwest of her current position. Given the lateness of the hour and the heaviness of the air traffic during the day, Fyfe opted to remain in the Babuyan Channel for the rest of the day and make the transfer that night. That decision proved fortuitous. Having surfaced at just about sunset, *Batfish* was slowly crossing below Camiguin Island northeast of Aparri when her electronics again tipped her to the presence of an enemy vessel.

1915	Radar signals on APR at 158 mgcs, 500 PRF. Since this is the same radar as we found on our submarine target last night, started searching very carefully on SJ and swung ship in order to find null in signal, thereby determining the approximate true bearing of the source.[23]
1951	Radar contact on SJ at 8,000 yards, bearing 310° True. Manned battle stations and commenced tracking. Since, if anything, it is darker than last night; and since we had found how ineffective the Jap radar was, decided to make a surface attack if possible and close target sufficiently to identify him by class.
2037	Sighted target from bridge at range 1,300 yards, identified as submarine with no shears, very low in water, and perhaps slightly smaller than our last target.[24]
2043	With range to target 1,200 yards, on a course for a 90° starboard track, had made up my mind to shoot when the gyro angles decreased 10 more degrees to 10° left.
2043-30	Signal on APR went off and target dove. Changed course to left and speeded up, in the meanwhile trying to reconcile myself to the fact that I had lost this one by trying to wait for the theoretically perfect set up.

There would be time enough later for self-recrimination. In the meanwhile, Fyfe had to deal with the fact that he might have gone from being the hunter to the hunted, and decided that distance in this case equalled safety. Earlier in the war, before the American superiority in radar technology made night not much different from day, the Japanese had been renowned and feared for their ability to fight at night. Excellent optics and regular night-fighting drills had frequently given them the edge in the vicious battles around Guadalcanal. By early 1945, however, over-reliance on radar that was clearly incapable of resolving a close-in target the size of a submarine, and lack of training had contributed to the inability of any of *Batfish*'s victims to detect the danger that was stalking them.[25] This was clearly the case with *RO-112*. There is no other explanation for what happened next.

2105	Just one half hour later heard a swishing noise from general direction of target that was universally accepted as the sound of a submarine blowing his ballast tanks.
2106	Sure enough, APR shows that 158 mgcs was back on and SJ made contact 8,650 yards, bearing 018° True. Whether the target heard us or thought he heard us; saw us or thought he saw us; had us on his radar or thought he did or just made a normal and routine night dive I don't know; but I do know that unless he has radar detector that will intercept our SJ, he's going to have a hard time finding us this time.
2109	Manned battle stations and started end around.
2150	With range to target 6,000 yards, dove to radar depth.[26]

2202	Commenced firing four tubes forward on a 100° starboard track, 880 yards range, torpedoes set to run at four feet using a 1 knot speed spread.
2202-50	First hit, timed as first torpedo. Target literally blew apart and sank almost immediately.
2211	One more explosion, very loud, which shook the boat considerably. Thought at first it was a close bomb, but then realized it was finale to the swan song of one Nip submarine.
2230	Taking sweep prior to surfacing, had possible plane contact at 5 miles. Dropped down to 100 feet.

Again, Fyfe was denied the chance positively to identify his victim, though this time there is no doubt who she was. The boat he sank has been positively identified as *RO-112*. She had departed Takao on 9 February on her eighth war patrol with the mission of picking up pilots stranded on Luzon by the destruction of their aircraft in Allied air raids. *Tai-i* (Lieutenant) Yuchi Toru and his sixty-one crew went down with the boat. In her year-and-a-half-long career, she had achieved no sinkings.

Batfish surfaced safely just before midnight and set out for her new patrol sector. The 12th was relatively uneventful until evening when Fyfe was ordered to make for the Batan Islands[27] to look for a downed US Navy flier. He was headed north at high speed after midnight when he again picked up a radar on his APR.

0227	Target tracks on base course 120° at 7 knots. Looks like another Nip sub so manned battle stations, submerged and commenced approach.
0241	With range to target 7,150 yards, he dove, why I'll never know, but he probably had a plane contact, or thought he did. Headed to a position ahead of him on his track so as to be in position when and if he surfaces.[28]
0310	APR signal at 157 back on again so submarine must be surfaced or taking a sweep.
0353	Finally regained contact after a few bad moments when we thought he was making an approach on us. Target now bears 336° True, range 9,800 yards. Commenced new approach.
0412	Dove on target's track at 6,800 yard range and went to radar depth.
0430	Swung for 90 track with stern tubes. Tide rips are making depth control and steering very difficult and I hope they don't adversely effect the torpedo.
0448	Commenced firing 3 tubes aft on an 80 starboard track, zero gyros 1500 yard torpedo run, using a 1 knot speed spread. Torpedoes set for six feet.
0449-30	Saw first torpedo hit and target sank immediately. Target could be seen blowing apart on radar screen and the explosion was

accompanied by a large yellow ball of fire and seen through the periscope. The second and third torpedoes missed, not due to errors in data, but because target sank so quickly.

0452   Surfaced and headed for oil slick.

This time Fyfe was determined to find out for sure what he had sunk.

0500   Ran through oil and wreckage debris. Attempted to use searchlight to search area and again this proved to be futile and unproductive ... so decided to stay surfaced until after daylight, planes permitting.

0620   After sighting several bits of wood and paper, lots of oil, but no survivors; our search for something tangible was rewarded when we recovered a wooden box that was found to contain Japanese navigation equipment and a book of tables. From the positions listed in the work book, it looks like this guy went from NAGOYA to FORMOSA before he headed down to LUZON to join his ancestors.

This boat is generally agreed to have been *RO-113*, under the command of *Tai-i* Harada Kiyoshi. *RO-113*'s career had been only slightly more successful than that of her sister, *RO-112*. Harada took his boat on two patrols in the Indian Ocean. On 6 November 1944 he sank a British freighter, the last Allied vessel torpedoed by a Japanese submarine in that ocean.[29] On the second patrol, he claimed two more sinkings in December, but those have not been substantiated. On 28 December, returning to Penang after that patrol, *RO-113* was attacked by HMS/M *Thule*. Under the command of Acting Lieutenant Commander A C G Mars, DSO, *Thule* lined up a good shot on *RO-113* and fired a full salvo of six torpedoes. A massive explosion followed, after which the Japanese boat was nowhere to be seen. Mars claimed the sinking, but it appears most, if not all, of the torpedoes exploded prematurely and *RO-113* survived this attack only to fall to *Batfish* a month-and-a-half later. Harada and his fifty-nine crew died in the sinking of his boat.

This success was Fyfe's and *Batfish*'s last. She headed back to Guam shortly afterwards in the company of *Blackfish*. After minor repairs, she returned to Pearl Harbor on 3 March. Fyfe gave up command of *Batfish* after this patrol. She went out on one more patrol, under a new commander, but by this point there were essentially no more targets and *Batfish*'s accomplishments on this mission were to rescue three US fliers and shell a Japanese fishing village. The war ended while she was on her way back to Midway. She was decommissioned in 1946 and placed in reserve, recommissioned in 1952 and served as a training boat until 1969. In 1972 she was stricken and acquired by the Batfish Memorial Foundation of Muskogee, Oklahoma, a town on the Arkansas River, a major tributary of the Mississippi River. There she sits today, in a city park, in a sea of grass, open to the public.

CHAPTER 23

Nearly Another Fratricide

USS *Hoe* and *Flounder* (and *U-537* too)

THE AMERICANS WERE MUCH MORE cautious than the Germans when it came to the risks involved in operating friendly submarines in close proximity to each other.[1] Nevertheless, the risks increased as the war progressed as a direct result of the very success enjoyed by those submarines. By February 1945, the area in which Japanese shipping could operate had shrunk, and the number of available US Navy submarines had increased to the point that the patrol zones of the US boats were getting dangerously close to each other. One of the places where that concentration was the densest was the South China Sea, especially along the coast of Indo-China, through which any shipping heading for the 'Home Islands' from the remaining Japanese possessions in Indonesia or Malaya was likely to pass. According to one report, there was a witticism repeated frequently in Singapore at the time that a person could walk to Japan stepping only on the periscopes of American submarines.[2]

USS *Hoe* was patrolling a sector in the South China Sea northeast of the naval base at Cam Ranh Bay in late February 1945. On the afternoon of the 23rd, she was submerged, looking and listening for any coastal traffic. *Hoe* was on her eighth war patrol, though this was only her second under the command of Lieutenant Commander M P Refo III. In her seven previous patrols, her success had been minimal. She had sunk one large tanker and one smaller freighter for all that time at sea.[3] Both of those victories had occurred before Refo took over command.

Hours earlier, Refo, believing *Hoe* to be approaching the southern edge of his zone, had turned his boat north and continued at a quiet, economical speed. What happened next, Refo recorded in his log:

1700   While at 60 feet, speed 1.8kt, course north . . . struck what I thought to be a rock. Ship took a four degree up angle and broached. Went to battle stations and blew all main ballast tanks. At the time of the supposed grounding, both myself and the executive officer were in the wardroom . . . On the way to the conning tower one look in the forward torpedo room showed that we had not holed the pressure hull. (The shock felt to me as though we had grounded forward on the starboard side.)

> 1706   A thorough inspection of the boat had now been made and no damage revealed.[4]

Refo popped the tower hatch and went up to take a look around. The only vessel in sight was a ship hull-down to the northeast; judging from the visible superstructure, it was a merchant ship of some type. Not an immediate threat. As his boat settled on the surface on an even keel, Refo set a course away from the merchant target. He wanted some time to assess his situation. He was to get very little.

> 1711   Sighted Jake type plane on starboard quarter, 40° port angle on the bow . . . Submerged with full left rudder.[5]

> 1723   Came up to periscope depth and commenced approach on target.

> 1735   Identified target as hospital ship.[6]

Refo was completely unaware that his activities of the preceding half-hour had caught the attention of another US submarine – USS *Flounder*. Despite having a lower hull number, she was almost a year younger than *Hoe*. She was on only her fifth war patrol in February 1945, all but the first under the command of Lieutenant Commander James E Stevens. Her success to date had been even slimmer than *Hoe*'s. She also could claim just two victories. One of them a small torpedo recovery vessel.[7] Her other victim, sunk on 9 November 1944, was more interesting.

U-537 was a Type IXC/40, a boat intended for long-range operations. She was commissioned in January 1943 under *Kapitänleutnant* Peter Schrewe and went through a relatively normal working-up before departing from Bergen on her first patrol at the end of September. This mission lasted just over two months and started with a special task. She carried two unusual passengers and the equipment to set up an automated weather station in a deserted spot in northern Labrador. The U-boat anchored in Martin Bay on 22 October, just south of Cape Chidley, the northernmost tip of Labrador. They inflated a pair of rubber rafts and, over a 24-hour period, manhandled ten waterproof cylinders ashore, each weighing 10kg and containing the weather instruments, a 150 W radio transmitter, a 10m tall antenna and multiple large dry-cell batteries.[8] In order to deceive anyone who found the apparatus, the cylinders were marked 'Canadian Weather Service' and the crewmen were given American cigarette packs and matchbooks to scatter around the site. In the event, these precautions were unnecessary as the site went undetected for 37 years. It was, it is believed, the only time uniformed German personnel 'invaded' North America during the Second World War. After this climax, Schrewe took *U-537* south to the region of the Grand Banks. He patrolled there for a number of weeks with no success before heading to Lorient, where he arrived on 8 December.

U-537 remained at Lorient for almost 4 months, preparing for the long trip to the Far East.[9] She left France on 25 March 1944, refuelling twice and making several unsuccessful attacks in the Indian Ocean, enduring a lengthy depth-charging lasting several days before arriving at Batavia on 2 August.[10] At first the plan was to send Schrewe back to Germany with much-needed cargo at the beginning of October, but the lack of refuelling prospects in the Indian Ocean led to her being reassigned to operations off Perth, Australia, where it was believed that easy pickings were to be had. She transferred in mid-October to Surabaya at the other end of Java, which was a better base of operations against western Australia. Five days before her planned departure on 9 November for Perth, details of her sailing, including her planned route and when she would be passing various landmarks, was radioed to Japanese garrisons throughout the area so she would not be attacked by 'friendly' aircraft or anti-submarine forces. The messages were intercepted and decrypted by US radio intelligence and made available to COMSUBSWPAC at Fremantle as part of the MAGIC system.

A pack of three US submarines was hastily assembled from boats that had put in for fuel at Darwin on Australia's northern coast.[11] *Flounder*, *Guavina* and *Bashaw*, under Stevens' tactical command, left Darwin on 6 November, making high speed towards the Lombok Strait between Bali and Lombok islands. The three boats passed the straits after dark on the 9th and took up positions between Bali and the Kangean Islands to the north, with *Flounder* at the northern end of the sweep line. Aware of the importance of the target he was after, Stevens ignored a small Japanese escort that passed in front of his periscope in the dark on the 10th. He was after bigger game. Just before 0800, his OOD observed through the periscope what he took to be a small sailboat off his port bow.[12] Within minutes, the image resolved itself into the tower of an approaching U-boat and Stevens took the boat to battle stations.

Schrewe was making 12 knots and zigzagging, but his zigzags were too regular, allowing Stevens to set up a simple submerged approach. *Flounder* was equipped with a few of the new Mk 18 electric torpedoes just being issued to the fleet.[13] Figuring that the wakeless feature of the new torpedoes would be an advantage in a daylight attack, Stevens turned away from *U-537*, because all of his Mk 18s were loaded aft. He launched all four of these torpedoes at a range of just under 1,000m. At least one, possibly two of them, hit the U-boat. The resulting explosion was spectacular, obscuring the boat in smoke and flame. Additional explosions were heard five and eight minutes later. Fearful that this might be Japanese aircraft dropping depth charges, Stevens took *Flounder* deep and away from the scene. Only when his sound operator said he also heard breaking-up noises was it clear that it was detonations inside the sinking *U-537* he was hearing. The boat went down with all fifty-eight of her crew and without being noticed by the Japanese. *U-537*'s loss was not noted by the Germans until she was listed as overdue in January.

Little did Stevens suspect that on *Flounder*'s fifth patrol, which began at Fremantle on 14 January 1945, it would be his turn to be on the receiving end of this kind of attention – not once but twice and on successive days. It did not really matter that in neither case were those attentions meant to cause *Flounder* any harm. Regardless of the intention, were it not for some skill and a large measure of luck, the results could well have been fatal for Stevens and his entire crew. It did not even matter that in the first of those incidents, the submarine whose attentions put them in such danger was none other than *Flounder* herself.

Late in the day on 21 February Stevens spotted what he took to be a Japanese patrol boat. This triggered a series of events *Flounder* just barely survived:

> 2330   Sighted target which was difficult to identify but appeared to be a patrol boat.

> February 22, 1945

> 0402   Range now 1,800 yards, target still not identified but definitely not a submarine . . . Opened fire and fired four bow tubes . . . As soon as the torpedoes started out we could see that the two fired from tubes #5 and #6 were running erratically. The torpedo from #5 started turning off to starboard while the one from #6 started turning off to port. They both started turning off as soon as they left the tubes, they did not broach. The torpedoes from #3 and #4 seemed to run normally.

> Speed was increased to everything we had in order to get away from our own fish. Suddenly one torpedo passed close under our stern and passed up our starboard side not <u>10</u> repeat <u>10 feet</u> away.

> . . . A few minutes later another torpedo broached on our port beam distance about fifty yards. This one was running slowly and had just about reached the end of the run. More and more radical maneuvers and finally enough time (two normal lifetimes) had passed for all torpedoes to have run their course. Sound could not hear anymore torpedoes running and we cleared the area at flank speed. This had been a terrifying experience and one which no member of *Flounder*'s crew from the captain on down ever wants to repeat.[14]

Only by luck and quick reflexes was Stevens able to manoeuvre the boat clear and narrowly avoid the fate that befell USS *Tullibee* and *Tang*.[15]

The very next day, *Flounder* again had another narrow scrape – literally.

> 1600   Changed course to 090° (T) to clear coast.

> 1700   All clear on sound, all clear by periscope, depth 65 feet. Suddenly the whole ship gave a peculiar shudder. Started deep. 30 seconds later ship gave another shake and water started entering boat through the APR cable. Shear valve was closed and stopped leak. Sound soon reported a tremendous rush of air and high speed screws, starting and stopping on our starboard bow. By this time we had figured out that someone had run into us. Screws began to get fainter so at

1711   Came to periscope depth and took a look. Calm seas, blue skies, nothing in sight. We were then convinced we had run into a Jap sub and we hope that he had sunk.

1724   Sound reported screws bearing 047° (T). Sighted large hospital ship (*Awa Maru*). . .[16]

Hoe and *Flounder* were again both now submerged and still in close proximity to each other, though still unaware of each other's presence. Within minutes of each other, they each looked around, sighted the hospital ship and let it pass unmolested. *Hoe* was still ignorant of what had caused the jolt she had felt. Refo took advantage of the few minutes he had on the surface to establish his position with enough accuracy to realise that he had not struck anything on the bottom, which was at 65 fathoms at that location, but his log reveals no other musing as to what exactly he might have hit. *Flounder* just happened to come to periscope depth only moments after *Hoe* had dived to avoid the Japanese floatplane passing overhead and thus Stevens could continue believing that he had encountered an enemy submarine. He may have hoped the Japanese boat had sunk, but he was not going to assume that had happened. He opted for caution. His log continued:

> Took stock of our damage. The hull and tanks seemed to be intact. The APR antenna seemed to be gone. SJ reflector seemed to be gone. Everytime we cut in the bridge repeater all repeaters would make about 10 RPM's. Number one periscope would raise but not train. From this we figured that a smaller submarine traveling at a shallower periscope depth had passed over us.
>
> Decided to wait until darkness in hope other sub would surface before we did.[17]

Hoe also chose to be cautious and spent two more hours submerged, surfacing at 1914 as the sun was setting. *Flounder* picked up the sounds made.

1920   Sound reported noise like air blowing on our starboard bow. Took a look through the periscope and sighted a surfaced submarine on our starboard bow, range about 3,000 yards, angle on the bow 75° port. Took another look and in the fading light identified him as a US submarine. At least he looked so much like one that I could not shoot. This submarine proceeded off to the northeast at high speed.

1932   Surfaced. She came up on an even keel and stayed that way, indicating that all tanks and piping were still sound.

Went to bridge to survey damage. Discovered a 25 foot gash in the superstructure on the starboard side just aft of the 4 inch gun. Looked closer and found the vent pipe to #2 normal fuel oil tank and the 10 pound blow line were badly bent but still holding. The staunchions and deck of the forward 20mm gun platform were bent, and the SJ mast badly bent, and the APR antenna was broken and badly twisted.[18]

Only at this point did the truth finally begin to sink in aboard *Hoe*.

1932   Pip on SJ radar bearing 270° (T), distance 8,200yds. Unable to
            exchange recognition signals via SJ radar.[19] Radar operator reports
            that he believes the other submarine is having trouble with his SJ. The
            interference on the SJ ceased suddenly without weakening. It was at
            this time that I first suspected we might have hit another submerged
            submarine.[20]

Meanwhile, Stevens reached the correct conclusion.

1934   Tried to call *Hoe*, who we strongly suspected now, by VHF and on
            Wolf Pack frequency but with no success.

2230   Sent message to CTF 71 reporting our collision and reported we were
            headed for Subic Bay.[21]

This at last revealed all to Refo.

2355   Broke message from *Flounder* to COM TASK FORCE SEVENTY-
            ONE stating that she had been rammed by another submerged
            submarine giving time and position of our supposed grounding.

            Sent *Hoe* serial one to COM TASK FORCE SEVENTY-ONE telling
            him that *Hoe* had struck *Flounder* and that we had sustained no
            damage.[22]

All in all, they had been very lucky. Had the two boats been as little as one
metre closer in depth to each other, the damage to *Flounder* could well have
been fatal. As it was, the damage was enough to send her to the nearest
repair facility, at Olongapo at Subic Bay in the Philippines, where she was
patched up in short order. She went out on one more war patrol in March
and April and then was sent back to Mare Island for a major refit. The war
was over by the time she was again ready for combat.

   Hoe's damage was so minor it did not require repair. It was nothing that
some paint would not cover up. Two days after the collision with *Flounder*,
Refo found and sank a Japanese escort south of Hainan.[23] That was to be
his last success. After that, he headed *Hoe* towards Pearl Harbor and out of
the war. Like *Flounder* and most other American submarines that had been
fighting hard for a year or two, she was in need of a refit and she ended up
at Mare Island alongside the boat she had scraped. Like *Flounder*, she re-
emerged too late to rejoin the fight.

The Last 'Official' Kills

USS *Besugo* and *U-183*; USS *Spikefish* and *I-373*

THE SURRENDER OF GERMANY in May 1945 and of Japan in August marked the end of a long and bloody war. For the last time, submarines of different nations would stalk each other under the auspices of official hostilities. It is difficult from a distance of more than sixty years to understand what would have driven men to make hazardous, well-nigh suicidal patrols in those final months, in support of states which had clearly lost the war on which they had staked their very national existence. Be it from patriotism, habit, fear of the consequences of disobedience or belief in the moral or spiritual correctness of their cause, crews went on board these last U-boats and I-boats, following the orders that took them out to sea and into the sights of waiting American submarines.

The last U-boat to succumb to attack by another submarine was *U-183*. She was another of the '*Monsun*' boats, the long-range boats that were sent from Germany to the Far East from mid-1943. These operations were intended to transport strategic materials, as well as being an attempt to find a theatre of operations where Allied defences were weaker and U-boats might again enjoy the relatively easy pickings they had found in the Atlantic several years earlier.[1] The plan was never as successful as Dönitz had hoped, for a number of reasons. Getting boats through the Atlantic was becoming more and more difficult as Allied code-breaking and aircraft combined to make the lifespan of U-boats in the open ocean shorter and shorter. While a few of the newest Type IXs could reach Penang unrefuelled, older boats like *U-183*, a Type IXC/40, needed to refuel before passing Cape Town, and the British made a priority of disrupting the resupply network the Germans had crafted in the South Atlantic. However, the main reason for the lacklustre performance of the '*Monsun*' boats was that merchant traffic in the Indian Ocean was sparse compared to the Atlantic, making the chances of significant success rather low.

U-183 had carried out two patrols in the Atlantic and Caribbean, sinking one victim on each of these missions. For her third patrol, starting in July 1943, she was selected as one of the eight first-wave '*Monsun*' boats. They were supposed to take on fuel from a *Milchkuh* near St Paul Rocks and proceed to individual patrol sectors in the Indian Ocean. There they would feast on the merchant shipping before putting in at George Town, Penang, where they would then be based. From the beginning the plan went wrong. The *Milchkühe* sent out in advance either failed to get out of the Bay of Biscay or was sunk in the Central Atlantic. Additionally, four of the ten original '*Monsun*' boats were sunk before ever reaching the planned refuelling point. Dönitz hastily arranged for five of the remaining boats to take on fuel from another outbound U-boat and from one of their own, leaving the rest with enough fuel to round the Cape of Good Hope. South of Mauritius they were met by a supply ship sent out from Penang and given enough fuel to carry out a full patrol before heading for George Town. *U-183*, under her original commander, *Korvettenkapitän* Heinrich Schäfer, operated for over a month between the Seychelles and the east coast of Africa but, despite sighting several good targets, had no success. Dönitz, most unhappy with Schäfer's passive conduct of this mission that had cost so many lives and resources to accomplish, replaced him as captain of *U-183* as soon as the boat arrived in Malaya. Her new commander was *Kapitänleutnant* Fritz Schneewind. He had come out to Penang in command of *U-511*, carrying a load of flasks of mercury, a pair of Daimler-Benz MB-518 marine diesel engines for use in a motor torpedo boat, blueprints for the Me 163 *Komet* rocket fighter and several German and Japanese engineers and dignitaries. She was codenamed '*Marco Polo 1*' by the Germans and '*Satsuki No. 1*' by the Japanese.[2] Arriving at Penang, *U-511* was formally turned over to Japan, becoming *RO-500*. In Japanese hands, she was extensively tested. The Japanese presented the Germans a list of critiques of the Type IX design, including low underwater speed, unreliable diesels, poor ventilation and inadequate range; however, they were impressed with the welded pressure hull and sound-damping engine mountings, and adopted those ideas for the advanced *I-201* class submarines then under development.[3] *RO-500* never saw combat in Japanese service. Schneewind sat at Penang, without a command, until tapped to take over *U-183* from Schäfer.

The boat spent two months in the yard at Singapore, which was the closest port to Penang with refit facilities. The keel plates were unbolted and the empty space in the keel filled with tin and tungsten, both in short supply in Germany. Empty space elsewhere in the boat was filled with rubber, quinine and opium. Schneewind then took his boat out of Penang on 10 February 1944 bound for a combat patrol near Ceylon and then on to France. He accounted for one British freighter and finished off a tanker already damaged by Japanese midget submarines, and then, in a change of plans, returned to Penang towards the end of March.[4] After that, *U-183* appears to have been plagued by mechanical problems, which led her to abort a patrol in early May. Then, after a seven-week patrol later in May and June that saw one more sinking, she left for Japan to have her batteries replaced. She was not ready to leave Kobe until the end of February 1945. Unable to reach France without refuelling and unable to refuel *en route* due to the complete collapse of the resupply network, *U-183* was ordered to make a combat patrol from Batavia, where she arrived at the beginning of

March. She was not ready to leave Batavia until 21 April 1945. Her patrol zone was supposed to have been off the south coast of New Guinea, not a terribly long distance for a boat of *U-183*'s characteristics. Yet, by some accounts, *U-183* was loaded to the gunwales with extra oil, filling even her ballast tanks, rendering her unable to dive.[5] The only possible explanation for this is that she was also being used as a tanker to carry fuel oil to a Japanese outpost, perhaps on the New Guinea coast.[6] In any case, she carried a large Japanese flag and had painted the *Hinomaru* on a white background on both sides of her tower in an attempt to prevent any attacks by Japanese defenders.[7] Unfortunately, as had been the case with *U-537*, the Japanese broadcast *U-183*'s planned departure time and route well in advance, giving the US Navy time to set up an ambush. (Actually, *U-183* could have dived, but only by venting the oil out of her ballast tanks in much the same way that air was normally vented to allow the boat to dive. The obvious problems with doing this were (i) that it would be a very slow process, at least compared to a normal dive, (ii) it would leave a massive oil slick at the point of the dive and a continuing trail behind the submerged boat, because the oil would not flush out of the tanks cleanly, and (iii) it would mean the failure of the resupply mission that was a major reason for braving the gauntlet of American submarines in the first place.)

The designated executioner in this case was USS *Besugo*.[8] A typical late-war US Navy submarine, *Besugo* was commissioned in June 1944 and left Pearl Harbor on her first patrol at the end of September. By that point in the war, targets had become few and far between and *Besugo* actually had more than average success under the circumstances. Her initial patrol off the Bungo-suidō, the southern entrance to Japan's Inland Sea, resulted in the damaging of two warships. Her second patrol off the Philippine island of Palawan resulted in multiple attacks, but the sinking of just one small landing craft. Her third patrol in the Gulf of Siam saw two sinkings, including a large tanker, and the damaging of a freighter. After this patrol, Lieutenant Commander H E Miller, took over from her former commander on 19 February 1945 at Fremantle.

Miller reported *Besugo* ready for her fourth patrol on 24 March 1945. Her assigned patrol zone was in the Java Sea and further east into the narrow Flores Sea. As would be typical in these waning days of the war, the sea lanes were busy with Allied submarines. On one day, still heading north towards the Lombok Strait, *Besugo* encountered two Royal Navy submarines and one American, all headed back to Fremantle after their patrols. North of Lombok, Miller met up with his pack commander in USS *Charr* and was assigned a patrol sector across the southern exit of the Makassar Strait. *Gabilan* had the sector to the north and *Charr* to the south. As MAGIC reports came in, the group was regularly moved around in an attempt to intercept the few significant targets left in the area.[9] *Besugo* spent two days, 5–6 April 1945, chasing a Japanese light cruiser and a few escorts through the Sape Strait and into the Savu Sea, waters where American submarines ventured rarely. Over the course of this chase, Miller fired off twenty-two torpedoes at the cruiser or its escorts, all but two of which missed. The first hit came as Miller fired four torpedoes (numbers 17 to 20 of the attack) at an escort which appeared to be carrying a full load of troops;[10] the hit sliced off the escort's bow but the larger aft portion of the ship showed no signs of sinking. After the twenty-first torpedo missed the drifting hulk, *Besugo*'s twenty-second (and last) finally hit and sank the escort. The cruiser was dispatched by *Gabilan* and *Charr*, which had waited at the northern end of Sape Strait.[11] Out of torpedoes, *Besugo* was ordered back to Fremantle to pick up a fresh load and to continue the patrol.

By 21 April, *Besugo* was again back in the war zone, transitting the Lombok Strait from south to north. She was directed to a patrol position in the middle of the Java Sea north of central Java. Her packmates, *Blower* and *Perch* had sectors east and west of her. *Besugo*'s log for 23 April tells the rest of the story:

0731(I)   Dived for submerged patrol during day.[12]

1350(I)   Sighted submarine bearing 262°(T), commenced submerged approach.[13] Target zigging radically about 50° each side of base course 085°(T), making 10kts over the ground. Turn count 240 RPM.

1414(I)   Identified submarine as German with Japanese merchant flag painted on upper side of conning tower and flying enormous Japanese warship colors.

1427-29(I) Commenced firing spread of six Mk. 18 torpedoes, set depth 8 feet. Range 1,500yds, speed 10, angle on bow 90° Port.

1429(I)   One hit. Looked no more than 4 second later, but sub had disappeared. Nothing visible but smoke, a slick of air bubbles and the beginning of an oil slick.

1436(I)   Surfaced to recover survivors.

1440(I)   Rescued German war prisoner Warrant Officer Karl Wisneiwski # UN2101/343, German Navy: who had been navigator of the sunken submarine and who identified her as the *U-183* of 740-ton class. He was the only survivor in the large oil slick and was treated for the following injuries: dislocated left knee, broken right collar bone, lacerated bridge of nose, lacerated lips and mouth, and three missing teeth.

1510(I)   Recover what we thought might be a 'burn' bag.[14] It turned out to be a large rubber boat in a canvas bag. The prisoner said his ship sank in one second, taking him far under water with her.[15]

As navigator on *U-183*, Karl Wisniewski held the rank of *Ober-steuermann*.[16] The navigator on a U-boat was technically a Chief Petty Officer, though he was treated as if he held a warrant.[17] The navigator and bosun were, along with the two technical chiefs, the leading enlisted personnel on a U-boat and had watch officer responsibilities. For the navigator and bosun, that meant they each generally stood one 4-hour tower watch in a 24-hour duty cycle. Additionally, the navigator was responsible for tracking the boat's position and the state of the consumables. In port, he was the boat's quartermaster, responsible for provisioning the boat. As watch officer, Wisniewski had been on the tower along with six lookouts when the torpedo struck.[18] He had just lowered his binoculars and was checking over the lookouts when a shudder shook the boat and a column of flame shot up the portside of the tower. He had time to look back at the tower watch and saw that all six men were collapsing in pain; he heard a single scream come up from below and then be cut short as the boat sank beneath him, driven down by the still-running diesels. He was sucked underwater and then bobbed up to the surface again, injured but still alive, the only one of fifty-six men to survive.

Wisniewski apparently received rather less courtesy than he expected onboard *Besugo*.

> The German officer was treated by the ship's pharmacist and nothing seemed wrong with him except his attitude. He thought as an officer he deserved better quarters than a bunk in the after torpedo room. As usual when a prisoner of war is aboard, a guard with a side arm such as a 45-caliber gun was assigned to guard the prisoner. In this case it was . . . torpedo man second class and a Buffalo, New York native, who after placing the '45' to the prisoner's head made it clear to him that his status in the German navy would not be honored by members of the *Besugo*.

> . . . On the evening of May 16, 1945, a course was set for Subic Bay in the Philippine Islands, where the patrol terminated May 20, 1945. A mooring was set alongside the USS *Antedon*, a submarine tender where a refit would be done while the crew enjoyed a much needed rest and relaxation. Upon tying up alongside the tender, the German Warrant Officer, again with a little persuasion from his guard, shaved and cleaned up to be ready for transportation for questioning and internment for the remainder of the war.[19]

Besugo sank one more small ship on this patrol and carried out one more patrol before the war ended. She remained in commission throughout the immediate post-war period and conducted two reconnaissance patrols from her base at Yokusuka, Japan during the Korean War. She was one of the few wartime submarines to be retained in commission but not modernised under the GUPPY programme. She settled into reserve training duties based at San Diego, California from August 1953. She was finally decommissioned in March 1958 and mothballed, but that was not the end of the story. She was towed to Mare Island in 1966 and given a minimal upgrade, adding a snorkel and streamlining the tower structure, and then transferred to Italy, where she served as *Francesco Morosini* (S514) until struck from the navy list in 1975.[20]

The last submarine of any combatant to be sunk in wartime by an enemy submarine was the Japanese *I-373*. She was a huge boat, of almost 2,000 tons surface displacement, designed to carry cargo and fuel to isolated island garrisons. As such, she had no torpedo tubes, but could carry 110 tons of cargo and 150 tons of fuel. No sooner was she commissioned on 14 April 1945 than she was taken in hand for conversion to an aviation gas tanker, in which form she finally joined the fleet in June. She departed Sasebo on 9 August on her first mission, heading for Formosa with a full load of avgas.

Almost as new to the war was USS *Spikefish*.[21] She had joined the fleet in June 1944 and was only on her third war patrol on 13 August 1945 when, after dark, she picked up a target on her SJ radar. She was just off the China coast. The target was heading southwest on a base course of 225° with a mean speed of advance of 10 knots. *Spikefish* closed the distance sufficiently to gain visual contact a few minutes later, but was well behind the target and would need several hours of chasing to gain a decent firing position. Although they were able to identify the target as a submarine, the night was too dark for *Spikefish*'s lookouts to establish the nationality of the other boat.

The chase went on for an hour when the target, still well ahead of *Spikefish*, suddenly submerged. Judging correctly that they had finally been spotted, *Spikefish*'s captain, Commander R R Managhan, guessed that the other submarine would loop back in an attempt to lose her pursuer. Managhan took *Spikefish* to radar depth and headed back in the direction they had come. His hunch proved correct; two hours later, the target reappeared on his radar, 8,000m away. While he had been following the target to the north, Managhan had contacted COMSUBPAC and had been assured there were no friendly submarines in the area. Nevertheless, Managhan decided to wait out the remaining hours until dawn, so he could make a visual identification. With the advantage of radar that the Japanese were unable to detect, he surfaced and performed a classic 'end around', submerging in the path of the other submarine as the sky began to lighten. One look in the pale pre-dawn light was enough to convince him that the target was indeed an enemy boat. The wait for the enemy to come within range was only a few minutes. When *I-373* had finally approached close enough, Managhan fired a full spread of six torpedoes. Two of them hit near the stern. The volatile avgas did not explode, but the damage from the torpedoes was sufficient to send *I-373* stern-first to the bottom. Incredibly, one survivor was picked up. In a final attempt to deceive the enemy, the survivor volunteered that his boat was *I-382*, a non-existent boat.[22] Like so much else that occurred at the end of this long war, the deception was utterly pointless and could do nothing to make up for the deaths of eighty-four officers and men who went down with their boat. It was the last futile sacrifice of warriors fighting in a cause long lost. The next day, Japan formally accepted the Allied terms for unconditional surrender.

CHAPTER 25

War by Another Name

Submarine Encounters since the Second World War

AS ALL SIDES LOOKED BACK on the war that had just ended, it was clear that the conflict had been a watershed event in many dimensions. So many aspects of warfare would never be the same again; airpower and the atomic bomb seemed to have made the nineteenth-century concept of nationalistic war for global or regional dominance too costly to seriously consider. Not that anyone thought that the Second World War was a 'war to end all wars' any more than the First had been. Less than a year after VJ Day, Winston Churchill gave a speech at Westminster College in Fulton, Missouri in which he declared that 'an iron curtain had descended' across Europe. No-one, in the West at least, doubted his assessment that a new kind of war had come along to replace the old. The potency of the new weapons forced the conflict between East and West, between communism and capitalism, to take a new form. The new war would often be fought by proxies. It would require the invention of a new word – 'brinksmanship' – to describe incidents like the Cuban Missile Crisis. It would see submarines playing deadly dangerous games as both sides tested the other's abilities and courage under the waves.

The principal use of submarines in the Second World War had been to target merchant shipping. The results had been, to say the least, mixed. In the Pacific, Allied submarines had swept the Japanese merchant fleet from the sea, but in the Atlantic, Dönitz's attempt to strangle Great Britain by breaking her lifeline of cargo shipping had failed utterly. The difference had not been the quality of the submarines or the submariners; it had been the quality and quantity of the anti-submarine forces that had been arrayed against them and their ability to exploit the weaknesses of the submarines of the day. Looking to the future from the perspective of 1945, it was far from certain that some decisive factors that had defeated the submarines in the just-finished war, specifically the breaking of enemy codes and the vulnerability of submarines to increasingly omnipresent airpower, would be repeated in any future conflict.

First of all, submarine technology had just begun a period of rapid change as the war was ending. Many technologies had progressed significantly during the war; a few had emerged so late that their full impact was not felt. One was guided missiles. Another was the development of 'true' submarines, vessels intended to spend more time and operate more effectively underwater than on the surface. This development came so late in the war that it was not possible to determine the effect of the German Type XXI or the Japanese *Sen Taka* on Allied anti-submarine capabilities, but there is no doubt that they would have had a serious impact. The advent of nuclear propulsion in the 1950s made it even less necessary for submarines to come to the surface and harder for aircraft and surface ships to detect them.

It was clear that the mission of the victorious navies in any future war against the Soviet Union would be far more like the Battle of the Atlantic than the Pacific. The Soviets had no merchant fleet worth sinking and did not depend on seaborne trade the way Britain had in the Second World War or the way the US would in any Third World War. What the Soviets did have was submarines – well-built and well-manned submarines – and plenty of them. The next battle, if it came, would be to defeat Russia's submarines before they could neutralise the vast Allied superiority on the ocean's surface and in the air above, and to do so without being able to depend on many of the elements that had led to victory in 1945. The lesson of the Second World War had been that the next war would be fought largely in the air and under the sea – and that the best anti-submarine weapon was another submarine.

The concept of an anti-submarine-submarine predates the end of the Second World War by 28 years.[1] Even before the end of the First World War, the Royal Navy was developing its 'R' class submarines, an idea well ahead of its time. Built to be faster and more manoeuvrable underwater than on the surface and with large hydrophones for tracking targets by sound while submerged, they were the world's first attempt at a true submarine. Eight of the class were built in 1917–19 and one of them, by repute, actually carried out an attack on a U-boat, but the salvo of six torpedoes all missed.[2] They were extremely unpopular, being so unstable on the surface that they were miserable to inhabit in any seaway and so underpowered that it was only possible to recharge the batteries by returning to port and using a shore-based charging station. By 1923, all but one had been scrapped; that one was used as a high-speed target for training ASW forces until 1934.[3]

The idea of a hunter-killer submarine – a submarine designed specifically to hunt other submarines – was not revived until after the Second World War with the US Navy's SSK programme. This was based around captured German technology. Having acquired two Type XXI U-boats as reparations, the US Navy discovered just how superior this design was to anything they were building or planning at the end of the war.[4] With Congress in no mood to fund the replacement of the entire fleet of war-built submarines, the US Navy submitted a modest building programme of new boats starting with USS *Tang* (SS 563) requested in 1947 and actually started in 1949. The *Tang*s, six of which were built over three years, were basically Americanised Type XXIs. Only four more diesel-powered attack submarines would be built before the nuclear programme took over. The US Navy estimated they needed sixty new submarines to maintain a minimal capability, but had to accept the fact that the funding was not there. They turned to their existing fleet of war-built submarines and began upgrading them by adding battery capacity and a snorkel and streamlining the hull and tower. The result was the so-called GUPPY boats, far from the boats the navy wanted, but better than nothing.[5]

The GUPPY boats filled a short-term need, but they were no better at the increasingly important task of hunting other submarines than before conversion because their sonar sensors had not been upgraded. The *Tang* class mounted a copy of the German *Balkongerät*, called BQR-2 in US Navy terminology; the GUPPYs had nothing similar. What was needed was a GUPPY-type conversion that included the BQR-2 and maybe even the improved BQR-4.[6] The US Navy converted a total of seven old *Gato* class submarines into SSK conversions.[7] Many more were planned, but those plans were shelved. The very success of the SSKs, which outperformed all other American boats in their ability to detect and attack targets, caused all previous GUPPY conversions to be scheduled for upgrade to the SSK standard, and the new nuclear boats were all to be built with SSK equipment. If every attack submarine was to be an SSK, the designation lost its meaning and was indeed dropped by the US Navy in 1959.

The task of these hunter-killer-capable submarines was a formidable one. The Soviet Union emerged from the Second World War scarred and damaged beyond belief by years of brutal war on its territory, but it was possessed of the world's most powerful land army and a large, capable air force. Only their navy was significantly less than world class. Stalin set about correcting that deficiency as soon as he was able. As did the Americans and to a lesser extent the British, the Soviets grabbed as much German technology, and as many technologists, as they could from the parts of German territory they overran. Like the American *Tang* class, the Soviets developed a class of submarines derived from the Type XXI, the Project 613 (NATO codename 'Whiskey').[8] The primary difference in the Soviet programme, compared to the American, was that while the US commissioned six *Tangs* in 1951–2, the Russians built 215 'Whiskey' class boats between 1951 and 1958.

Ideology aside, from the Soviet point of view, the West was an aggressive cultural as well as military force that was intent on hemming in and eventually subjugating the Soviet state. From the American point of view, the Soviet Union, with its godless, collectivist ideology and militaristic economy was a viral threat to everything the West held dear. To both sides, this war, 'cold' only in the sense that there never was an official declaration of hostilities, was a fight to the death between two irreconcilable ways of life. Because neither wished to ignite a nuclear war that no-one would win, the war was fought in out-of-the-way places like Korea and Vietnam, and it was often fought out of sight in the cold ocean depths by this new generation of increasingly capable submarines and submariners.

(The remaining sections of this chapter tell some of the stories of encounters between these submarines, to the extent that those stories are known. There is in fact a long list of these incidents and the list looks rather different from the Soviet/Russian side than it does from the NATO point of view. The incidents described below were selected because they were better documented than most or simply more interesting than the rest.)

USS *Grenadier* was a *Tench* class boat, in fact the last of the series of war-built fleet submarines to be completed. Even though she was laid down and launched in 1944, she remained incomplete at the Boston Navy Yard for six years, before being taken in hand and completed as one of the first GUPPY boats in 1951. Her assignments were typical of boats of the time: plenty of time spent exercising the fleet's ASW assets and a lot of port calls at interesting places around the world. But in May 1959 the peacetime routine briefly turned very serious.

American submarines had been creeping close to Russia since *Sea Dog* first snooped along the Bering Sea coast in May 1948. It is not clear how soon the Soviets realised they were being watched, but it was no later than 19 August 1957, when Soviet ASW forces trapped USS *Gudgeon*, a diesel-powered *Tang* class boat under the command of Lieutenant Commander Norman B 'Buzz' Bessac, near the entrance to Vladivostok.[9] The US recognised only 3-mile territorial waters, while the Soviets claimed a 12-mile zone. By all accounts, *Gudgeon* was just outside the 3-mile limit when she was detected by a Soviet picket boat. Already nearing the end of a long day of submerged snooping, *Gudgeon* was ready to put up her snorkel to start ventilating the boat and charging her batteries, but a squadron of Soviet patrol boats kept her down for 30 hours. At one point, *Gudgeon* approached the surface close enough to put up her snorkel, but the Russians detected the head valve and forced Bessac to go deep again. At several points during this episode, the Russians dropped practice depth charges that exploded near *Gudgeon*; these acted like a real depth charge except that they contained only a token amount of explosive, enough to make a loud noise, but not enough to cause any damage. Finally, Bessac realised the boat and crew had both reached the limit of their endurance and he brought *Gudgeon* to the surface. Sidearms had been passed out to the men, torpedoes had been readied and torpedo doors opened and classified papers had all been burned. On the surface, he found a ring of boats that parted in front of him as he set course away from land. The Soviets had no desire to see the incident escalate any further. The point had been made; they were 'one up' on the Americans.

It took *Grenadier* to even the score. A year after the *Gudgeon* incident, CINCLANTFLT issued a challenge to his ASW forces, promising to award a case of a famous American whiskey to the unit that 'wore out' any unidentified submarine found approaching the United States.[10] The winner of the whiskey was *Grenadier*, under the command of Lieutenant Commander Theodore Davis. In May 1959, Davis was patrolling submerged near Iceland when sonar picked up the sound of another submarine where none should have been. The Soviet boat was soon aware of *Grenadier*'s presence and tried evasive manoeuvres, but to no avail. Davis 'held down' the Russian by maintaining good position near the other boat. Finally, after nine hours the Soviet boat, a 'Zulu V' class diesel-powered ballistic missile submarine, was forced to the surface to recharge batteries and replenish air.[11] A US Navy patrol plane, alerted to what was going on, got photographs of the 'Zulu', the first view in the West of the world's first ballistic missile submarine.

After that, incidents continued to occur on a regular basis. In 1960, USS *Swordfish*, one of the first American nuclear submarines, was reportedly struck from below by another boat while at periscope depth. The other boat must have been surfacing, because its lights were then seen close by through the periscope, but by the time *Swordfish* surfaced, the boat was gone. This was not the last time *Swordfish* would scrape with a Soviet submarine.

On 15 November 1969, USS *Gato*, a nuclear submarine barely a year old, was chasing a Soviet 'nuke' under the Barents Sea.[12] The Soviet boat turned out to be one of the unluckiest boats in any navy, or maybe just one of the most poorly built.[13] She was *K-19*, the first 'Hotel' class nuclear-powered ballistic missile submarine.[14] She suffered a series of reactor accidents.[15] In the second of those accidents, in July 1961, the failure of a weld in the primary coolant circuit of one of her two reactors caused a radiation leak that killed as many as twenty-two crewmen.[16] Subsequent to that, *K-19*'s entire reactor compartment was removed and replaced, an operation which took two years, but this did not repair the boat's reputation. She was known derisively in the Soviet fleet as 'Hiroshima'. Nevertheless, she was returned to service and upgraded in 1969 with more advanced missiles. In this form, she was on station in the Barents Sea when she and *Gato* collided.

No sooner had Soviet submarines come out into the open ocean, than it became the primary challenge to NATO submarines to track them as they patrolled. The emergence of ballistic missile submarines in the 1950s only made this more important, as the only real defence against 'boomers' is to sink them before they can launch their missiles.[17] If all was right with the world, every Soviet boomer should have had a NATO attack submarine on its tail from the moment it was detected heading out on patrol.[18] Such was the case with *K-19* in November 1969. *Gato*'s mission was part of an operation codenamed 'Holystone' that monitored Soviet submarine activities.[19]

There is an art to trailing an enemy submarine without being detected.[20] Obviously, the quieter submarine has an advantage in this situation, and for much of the Cold War, NATO submarines were quieter than their Soviet counterparts.[21] A patrolling submarine is generally not in a rush and is definitely interested in remaining undetected, so most submarine 'chases' took place in slow motion. This is important because, as a general rule, the slower a submarine moves, the quieter it is. Thus the art of tracking an enemy submarine involves the ability to differentiate the sound of a very quiet submarine from the background noise of the ocean. (This includes not only man-made noise from other sources, but also a variety of naturally occurring noises, such as waves and fish sounds.) This frequently requires the trailing submarine to get extremely close to the target in order to hear it, sometimes following by less than a boat length. The danger involved as football-field-length behemoths displacing anywhere from 5,000 tons to more than 20,000 tons manoeuvre in this proximity should be obvious. The trailing submarine tried, as much as possible, to stay in the target's 'baffles', which meant staying in the narrow band directly behind the leading boat where that boat's listening devices were ineffective. Submariners were taught to periodically 'clear their baffles', meaning to alter course enough to be able to hear any boat that might be hiding in this shadow. Some Soviet submariners became so good at doing this at such random intervals and extreme angles that the manoeuvre became known as a 'Crazy Ivan'. If caught unprepared by a 'Crazy Ivan', the trailing submarine could not only be detected, but there was also a very real risk of collision. This may very well be what happened between *Gato* and *K-19*.

What is known for certain is that the two boats did hit. The version officially acknowledged much later by the US Navy was that the Soviet boat slid over the American and then cleared off to the side, neither boat suffering much more than scraped paint or dislodged tiles.[22] From the Soviet side, the collision appeared far more serious. *K-19*'s sonar dome, a bulbous fairing under her bow, was crushed and all four of her torpedo tube doors were bent in, jamming them shut. This is one of the rare instances when participants in the event have spoken, so it is possible to test the veracity of the official statements.[23] Based on these statements, it certainly appears as if the collision was a result of a 'Crazy Ivan' that never happened. It appears that about 2100 on 15 November, *Gato*'s sonar first picked up the sounds of the Soviet boat. *K-19* was passing from the White Sea into the Barents Sea, outbound from the big submarine base at Severodvinsk. *Gato*'s sonar operators appear to have misjudged the speed of *K-19*, believing she was going somewhat faster than she really was. Speed was set based on that incorrect estimation, with the result that *Gato* was rapidly overtaking the Russian boat rather than maintaining a trail position. *Gato* was apparently coming up along *K-19*'s port side, but since the soundmen believed they were still behind her, they misread the changing bearing of the sounds coming from *K-19* as evidence that she had turned to starboard. In fact, *K-19* appears to have kept a steady course. Believing *K-19* was pulling a 'Crazy Ivan', *Gato* made a sharp turn to starboard to stay in her baffles, but in fact by this time *Gato* was slightly ahead of the Soviet boat and actually turned into her path.

The resulting collision caused fatal damage to neither boat, because the speeds involved were relatively slow. *K-19* appears to have struck *Gato* right along her reactor compartment, where the hull is the strongest, so no serious damage was inflicted to *Gato*. The Soviets appear not to have been aware of *Gato*'s presence until the boats collided and even then not to have known at first exactly what they had hit. Only after turning on their fathometer (an active depth-finding sonar system) and finding they were well clear of any underwater obstructions, did they realise that it must have been an American submarine they had collided with. *K-19* surfaced immediately and began calling for help; *Gato* exited the area as rapidly as possible.

While in no danger of sinking, 'Hiroshima' had clearly come off worse from the encounter. Based on reports by *K-19*'s captain, the Soviets believed for a while that *Gato* might have been sunk in the collision and they spent some time and effort looking for her wreck on the ocean floor, but they soon realised that she too had survived. Nor did 'Hiroshima's' luck change after the incident with *Gato*. In 1972, a leak of hydraulic fluid led to a fire while the boat was submerged. Before the boat could be surfaced and the fire contained, twenty-eight crew members died. Amazingly, the boat was repaired and again returned to the fleet, serving until 1991. As of 2003, she had not yet been scrapped.[24]

USS *Swordfish* may or may not have been involved in the sinking of the Soviet 'Golf II' class submarine *K-129*.[25] It is a matter of which side you are looking from. From the American point of view, it is a story of typically sloppy Soviet engineering.[26] *K-129* was on patrol in the Pacific northwest of Hawaii. She had left Petropavlovsk, the main Russian submarine base on the Pacific coast located on the Kamchatka Peninsula, in late February 1968. While *en route*, there had been an explosion of unknown cause on 8 March and *K-129* had sunk to the bottom at a depth of over 4km.[27] Speculation suggested that there had been a mishap in the handling of the volatile liquid propellant for one of the 'Serb' missiles with which she was armed, and that the resulting explosion had sent her to the bottom.[28] From the beginning, the Americans had used only solid propellant for their SLBMs (Submarine-Launched Ballistic Missiles). From the American point of view, it was just a matter of time before an accident like that which sank *K-129* happened. It all sounded believable enough.

Except that the Soviets never believed it. Their official position was, and still is, that *K-129* sank as the result of a collision with *Swordfish*.[29] This was, as far as they are concerned, another case of an American submarine trailing too close behind a Soviet boomer. Being a diesel-powered submarine, *K-129* had been either on the surface or snorkelling on the night of 8 March. *Swordfish*, according to this version of events, hit *K-129* forward of her missile compartment, slicing into the compartment where the control room was located. The damage was fatal. *K-129* sank immediately; all those in the central compartment died quickly, the rest of the 98-man crew perishing as the remaining compartments collapsed as the boat fell to the bottom. Since no-one admits to having witnessed *K-129*'s demise, there is no way to choose between these stories, though there is one fact that casts at least a little doubt on the American version. Shortly after the loss of *K-129*, *Swordfish* showed up at Yokusuka, Japan with damage to her sail. The US explanation was that *Swordfish* had encountered ice in the Sea of Japan. The Soviets never believed it.

What is generally agreed is that the Americans were rapidly able to locate the wreck of *K-129* and that the *Hughes Glomar Explorer*, a deep-sea recovery vessel ostensibly built to scrape manganese nodules off the ocean floor, was in fact funded by the CIA and sent out in 1973 to recover the wreck of *K-129*. The most common account of what happened next is that the recovery started well enough, but that it failed part way through due to mechanical failure and that only part of the wreck was actually recovered, the rest falling back down to the sea floor. A number of Soviet sailors' bodies were recovered and given ceremonial burials at sea by the crew of the *Glomar Explorer*. Videotape of the burials was reportedly turned over to the Soviet authorities some years later.[30]

One other theory of *K-129*'s demise has been put forward, namely that her commander had decided to attack Hawaii without authorisation and was in the process of launching his missiles when an accident caused the first missile to explode and sank the boat.[31] As always, it is hard to disprove speculation like this, but there seems to be little to support it either.

USS *Tautog* was the second submarine to carry that name. The first was famous, having fought in the Pacific from Pearl Harbor, where she was credited with shooting down a Japanese torpedo plane, through thirteen war patrols until she was finally assigned to training duties in February 1945. The official history of the war credits *Tautog* with sinking two Japanese submarines in early 1942, but only one is now acknowledged.[32] The second *Tautog* was launched in 1967 and joined the fleet a year later. She was one of the *Sturgeon* class nuclear attack submarines whose design specifically includes intelligence gathering capabilities, so it is not at all surprising that, on her first patrol into the WESTPAC took her near Petropavlovsk in June 1970.

Tautog was particularly interested in picking up the trail of an 'Echo II' class submarine.[33] These were still fairly new; twenty-nine of them had been built between 1963 and 1968, and they represented a particular threat to the carrier battle groups deployed off the coast of Vietnam because they mounted eight anti-ship cruise missiles. *Tautog* found what she was looking for. The 'Echo' was going through a seemingly random series of abrupt course and depth changes; this was a manoeuvre often performed by submarines of all nationalities at the beginning of a patrol in an attempt to shake loose any improperly stowed equipment and identify any unexpected noise sources. *Tautog* was following very closely, perhaps too closely given the kind of manoeuvring the 'Echo' was doing.[34]

One of those manoeuvres had caused the 'Echo' to ascend close to the surface and slow down dramatically. *Tautog*, caught unawares, slipped below the Russian, out of her baffles. *K-108* (known as '*Black Lila*' – she was one of the few Soviet-era submarines given a name) must have thought she detected something, because the next thing *Tautog* knew, the Soviet boat was diving, speeding up and then pulling the craziest of 'Crazy Ivans', doing a complete 180° turn and heading back on her former course at high speed. *Tautog*'s crew had no time to react (other than emit a few expletives). There was a sudden shock, a loud scraping sound and within seconds the boat's forward progress was halted and she started to roll to starboard and head deeper stern-first. The scraping ended with a loud crunch and then there was an eerie silence.

There could be no doubt what had just happened. *Black Lila* had obviously not had time to locate *Tautog* after her turn and she had scraped her keel along *Tautog*'s sail.[35] The last crunch could only have been one of the 'Echos' screws digging into the tower structure, leaving part of a blade to be found later. A quick inspection showed no serious leaks and only minor injuries to *Tautog*'s crew, though she would retain the starboard list until she reached port. As they were leaving the scene, the sound operator announced that he heard sounds like a runaway turbine, sounds that would be made if *Black Lila* had lost one of her propellers and her crew was unable to shut down the reactor on that side. This was followed by popping sounds reminiscent of popcorn. Then more silence. There had been no pumping noises, nothing to indicate the Soviet boat had blown her ballast tanks and risen to the surface. As *Tautog* headed back to base, all onboard were convinced that the Soviet submarine had sunk to the seabed, taking her crew with her.

It was more than 20 years later before they learned the truth – *Black Lila* had survived. Unsurprisingly, the Soviet version of the event was rather different from the American.[36] In this account, *K-108* had completed her 'shaking out' and was approaching the surface and slowing down in order to make radio contact with her base. A thermal layer hid the two boats from each other and it was at that point that *Tautog* unknowingly slipped directly below *K-108*.[37] Having completed her transmissions, *Black Lila* started to dive back to her former depth. As soon as she dropped below the inversion layer, she detected the sounds of a submarine close on her starboard side and moving faster than she was. The sounds disappeared almost immediately, because *Tautog*, which must have reacquired *Black Lila* at the same time as she was detected, appears to have turned sharply to port to hide again in her baffles. Apparently, *Tautog* misjudged how close she was to *K-108* because the next instant, the American's sail struck her stern. *Black Lila* took a sharp down angle after the collision and when attempts to blow her ballast tanks failed to stop her plunge, the boat was brought back to the surface by the simple expedient of reversing the one remaining propeller. She had a jagged gash in her outer hull, but unlike American submarines of the era, 'Echos' were double-hull boats, and the inner, pressure hull remained intact. The sound of the lighter metal of her torn outer hull rattling as the boat moved upwards must have been the source of the popping sound heard on *Tautog*. The Soviet crew heard the sounds of *Tautog* leaving the area; they never believed the American boat had been lost, despite the fact that when *Black Lila* was docked, they found two metres of *Tautog*'s periscope wrapped around the damaged starboard propeller shaft. The real losers were the two commanders, both of whom had their promising careers overshadowed by the incident.

It was not only the Americans who were playing tag with the Soviets. Twice, British nuclear submarines are believed to have tangled with their Soviet counterparts.[38] In 1981, HMS *Sceptre* was apparently following too closely when the boat she was trailing slowed and turned and *Sceptre* was nicked by one of her screws. On 24 December 1986, HMS *Splendid* scraped along the side of a Soviet boomer, identified by at least one source as *TK-12*, one of the big 'Typhoon' class boats. Little more than that is known. *Splendid*'s name turns up again in this chapter, as a possible witness to (or cause of) the sinking of the *Kursk*.

Such incidents appear to have continued well after the Cold War officially ended with the collapse of the Soviet Union in 1991. The new Russian state inherited the bulk of the old Soviet Navy and the intense interest of NATO in its activities.[39] On 11 February 1992, *K-239 Karp*, a Russian 'Sierra' class nuclear attack submarine, the latest and most advanced of late Soviet submarine designs, and USS *Baton Rouge*, a *Los Angeles* class nuclear attack submarine, the latest and best in the US Navy's inventory, collided 12 miles off the coast of Kildin Island in the Barents Sea.[40] This was an area that the Russians considered to be in their territorial waters and the Americans claimed was not. Submarines transiting in and out of the main Russian Northern Fleet bases would have to pass through this small patch of water. The details of the incident are skimpy, but what is known is generally agreed on by both sides.[41] (This is one of the rare instances when the US Navy has acknowledged involvement in a submarine collision.) *Baton Rouge* was at periscope depth when *Karp* came up from below and her sail struck the underside of the American boat. There were no injuries or deaths on either boat and both made their respective ports without requiring assistance. The Russians claim to have recovered samples of American anti-sonar tiles from *Karp*'s dented sail. The Americans claim that when *Baton Rouge* was docked, the damage was limited to some minor tears in one of her two main ballast tanks. However, because American boats are of single-hull design, these tears were ruptures in her pressure hull, and thus represented significant damage.

Even the Russians, normally ready to give credence to theories that blame the Americans for any Cold War submarine incident, seem genuinely willing to concede that this collision was most likely an accident, though they still question why an American submarine was in contested waters so close to Russian sea lanes. In turbulent, shallow waters, such as those found in the Kola Inlet, passive sonar is largely ineffective, especially if the target being tracked is a 'Sierra', one of the quietest classes of Soviet submarines.

From the relative positions of the two boats, it is highly likely that neither was aware of the other's presence in the immediate vicinity. It is unclear why *Baton Rouge* was at periscope depth in those waters or why the Russian boat was approaching that same depth, but it simply appears to be bad luck that they tried to do it in the same space. What is known is that *Karp* was repaired and back in service again in less than a year. *Baton Rouge* was decommissioned the next year and stricken in January 1995, the first *Los Angeles* class boat to be retired.[42] The US Navy has never acknowledged any connection between the collision and the early disposal of *Baton Rouge*.

The last collision generally agreed to have occurred between a NATO and a Russian submarine took place on 20 March 1993. In that incident USS *Grayling*, a *Sturgeon* class boat, was trailing *K-407 Novomoskovsk*, a 'Delta IV' class boomer, when the two boats collided in the Barents Sea.[43] At least one source says that Russian boat involved was an earlier 'Delta III' class SSBN, perhaps *K-496 Borisoglebsk*, though this seems unlikely. The Russians believe the two boats collided head-on, but fortunately with only a glancing blow, an indication of how much quieter submarines had become and how much more dangerous the game of underwater tag had become as a consequence.[44] Both boats survived the encounter. The incident was a major embarrassment for President Clinton, who was scheduled to meet Boris Yeltsin shortly after the Russians made the incident public. The US Navy was ordered to find other, less dangerous ways to fulfill its mission of preparedness for any future eventuality.

Grayling was retired four years after this incident, but she was by then more than 28 years old and retirement was appropriate. *K-407* returned to service and has been used for numerous missile tests, including being used as a satellite launch platform. As far as can be discovered in open sources, there have been no further incidents of underwater submarine encounters, except for possibly one other . . .

The most famous recent submarine disaster is certainly the sinking of the 'Oscar II' class nuclear cruise-missile submarine *K-141 Kursk* on 13 August 2000.[45] It is known that *Kursk* was participating in a Russian fleet exercise and it is likely that NATO submarines were on hand to monitor the activities. (Russian sources claim that two American boats, USS *Memphis* and *Toledo*, and the Royal Navy's HMS *Splendid* were in the vicinity when *Kursk* sank.) It was not the cruise missiles *Kursk* carried that attracted so much attention, but rather the fact that she was believed to be testing the VA-111 *Shkval* (Squall) supercavitating torpedo reportedly capable of reaching speeds of over 175 knots underwater.[46]

It is generally accepted that *Kursk* suffered an explosion of a torpedo she was preparing to fire, which set off the rest of her torpedoes' warheads and that she sank. The cause of the initial explosion will never be known. There are Russians who believe, based on past history, that the cause was a collision with a NATO submarine.[47] Further, they believe that the failure of the Putin government to follow up on this possibility was part of a grand conspiracy, that the Russian government had been bought off or intimidated by their Western counterparts. As with most grand conspiracy theories, this is highly unlikely. Regardless, 118 submariners died that day, perhaps the last casualties of the Cold War.

Afterword

The loss of *Kursk* brings this story up to the present, but it does not bring it to an end. There are today more nations than ever with submarines capable of tracking and sinking each other, and the end of the Cold War seems to have, if anything, made it more likely, not less, that regional conflicts can boil over into a shooting war. For the moment, the forces of irrational religious fundamentalism do not possess or seem to want the military infrastructure necessary to deploy submarines, but that might change.

Five nations, maybe six, possess nuclear submarines; many more have modern diesel-electric boats. New propulsion options, such as hydrogen fuel cells, allow even conventional submarines extended underwater endurance at high speeds. All are equipped with ever more capable torpedoes, some wire guided, some with sophisticated active homing, some capable of incredible speed, some armed with nuclear weapons. The net effect is that the world's oceans are busier than ever, populated by deadlier submarines in ever greater numbers. It is more likely than not that submarines will again hunt each other under the waves.

APPENDIX

Gun Calibres

Throughout this book, gun calibres are given as they were denominated by the navy of the boat being described. This means that several different nomenclatures can appear in some chapters, as there were three basic systems in use simultaneously at least up to the end of the Second World War: the British, American and Metric (used by almost everyone else).

The Royal Navy used the 'pdr' (pounder) designation of gun sizes for most of the time period covered by this book. It is a system dating back to the beginning of artillery design and designates a gun by the weight of the projectile it fired. In the earliest days, every gun was different and the shot that fitted one cannon might not fit any other in the world. The onset of the Industrial Revolution and the mass-production of guns led to standardisation on a few basic gun calibres. This led to certain 'pdr' designations being associated with specific gun calibres, even though shell weight might vary considerably for any given calibre depending on the type of shell. However, the 'pdr' designations were not dropped until after the Second World War. To make matters worse, for guns larger than 25pdr, and even a few smaller ones, the British used imperial or metric designations, sometimes interchangeably. In recent years, the Royal Navy has adopted solely metric gun designations.

Most European nations referred to guns solely by calibre (shell diameter) using the metric system throughout this period. The US Navy also referred to guns by calibre, but used (and still uses) inch measurements (with some notable exceptions, such as anti-aircraft guns, which were sometimes given metric designations, depending mainly on where the design originated). Very small guns of less than an inch bore diameter were given 'calibre' designations, such as the Browning 50-calibre machine gun. A calibre, in this system, was 1/100 of an inch, so that 50-calibre was half an inch (or 12.7mm).

The following table covers most of the gun calibres mentioned in this book and, for the sake of completeness, some that are not. Please note that the listed equivalents are approximate and that these are gun designations and not necessarily actual shell diameters. Also note that these equivalents between nomenclatures changed over time, so that a 12pdr of the Napoleonic era was quite different from a 12pdr of the Second World War.

1pdr	37mm	1.46in
2pdr	40mm	1.57in
4pdr	50mm	1.97in
6pdr	57mm	2.24in
9pdr	65–70mm	2.55–2.75in
12pdr	75mm	2.95in
17pdr	76.2mm	3.00in
18pdr	83.8mm	3.30in
25pdr	87.6mm	3.45in

Endnotes

Chapter 1: First Blood – *U-27* and HMS/M *E.3*, and the '*Baralong* Affair'

1. The Royal Navy was just as happy that the Germans chose not to challenge the Grand Fleet in the early days of the war. As Winston Churchill put it, Admiral Jellicoe, the Commander of the Grand Fleet, was 'the only man on either side who could lose the war in an afternoon'.
2. The first ship sunk by a submersible was USS *Housatonic*, a screw sloop blockading Charleston, SC, on 17 February 1864 during the American Civil War. The submersible CSS *Hunley*, named after its inventor and builder, sank the Union ship with a spar torpedo but was swamped by the resulting explosion and sank as well.
3. When war broke out, the Royal Navy had seventy-five submarines, compared to Germany's thirty. Many of the submarines in both fleets were several years old and already obsolescent, but the newer boats of each were qualitatively equivalent and the Royal Navy had more of them. The two submarines whose story comprises this chapter, *U-27* and *E.3*, were remarkably similar in their capabilities. The only significant differences were that the German boat had greater range, while the British had more torpedo tubes and carried more torpedoes.
4. From the earliest days of torpedo development, it was understood that they represented a threat to the firing boat if allowed to explode too soon after launch. Therefore, torpedoes were fitted with an arming device, generally a free-rotating propeller, which prevented the warhead from arming until the torpedo had travelled a safe distance.
5. British records show the sighting taking place at 10.25. This discrepancy between the times that events are reported by different sources is caused, in this case, by the fact that Germany was in a different time zone from England and boats of both nations maintained their local time while operating in waters close to home. This problem of differing timekeeping by the two sides of events shows up repeatedly in this book, sometimes causing events to be reported as happening on different days. I found no one correct way to handle this, so I simply note when it happens as appropriate.
6. This excerpt and those that follow in this chapter are from *Auszug*, found in *U-27*'s *KTB* (*Kriegstagebuch* – war diary). (It was the responsibility in all navies for the captain of a vessel to maintain a written log of his ship's activities. These often are the most straightforward description of events as seen from a particular combatant's point of view and I have sought them out when available and use them extensively in this book. They vary considerably in literary style.) The Germans in both wars supplied their captains with specially formatted paper to use for this purpose. The first column was for date and time, the second for environmental information and location and the

third for the narrative. (American war diaries that I quote later in the book used a simpler, two-column format.) I have maintained this format in my excerpts. Germans always use a day-month-year format to show dates, sometimes using roman numerals for the month, often leaving off the year. In the First World War, the Germans often used a 12-hour clock to show time; I have changed all such times to a 24-hour clock for the sake of consistency.

7. This section gives both wind state ('NW 3–4') and sea state ('Sea NW 3'). This tells us that the wind and waves were both coming from the northwest. The wind state is given using the Beaufort Scale, which categorises winds in twelve (sometimes seventeen) gradations of increasing force. For example, wind state 3 is described as a 'Gentle Breeze – 7–10kt' which causes 'Large wavelets and crests begin to break. Possible scattered white horses.' The sea state is given separately using the Douglas Sea Scale, which used one or two numbers, each with a 0–9 scale, where the first number indicated the height of the waves and the optional second number indicated wave form. A sea state of 3 is described as 'Slight – waves 0.5 to 1.25 m'.

8. AK – German for flank speed (*Äußerste Kraft*).

9. Cf., Chapter 3 for more about the development of this idea of U-boat traps, also called Q-Ships.

10. Cf. Appendix 1 for a discussion of gun calibres.

11. The various accounts of this incident, including Herbert's official report and interviews given to the American press by several of the muleteers, agree up to this point, but then begin to diverge widely. I have attempted to piece together a consistent story from these various accounts, but have noted major discrepancies as appropriate. The fact that none of the Germans survived means that their side of the story remains a matter of speculation.

12. The Royal Navy seemed to be the only party involved that failed to notice the absurdity of these survivors scuttling the ship that represented their only safe refuge.

Chapter 2: Fratricide I – *U-7* and *U-22*

1. This specifically excludes the unfortunately more numerous cases of training accidents when one submarine accidentally sank another of the same navy.

2. These excerpts are from *Gutachten*. This was an eight-page document attached to *U-22*'s *KTB* containing the findings of the inquiry conducted by Hoppe's flotilla chief.

3. A 'point' is 11¼°, thus four points is 45° and six points is 67½°.

4. The German signal flares (*Leuchtpatrone*) were intended to be fired straight up. At or near the highest point of their trajectory, they would separate into several individual 'stars' of specified colours, different flares having different colour combinations.

5. Hoppe was looking for two tell-tale signs that might identify the boat he was following as being German. One was a characteristic forward extension of the tower structure to form a breakwater. The other was the narrow exhaust pipe that all early U-boats, including *U-22*, erected on the surface. It was only with *U-23* that the Germans, having switched over to diesel engines that produced far less smoke, omitted the exhaust pipe.

6. At this point, the report becomes unreadable for most of a page. The author indulges in some speculation to fill in the blank, based on the drawings included with the report.

7. As part of the elaborate cat-and-mouse game of Q-ship vs. U-boat, the British took to filling the holds of the small steamers used as decoys with cork or wood or some other inherently buoyant material so that they would remain afloat after being torpedoed.

Chapter 3: U-boat traps – HMS *Taranaki*, HMS/M C.24 and U-40

1. The complete text of the German announcement, translated into English by the German Foreign Ministry, is as follows:

> *All the waters surrounding Great Britain and Ireland, including the whole of the English Channel, are hereby declared to be a war zone. From February 18 onwards every enemy merchant vessel found within this war zone will be destroyed without it always being possible to avoid danger to the crews and passengers.*
>
> *Neutral ships will also be exposed to danger in the war zone, as, in view of the misuse of neutral flags ordered on January 31 by the British Government, and owing to unforeseen incidents to which naval warfare is liable, it is impossible to avoid attacks being made on neutral ships in mistake for those of the enemy.*
>
> *Navigation to the north of the Shetlands, in the eastern parts of the North Sea and through a zone at least thirty nautical miles wide along the Dutch coast is not exposed to danger.*
>
> *Reichsanzeiger, 4 February 1915*

2. It has been estimated that 614 fishing vessels, mainly trawlers, of approximately 62,000 tons were sunk by U-boats between May 1915 and the end of the war (*Tarrant*, p 153).
3. 'Eel' – *Aal* in German – was common slang for a torpedo, which after all, as is often forgotten, was the name of a fish (otherwise known as an electric ray) before it was the name of a weapon. The Americans, more generically, called a torpedo a 'fish'.
4. The account of *U-14*'s loss comes from a deposition given by *Kapitänleutnant* Mühlau after the war, quoted extensively in *Messimer*, pp 31–2.
5. The sources do not agree on what size gun *U-14* might have carried. It is clear that, as built, these early U-boats carried no deck gun, but survivor accounts indicate that the boat mounted a gun and that it was used to fire a warning shot.
6. After the war, Werner Fürbringer, the brother of *U-40*'s commander, wrote a popular account of his brother's career in U-boats, in which he states that Gerhard complained upon being rescued that the sinking of his boat had been a dirty trick. What bothered the Germans most about Q-ship tactics was the 'false surrender' aspect. The Germans believed that by heaving to and putting the 'panic crew' into boats, the target had surrendered and that, therefore, opening fire later was an action prohibited by the rules of war. The British position was that as long as the flag (albeit false) had not been struck, no actual surrender had taken place.
7. Dobson, by then a Commander, was in charge of a squadron of eight coastal motor boats in the so-called 'Scooter Raid' on the Kronstadt Naval Base near St Petersburg (later Petrograd and Leningrad, and now St Petersburg [actually Sankt-Peterburg] again) on 17–18 August 1919. He was promoted Rear Admiral after he retired in 1936.

Chapter 4: Almost an Ace – Heino von Heimburg

1. The passage of *U-21* under the command of Otto Hersing in May 1915 from Wilhelmshaven to the Adriatic proved the voyage could be made safely.
2. The Germans in the First World War had numerous parallel lines of U-boat development. Too many. The technology was evolving so rapidly that the Germans were reluctant to settle on a single design to build in quantity. For

example, *U-93* (a successful mid-war design) was one of just three boats in its class. Constantly building boats to new, improved designs made them expensive and slow to build. There would never be enough of them.

The 'UC' small minelayers and the 'UB' coastal boats were designed in response to the need for smaller, simpler, standardised designs that could be built in quantity. The early examples of each type were too small and clearly inadequate, but both designs evolved rapidly through several major revisions into the 'UC-III' and 'UB-III' types, which were highly capable medium-sized boats and were ordered in large quantities. The orders came too late for enough of these boats to be built to make a difference in the war. The 'UB-III' design served as the design precursor of the Type VII boats of the Second World War, more than 600 of which were built.

3. Cattaro (now Kotor in Montenegro) and Pola (now Pula in Croatia) were the primary Adriatic bases used by the German navy to conduct the U-boat war in the Mediterranean. These boats remained part of the German navy and were operated as part of the *Deutsches Marine Spezial Kommando* based at Pola. However, when they were operating in the Adriatic, they adopted Austrian identity, because, although Italy and the Austro-Hungarian Empire had been at war since 23 May 1915, Germany was not technically at war with Italy until August 1916. Therefore, for a period of 15 months in 1915–16, German U-boats based in the Adriatic carried Austrian markings and flew the Austrian flag.

4. The Germans maintained an office at Pola for the purpose of smoothing the transfer of boats to Austrian service. *Deutsche Marine Spezial Kommando* retained control of these early boats for their first patrols as the Austrians got used to their handling.

5. The Austro-Hungarian navy designated its U-boats using a similar naming system as the Germans. Since their boats operated alongside German boats in the Adriatic and even after August 1916, it was customary for German U-boats operating even temporarily from Adriatic bases to have an Austrian number as well as a German one, there was frequent confusion over which boat was indicated by a particular name. The Germans tried to address this by giving Austrian boats Roman numeral designators in their logs and orders (*eg*, *U-6* = *U-VI*), but the Austrians appear not to have adopted this convention.

6. He was able to take *U-11* out on patrol so soon after being recommissioned because he and the crew had already worked up the boat. *UB-15* was commissioned into the German navy at the AG Weser Werft Bremen on 4 April 1915. They had a month to familiarise themselves with the boat and each other before the boat was decommissioned on 6 May, disassembled at Kiel and sent out by rail on 12 May. Sources differ as to exactly when the boat became Austro-Hungarian and whether *UB-15/U-11* was technically German or Austrian on this first patrol.

7. Cf., *Gefechts* for these excerpts.

8. Salvore is now Savudrija in Croatia at the tip of the Istrian peninsula.

9. Although the Turks conquered Constantinople in 1453 and began calling the city Istanbul almost immediately, the name was not 'officially' changed until 1930. Curiously, the name Istanbul is not of Turkish origin. Rather, it is a corruption of a Greek word meaning 'in the city'.

10. Some reports put the base not at Bodrum itself, but in a bay called Orak some 9 miles east of Bodrum.

11. Chanak, now known as Canakkale, is a port city on the eastern (Asian) shore of the Dardanelles right at the narrowest point of the straits.

12. These appear to have been a rather crude form of depth charge. They were fitted with a waterproof fuse that would be cut to the appropriate length, lit

and the mine would be tossed over the side. Since the mine would drop
through the water at a known rate, as long as the fuse burned at the correct
rate, the depth at which the mine would explode corresponded directly to the
length of the fuse.

13. In July, *E.7* penetrated the Sea of Marmara and, using her deck gun, shot up
the railway line that ran along the Asian shore and two trains that had been
stopped by the damaged track.

14. It appears to be impossible to determine which date was the actual date of the
event. Records seem evenly divided between the 5th or 6th. Even von
Heimburg's *KTB* is ambiguous, as the written log, excerpted here, states 6
November, while the accompanying chart, says 5 November. I have, in this
telling, stayed with the 5th, without any particular conviction that it is more
correct than the 6th.

15. *Evans*, p 68. This account, in common with most British accounts, is very
critical of the French, perhaps understandably so given the fate of *E.20*.

16. The chart below indicates this course change took place at 1540 (3.40pm).
This kind of imprecision was normal as exact timekeeping for the purposes
of the *KTB* was not critical.

17. *Grayl*, p 172. Von Heimburg apparently was a renowned storyteller, who,
as with many of the type, valued the interest of a tale over its strict adherence
to historical fact, and he reportedly told this story after the war to anyone
who would listen.

18. The Turkish name for *Turquoise* is rendered into English several different
ways, including *Mustadieh Ombashi*, *Mustedieh Onbashi* and *Mustecip
Ombasi*.

19. These excerpts are from *UC-22 KTB*.

20. The *Pour le Mérite* was popularly known in English as the 'Blue Max',
though this nickname ('*Blauer Max*') originated in Germany. The name
derives in part from the distinctive blue colour of the Maltese cross worn at
the collar. The 'Max' part of the popular name originated in the First World
War among German pilots, because the first award to an aviator was to Max
Immelmann.

21. Dönitz's new tactics also included the idea of meeting concentration with
concentration. The convoy system was effective in part because it
concentrated the limited numbers of escorts in a way that maximised their
effect. Dönitz, and others, concluded that concentrating U-boat resources by
having them operate in groups would stretch and potentially overwhelm
convoy escorts. On the mission on which *UB-68* was lost, Dönitz had
planned to rendezvous with *UB-48* commanded by *Kapitänleutnant*
Wolfgang Steinbauer, with whom he had been discussing his ideas. But the
planned meeting on 3 October 1918 southeast of Capo Passaro never
happened because *UB-48* was delayed by mechanical problems and *UB-68*
carried out the attack that night on her own.

22. Only one other commander could be credited with sinking three enemy
submarines, Lieutenant Commander Jake Fyfe of uss *Batfish*. Cf. Chapter 22.

Chapter 5: The Sound of Torpedoes?

1. In the lowest ranks of European aristocracy, certain honours could be
granted to an individual which were not inherited by any offspring. In
German and Austrian practice, as in England, such was the case when a
person was knighted. This carried with it the right to add the honorific '*Ritter*
(Knight) von' before their surname, similar to 'Sir' in British practice. This
was the case with Georg's father, August *Ritter* von Trapp, but because the
honour was not hereditary, his son was simply Georg Trapp until he won the

right to be called Georg *Ritter* von Trapp in his own right.

2. I use the terms 'Austrian' and 'Austro-Hungarian' interchangeably when talking about the First World War period.
3. Fiume is now the Croatian port of Rijeka.
4. Holland-type submarines were those related to the original designs developed by the Irish-born American engineer John Holland for the US Navy. Experiments were going on in a number of countries at the end of the nineteenth century, but Holland's design is generally conceded to be the first truly practical submersible in part because it employed dynamic depth control by means of diving planes, rather than using a diving screw and/or ballast to maintain depth.
5. Now the Croatian island of Palagruza.
6. *U-14* survived the war and was returned to France and recommissioned as *Curie* on 17 July 1919. *Curie* remained in service until 1929, being broken up the next year.
7. The reasons for von Trapp's anti-Nazism are not completely clear, but seem to have roots in his devout Catholicism. He considered the Nazis to be anti-religious, attempting to put their political 'mythology' in the place of Christianity.
8. Zara is now Zadar in Croatia.

Chapter 6: The First 'Cold War' – *U-34* and *C-3*

1. It appears that approximately 160 all-big-gun battleships and battlecruisers were laid down before or during the First World War by ten countries. Not all of these were completed before the end of war, many were never completed at all, but all took valuable money, manpower and resources away from other needs.
2. Cf., Chapter 1, note 1.
3. As late as April 1940, one month before the invasion of the Netherlands by the German Army, *IvS* was developing plans for the Dutch navy for a proposed battlecruiser project. *IvS* was funded by a consortium of German shipyards which were all suffering from the restrictions in the Versailles Treaty and all looking forward to renewed naval construction.
4. The *E-1* design was developed for Spain starting in 1927. Actually, Spain played the part of a surrogate at the beginning, as the impetus for the project came from Germany, as did all the initial funding, but the Spanish navy meddled with the design process, insisting on changes to suit their needs. *E-1* had started out as a repeat of the late-First World War 'UG' design, an improved 'UB-III' that had been developed in 1918 and ordered into production too late for any to be laid down before Germany's surrender. But by the time *E-1* was built she had changed into a larger, less manoeuvrable boat. In the end, the Spanish didn't want the boat when she was launched in 1930, so she remained in something of a legal limbo, nominally part of the Spanish navy, but manned by a German crew, until she was sold to Turkey in 1934 and renamed *Gur*.
5. The 'Z Plan' of 1939, which was supposed to give Germany a large surface fleet by 1945 was a paper exercise intended to keep the naval staff busy while Hitler took Germany to war.
6. These were the first twelve of twenty Type IIBs, slightly larger than the IIAs, with almost double the range, though still of very limited combat potential.
7. The intervening type numbers belonged to projected U-boat types that were never built. They were a large minelayer of 1,500 tons (Type III), a 2,500-ton resupply boat (Type IV), a prototype powered by the Walter closed-cycle drive (Type V) and a larger steam-powered boat (Type VI).

8. The Type VII series started with *U-27*, the first of six ordered from AG Weser (Deschimag). The Germaniawerft series started with *U-33* and was four boats. Plans changed again after these orders were placed. The Anglo-German Naval Agreement was modified in the light of the London Naval Arms Treaty to allow Germany 45 per cent of British totals. The Germans responded by next ordering eight Type IXAs, boats of similar size as the Type IA, but of a new and much improved design.

9. It seemed to make little difference whether the state was nominally leftist, as in Soviet Russia, or rightist, as in Fascist Italy. Both types of state were equally authoritarian and repressive, and used elaborate state-sponsored propaganda machines to drum up the appropriate level of hatred of enemies internal and external and distract the mass of the populace from the elimination of any internal opposition.

10. Alfonso XIII fled Spain in 1931, but never formally abdicated, laying the foundation for the re-establishment of the Spanish monarchy by his grandson Juan Carlos in 1975.

11. This airlift used German and Italian aircraft, marking the start of the foreign intervention that characterised the Spanish Civil War from the beginning.

12. Naval officers removed from command by the Republic were rarely executed. Most often they were simply imprisoned and later exchanged. The death rate among officers in the other services found on the wrong side of the conflict, on both sides, was very high.

13. Melilla and Ceuta are port cities on the north coast of Morocco, which were Spain's primary bases for their long, largely unsuccessful attempt to colonise the country. Both cities and their suburbs remain Spanish enclaves to this day, as frustrating to the Moroccans as Britain's continued possession of Gibraltar is to the Spanish. The Spanish reject this comparison, claiming that the cities are not colonies, but are actually part of Spain, making them the last European territory on the African mainland.

14. The initial push by the Nationalists left them in charge of a contiguous band of territory that included Navarre, Léon, Old Castile and Galicia in the north and Extramadura and most of Andalucia in the south and west. The Republicans held two separate zones: Asturias and most of Viscaya in the north, centred on Oviedo, Santander and Bilbao, and most of the centre and east of the country including New Castile, La Mancha, Murcia, Catalonia and most of Aragon, centred on Madrid, Barcelona and Valencia. Most of Spain's population, minerals and industry were in the Republican zones, but the Nationalists held most of the food production and had the tremendous advantage of being able to attack the separate Republican zones individually.

15. The diesels were made by Vickers and were notoriously unreliable. After the Civil War began, British 'neutrality' made spare parts impossible to obtain.

16. '*Saltzwedel*' was the second flotilla formed after Germany started building U-boats again. The first, the '*Weddigen*' flotilla, was formed at Kiel around the smaller Type IIB boats that were essential to training the new U-boat force. The second flotilla was formed at almost the same time, September 1936, around the bigger Type Is and Type VIIs (and later Type IXs) just emerging from the shipyards.

17. Hitler completely failed to understand that the Spanish Civil War was, to Franco, only peripherally a military conflict. Franco actually favoured a war of attrition over a rapid military victory, as this gave him a chance to kill more Republican troops and do a more thorough job of the *limpieza* (cleaning – the systematic imprisonment or killing of anyone suspected of leftist sympathies) of conquered territories.

18. Except for trade unionists and the rare socialist politician, the British government in 1936 was not-very-secretly pro-Franco. (This included the

later prominent anti-Fascists Eden and Churchill.) They pressured the French into closing their border to arms shipments, forcing the Republicans to rely solely on Soviet Russia for equipment. In the US, public opinion was strongly pro-Republican, but the powerful American Catholic lobby pressured Roosevelt into maintaining a strict neutrality that precluded trading with either side, which only hurt the Republicans.

19. Cf., Chapter 4. *FdU* – *Führer der Unterseeboote* (Leader of U-boats) was Dönitz's title from 1 January 1936 to 19 September 1939. On that date, his title was changed to *BdU* – *Befehlshaber der Unterseeboote* (C-in-C U-boats).
20. At the time when this planning was being done, early November 1936, there were five Type VIIAs (*U-27, U-28, U-30, U-33* and *U-34*) and two Type IAs (*U-25* and *U-26*) in commission. Despite the fact that the Type IAs were bigger and had better range, they were not liked by Dönitz and were never seriously considered for this operation. *U-30* had just been commissioned and was also not considered. That left the choice between four Type VIIAs.
21. *The Saltzwedel Flotilla in Spain*, p 3.
22. In an attempt to make up for the lack of skilled officers, and to find use for the many merchant sailors out of work due to the increasingly tight blockade of the Republican coast, a number of merchant officers were drafted into the Republican navy.
23. It seems that every source gives a different number for the size of the crew of *C-3* that day. Somewhere between thirty-five and forty-seven men lost their lives in *C-3*.
24. GHG – *Gruppenhörchgerät* (Group Listening Apparatus) – A fixed semi-circular hydrophone array mounted on either side of the bow of all but the last Type VII U-boats. On a small boat, like a Type VIIA, the radio operator (*Funker*) doubled as the sound man.
25. *Tabacalera* was the Spanish tobacco monopoly. Before the Civil War, smuggling tobacco was a lucrative sideline for fishermen along the Mediterranean coast and the monopoly maintained a small fleet of patrol boats to combat this illicit traffic. When the war broke out, these boats were incorporated into the Republican navy.
26. This message and the next is reproduced in several sources, including *Mollá*. The location is given in a grid system similar to, but not the same as, the one the Germans used in the Second World War. This system divided the world's oceans (and the European landmass) into grid squares 8° on a side. At the latitude of Great Britain, the grid squares were 486nm square. Each major square was given a two-letter code. It was then divided into nine sub-squares and redivided three more times to give squares described by two letters and four numbers that were, at that latitude, 6nm on a side. As the system approaches the poles, the grids get elongated and become quite irregular in shape. Following the Germans' Second World War system, the square AQ 1419 was in the middle of European Russia. Grosse was either using an earlier version of the grid system or encoded his grid location for greater security. Following the Second World War system, *U-34*'s location at the time she sank *C-3* would have been in grid CG 9399.
27. When lead-acid batteries are overcharged, they can give off hydrogen gas, which is very explosive. When sea water contacts the hydrochloric acid in the batteries, chlorine gas is generated which is highly toxic but not explosive.
28. The transfer of the two submarines, originally the Italian *Archimede* and *Evangelista Torricelli* was announced as a purchase to cover up the fact that they were given to the Nationalists as part of the ongoing supply of massive quantities of arms to Franco by Italy and Germany. They were officially renamed *General Sanjurjo* and *General Mola* and served in the Spanish fleet until stricken in 1959.

Chapter 7: First Shots of a Long War – ORP *Sep*, U-14 and HMS/M *Spearfish*

1. Memel is now Klaipeda in Lithuania.
2. This movement of units of the Polish fleet to England was codenamed '*Pekin*'.
3. Gdynia was a small fishing village and a popular tourist destination before the Versailles Treaty gave the 'Polish Corridor' to Poland. The Poles developed the village into an active and modern seaport during the 1920s in an attempt to rival the German-dominated Free City of Danzig barely 10nm down the coast. When the Germans occupied the city in September 1939, they renamed it Gotenhafen rather than call it Gdingen, which was the old German version of Gdynia. After the Second World War, Gdynia reverted to Poland, along with the western half of East Prussia. Danzig is now known by its Polish name, Gdansk. Polish warship names were formally preceded by 'ORP' which stands for *Okret Rzeczpospolitej Polskiej* – Vessel of the Polish Republic.
4. Hela is a small port at the tip of the Hela Peninsula that helps separate the Gulf of Danzig from the Baltic. Both the port and the peninsula are now known by their Polish name, Hel.
5. One source, *WLB_Stuttgart*, states that the target of *U-14*'s attack was the submarine *Zbik*, but all others agree that she was *Sep*. *Zbik* was attacked by *U-22* four days later in a manner that precisely mirrored the details of *U-14*'s attack on *Sep*, down to the mistaken claim of success.
6. This problem is covered in detail in *Stern*, pp 79–84.
7. U-boats dedicated to training new crews were called *Schulboote* – school boats.
8. *U-18* had an interesting history. She had been sunk and raised once as a result of a training accident in 1936. After her brief stint as a *Frontboot* in 1939–40, she returned to training duties until 1942, when she was selected for transport to the Black Sea, along with five other Type IIBs, in a manner similar to the way that 'UB' and 'UC' boats had been transported to Pola in the First World War. Operating out of Constantia, she made eight patrols and sank at least four Soviet targets. She was scuttled in Constantia harbour along with *U-24* in August 1944 when Romania surrendered. Most accounts have the Soviets raising both submarines. For *U-18*, this was the second time she was salvaged from the bottom of the sea. Accounts differ as to when *U-18* was raised and what her fate was afterwards. The most interesting account states that she was raised again in late 1944 and was eventually sunk as a target by the Soviet submarine *M-120* on 26 May 1947 off Sevastopol. (This account is from *Niestlé* p 32 and uboat.net.) If this account is true, this makes *U-18* one of the most unusual instances of a submarine being sunk by another.
9. This was the pre-arranged signal to all units that hostilities had begun with Germany and any German warships were to be engaged on sight.
10. It is this author's opinion that the former explanation is far more likely.

Chapter 8: Fratricide II – HMS/M *Triton* and HMS/M *Oxley*

1. The exception was the fleet of ore carriers discussed in the next chapter.
2. This approach obviously applied only until the German conquest of Norway and France opened up a much longer coastline under Nazi control.
3. The quote is from *The Times*, reporting on an incident that took place on 29 June 1939, found in an article at www.fogbugz.tkwebservice.com/default.asp?ahoy.2.421.20.
4. Most of this account comes from *Evans*, pp 195–9.
5. Like other navies, the Royal Navy had developed a dedicated system for short-range underwater sound communication, calling theirs the HTD. The two boats had communicated their positions via HTD at 1600 that day and

at that time, *Oxley* had estimated *Triton*'s bearing and range. A later, interrupted communication showed *Triton* much closer, but was not believed by Bowerman due to the lack of success in maintaining contact. Cf., also Chapter 17, Note 5.

6. It was standard practice, in the days before electronic IFF, for ships in a navy to have challenge-response signals they could send to one another to ascertain nationality. These would be changed regularly in case the enemy had managed to obtain the current sequences. (The stealing of recognition codes was a constant pre-occupation of both sides and took many forms, including capturing enemy small craft and the salvaging of sunken boats.) On 10 December 1939, the challenge was 'FO' and the proper response would have been 'DY'. Failure to respond, or an incorrect response, indicated (but did not prove) that the ship being challenged was not of the same navy.

7. *Oxley* also had a very un-German-looking conning-tower structure, but it was determined that at night and in the mist, *Triton*'s lookouts could understandably have failed to note this distinction.

Chapter 9: Tit for Tat – HMS/M *Thistle* and *U-4*

1. Dönitz, in fact, was well off in his projections, because he never counted on the ability or willingness of the Americans to mass-produce merchant ships. By the end of the war, US shipyards had delivered over 56 million GRT of cargo shipping. When the Liberty Ship programme peaked in December 1943, new construction exceeded losses by 1.4 million GRT that month alone.

2. Experience during the war was to show that with refuelling and careful management of stores, Type VII boats could operate effectively off the US east coast.

3. All the prewar U-boat construction was done at three yards: AG Weser (Bremen), Germaniawerft (Kiel) and Deutsche Werke (Kiel).

4. *U-1* was last heard from on 6 April, when she was leaving Wilhelmshaven. The best guess is that she hit a mine that same day in a newly laid British minefield north of Terschelling and was lost with all hands. For many years the British maintained that *U-1* was sunk by a torpedo fired by HMS/M *Porpoise* on 16 April, but the boat that *Porpoise* attacked that day was *U-3*, which was unharmed. *Porpoise* had the unfortunate distinction of being the last Royal Navy submarine lost in the Second World War, when she was sunk by Japanese aircraft in the Malacca Straits on 19 January 1945. She will appear in this narrative several more times.

5. The *Altmark* Affair on 16 February 1940 stiffened Norwegian resistance to British pressure. In this incident, a German supply ship, which had been supporting the 'pocket battleship' *Admiral Graf Spee* and was on its way back to Germany with a full load of prisoners taken from the ships the raider had sunk, was chased into Norwegian territorial waters by HMS *Cossack* and the prisoners rescued.

6. There is no question that Hitler would rather not have invaded Norway, being much more interested in his plan to invade France and the Low Countries, but he was also unwilling simply to let the British occupy the country without opposition. He was able to squeeze in the invasion of Norway with only minimal disruption to his plans in the west. When he similarly inserted an excursion into the Balkans into his plans in the east the next year, the effects were far more serious.

7. The best account of the British side of this incident is in *Jones*, pp 39–42, from which I have obtained much useful detail.

8. *Jones*, pp 39–40.

9. The Germans captured Stavanger in an operation carried out entirely by air. A single unescorted cargo ship was sent in support with the paratroopers' heavy equipment. This ship, *Rota*, was intercepted and sunk on 9 April by the Norwegian torpedo boat *Aeger*, which was based at Stavanger. *Aeger* was sunk by air attack later the same day.

10. 'T' class boats were big. As built, they had ten torpedo tubes, six internal tubes at the bow and four external tubes (two at the bow and two forward-firing under the tower). They carried a total of sixteen torpedoes, meaning they had a reload for each internal tube. For *Thistle* to have only two torpedoes left after firing six at *U-4* means that eight had been fired at other targets earlier or that she had left port with less than a full load.

11. These excerpts are from *U-4 KTB*.

12. Type II boats had three torpedo tubes, all forward.

13. The G7e and G7a were the two standard German submarine torpedoes of the Second World War. They were virtually identical in size and weight, a necessity given that they were to be fired from the same tubes. They differed in the method of propulsion. The G7a burned a naphtha-based propellant in air to produce steam which turned a turbine; the G7e was electric-powered. The former was faster and had a longer range, but the later left virtually no wake, which made them popular.

14. *BdU KTB*, PG 30262, p 13 – entry for 14 April 1940. 'W/T' was 1940s shorthand for radio, standing for 'wireless telegraphy'.

15. The likely cause of the torpedo failures described in Chapter 8.

16. The impact fuse was massively over-engineered. Designed to address a problem with the First World War fuse, which would sometimes fail to detonate if it hit a target at an angle, the new fuse worked extremely well in those cases, but had an increasing chance of failure as the impact angle approached the perpendicular. In other words, the better approach a captain made, the worse his chances of success.

17. *BdU KTB*, PG 30264, pp 71–2 – entry for 23 May 1940.

Chapter 10: This War was Anything but Phoney – *Doris* and *U-9*

1. Known in England as the 'Phoney War' or the 'Bore War', in France it was '*La drôle de guerre*'.

2. In fact, a total of twelve French submarines were serving with the Royal Navy in early 1940. The other four were larger 1,500-ton boats, which operated with the RN 9th Flotilla from Dundee.

3. The other four boats sent to Harwich (*Orphée*, *Antiope*, *La Sibylle* and *Amazone*) were built to the later, somewhat larger design, known as the '*630-tonne*' class, which was an attempt to address some of the shortcomings of the '*600-tonne*' boats.

4. Unlike the sailors on larger surface units, submariners were universally provided shore accommodation while their boats were in port. Living in the cramped, damp and smelly interior of a submarine was accepted as necessary during a patrol, but was acknowledged as an undue hardship when the boat was in port. On top of that, all navies, including even the US Navy, whose submarines were far more comfortable to live in than any others in the Second World War, practised 'hotbunking' whereby three enlisted men shared two bunks since at sea one of the three would always be on duty.

5. The Maginot Line, which provided a wide belt of fortifications along the German border, was never completed along the Belgian border, in the belief that a mobile French army would advance into Belgium and hold the Germans north of the border. The fortifications were weakest behind the Ardennes, a region of hills and forests in southeastern Belgium, which was

considered impenetrable by a modern mechanised army. The plans the French obtained showed the Germans attacking exactly there; since that was obviously impossible, the Allies reasoned, those plans must have been intended as a ruse. In fact, that's where the Germans indeed attacked with the bulk of their armour, driving to the Channel behind the British Expeditionary Force and the best units of the French army, trapping those troops in Belgium.

6. They were ORP *Orzel*, which was sunk in the North Sea in June 1940, and *Wilk*, which was used only for training after September 1940 and survived the war. *Wilk* will show up again in this book.

7. The Dutch had ten seagoing boats in service operating from Den Helder on the channel between the mainland and Texel, the southernmost of the Frisian islands. There were also four brand-new boats just completing and not yet ready for service.

8. Both two-stroke and four-stroke engines were widely used in the 1930s, but increasingly the four-stroke became the more used type because it was less complex and therefore tended to be more reliable (or easier to repair) in submarines. Both types are still being made today.

9. *Amiral* (Admiral) Jean-François Darlan is an ambiguous figure in French history. To his supporters, he was a fierce patriot and, at the same time, a pragmatist who accepted the fact of France's defeat in June 1940 and worked within the state that remained in France to preserve what was left of the integrity of France and its empire. (In the process, he rose to post of *vice-première* in the Vichy state.) To his detractors, he was a willing and enthusiastic collaborator with the victorious Nazis and a crass opportunist who changed sides without the slightest hesitation when caught in North Africa by the 'Torch' landings. He was appointed head of the Free French forces by General Eisenhower – with the support of both FDR and Churchill – much to the disgust of De Gaulle and many of his supporters. He was assassinated on 24 December 1942 by a French royalist resistance fighter.

10. *Amazone* patrolled the adjacent sector to the north. Other boats involved in the barrier patrol at the beginning of May 1940 (besides *Doris* and *Amazone*) were: *Thétis, Calypso, La Sibylle, Antiope, Sturgeon, Snapper, Seawolf* and *Triad*. The first four on that list were French, the rest British.

11. One analysis of U-boat attacks on British warships during the Norwegian operation concluded that out of twenty-seven attacks north of 62°30'N (well north of Bergen), twenty had had a high chance of success. Of these, none had succeeded due to problems with the torpedoes. (*MoD*, p 26)

12. *BdU KTB*, PG 30264, p 66 – entry for 5 May 1940. Only one ship was sunk in this minefield, that being the large tanker SS *San Tiburcio* of 5,995 GRT, which sank on 4 May 1940.

13. These excerpts are from *U-9 KTB*.

14. The gyro angle was the angle a torpedo was commanded to turn to after a brief straight run out of the tube. This allowed a submarine to fire torpedoes at targets that were not directly in front of the tubes (and made unnecessary the aimable tubes such as *Doris*'s). This feature was introduced to the torpedoes of all major navies between the wars.

Note that the G7e was set to run 1m shallower than the G7a and that it still missed, most likely because it ran under the target. The G7e was notorious for running deeper than set. This problem was not resolved until mid-1940 when it was discovered that high-pressure air from inside a U-boat was leaking into the torpedo's air chamber used to drive the depth-keeping gyroscope and causing it to malfunction.

15. The *Grampus* class were large Royal Navy minelaying submarines derived from HMS/M *Porpoise*. Despite being at least 50 per cent bigger in all

dimensions, there was enough resemblance to *Doris* to excuse mistaking the two types in a night engagement.

16. Scheveningen is a fishing port and seaside resort that is part of the city of Den Haag.

17. This is another occasion when differences in the time kept on opposing boats occurred. French records show the sinking taking place on 8 May, just before midnight.

18. The ships she sank were ss *Viiu* (Estonian, 1,908 GRT) and ss *Tringa* (British, 1,930 GRT), both sunk on the 11th.

19. Pillau is now Baltiysk, now part of an isolated Russian enclave in what used to be East Prussia.

20. There was in fact one higher grade of Knight's Cross, the 'Golden Oakleaves, Swords and Diamonds', which was given only to one man, Hans-Ulrich Rudel, a pilot and ardent Nazi. That grade of the award was created specifically to be awarded to Rudel, who was a personal favourite of Hitler, and is therefore not considered to have been achievable by any other person.

Chapter 11: What did ORP *Wilk* Hit?

1. One Yugoslav boat, *Nebojsa*, operated with the Royal Navy in the Mediterranean. The Norwegian submarine *B-1* escaped to Britain in 1940, but was never used operationally after arriving there. Three British-built 'U' class submarines operated under the Norwegian flag from 1941. Five Greek submarines also operated under RN command in the Mediterranean after the fall of that country in April 1941. Dutch boats operated with the British in the Pacific as well.

2. Besides the seven obvious major powers which designed and built their own submarines in the first half of the twentieth century (UK, USA, USSR, Germany, France, Italy and Japan), there were seven other nations that built submarines during this period. Three of those (Sweden, Denmark and the Netherlands) designed their own boats; the other four (Spain, Romania, Finland and Norway) built boats to foreign design.

3. In 1936, the Dutch dropped the distinction between overseas boats and home defence boats. Starting with O 16, all Dutch boats built up to the outbreak of the Second World War were given 'O' designations.

4. The purpose of this extended refit was to modify or replace weapons and electronics so they would handle standard Royal Navy munitions (in particular torpedoes) and communicate with Royal Navy boats and land stations. Despite this, foreign-built submarines tended to have relatively short careers because their major systems, particularly their engines and motors, would be non-standard and therefore difficult to maintain.

5. There is considerable confusion as to whether this incident occurred on 20 or 21 June 1940. Reports from the time exist with both dates. I have used the later date for no reason other than it seems to fit the known data somewhat better. In the North Sea, where regular air activity forced submarines to submerge during the day, it is reasonable to assume an average speed for *Wilk* of no more than 6 knots, which would account for her being approximately 250nm from base after two days.

6. The following description is as detailed in *Wilk*, pt. 1. It is reportedly derived from an account of the incident published by Romanowski during the war.

7. The location of the collision is given as 56° 50' N, 3° 30' E. The minefield, known to the Germans as '16B', was at 56° 55' N, 3° 00' E. It was laid in early May 1940, but not discovered by the British until later. The possibility also exists that *Orzel* was lost in a minefield laid by the British at 57° 00' N, 3° 40' E laid on 25 May, two days after *Orzel* left on patrol.

8. This was crash-dive time from the moment of sounding the alarm to the moment that the last parts of the boat were completely underwater, generally the trailing edge of the conning tower or the after deck casing. Depending on the weather and the state of the sea, it could take up to another 30 seconds for surface disturbances to subside to the point that no trace of the boat was visible.

9. This refers to the account by the veteran Jan Jaworski, reported in *Wilk*, pt. 2.

10. According to British records, a U-boat made a long signal from a point in the North Sea not far from *Wilk*'s location at 1630 on 20 June. Long signals were rarely made by U-boats, generally only when boats were returning from patrol or if they had specific problems to report. German records report no messages received from any U-boat at or near that location at that time.

11. *BdU KTB*, PG 30267, p 81.

12. Ibid. It is believed that this attack was by an Arado floatplane launched from the *Scharnhorst*.

13. *BdU KTB*, PG 30266, p 78.

14. This was actually *U-122*'s second patrol, but the first had been a supply run to Trondheim and back.

15. *BdU KTB*, PG 30268, p 88. U-boats on patrol regularly made weather signals, a standard short message format, as Dönitz relied heavily on current weather information to plan anti-convoy operations.

16. *Niestlé*, pp 236–7.

17. *Wilk*, pt.1, p 3.

18. Some sources say *Wilk* was returned to Poland in 1951.

Chapter 12: One Busy Week – 29 July to 3 August 1940

1. *BdU KTB*, PG 30269, p 90.

2. The victim had been SS *Pearlmoor* (4,581 GRT), which had been part of Convoy SL.38 from Freetown, Sierra Leone. That sinking, and the sinking of the destroyer HMS *Grafton* in late May during the evacuation of Dunkirk had been *U-62*'s main successes.

3. Submarines of the Second World War were, with a few notable exceptions, designed for surface operation, with little thought given to efficient or quiet underwater operation. For a submarine to move silently, it had to reduce speed to a point where the screws and motors made the least noise possible. This could only be determined by experimentation and varied from design to design and even between boats built to the same design. For a typical German Type VIIC, silent speed (*Schliechfahrt* – creeping speed) was achieved by running the motors at 90 rpm, which gave a speed of about 2.5 knots.

4. Route '1' headed northwest from Emden into the middle of the North Sea and then turned north. A map showing these routes in detail can be found in *War*, p 54.

5. *Luchs* was a torpedo boat sunk by HMS/M *Thames* on 26 July near Stavanger. Some sources credit HMS/M *Swordfish* with this sinking, as *Thames* was lost on this patrol, but it appears more likely that *Thames* was responsible.

6. Cf., Chapter 10, Note 6.

7. *BdU KTB*, PG 30270, p 93. HMS/M *Seal* was captured by the Germans on 4 May 1940 in the Skagerrak after striking a mine and being damaged to the extent that she could no longer dive.

8. O 21's zone was centered at 55° 30' N, 2° 20' E; O 22's at 56° 10' N, 2° 30' E.

9. It is widely stated in English-language histories of the U-boat war that 'Adi' Schnee was Dönitz's son-in-law. (Including a book by this author.) In fact, this was not the case. Dönitz had only one daughter, Ursula, who married

Günther Hessler, who was also a young, handsome and successful U-boat commander, also served on Dönitz's staff and who, after the war, was the primary (uncredited) author of *The U-Boat War in the Atlantic 1939–1945*.

10. Cf., Chapter 9.
11. *Wynn* splits this last patrol into two separate ones because *U-34* put into Lorient to replenish between 18 July and 23 July.
12. Cf., Chapter 8.
13. Analysis of Eaden's decision to put *Spearfish* on the bottom and try to ride out the ensuing barrage of depth charges was to serve as an example to many others of how NOT to react to attack by surface units. It became common wisdom among submarine captains that it was essential to keep moving, even if only at silent speed, as this offered a far better chance of escaping the attackers.
14. The Skaw is the English sailor's name for the Skagens Odde, the cape at the northern tip of Denmark.
15. These excerpts are from *U-34 KTB*.
16. *Sterlet* was a sister of *Spearfish*, so Rollmann's identification was accurate.
17. *Wynn*, p 24. Pester is the name given in *Evans*, p 243. The story of his experiences during and after the sinking comes from *Jones*, p 59.
18. This was according to the letter of international law. The German pocket-battleship *Admiral Graf Spee* was similarly allowed 48 hours for repairs in Montevideo before she had to leave and face the Royal Navy again.
19. Most submarines of this era carried active sonar, though it was rarely, if ever, used because it could be traced back to its source. The only time it was useful was in an instance such as this, when there was no value in concealment and a great need to pinpoint the location of the other submarine.
20. Cf., Chapter 14.
21. *U-25* was lost, probably on 3 August, to a new British minefield just north of Terschelling, on the southern stretch of route '1'.
22. *BdU KTB*, PG 30270, pp 84–5.

Chapter 13: Fratricide III (and more) – R.SMG *Gemma* and R.SMG *Tricheco*; HMS/M *Upholder* and R.SMG *Ammiraglio Saint Bon*

1. The Atlantic had its famous 'air gap' at the beginning of the war, a stretch of water that was out of range of any air surveillance. This was not closed until 1943 with the emergence of escort aircraft carriers and very-long-range Liberator bombers.
2. Cf., Chapter 14, Note 1.
3. Royal Navy Flotillas in the Mediterranean were:
    1st Flotilla – based at Malta (until April 1940), Alexandria (until June 1942), Beirut (until February 1944) and Malta again until the unit was disbanded in November 1944 and its constituent submarines assigned to the 8th Flotilla.
    8th Flotilla – transferred from Colombo to Gibraltar in December 1940 (until November 1942) and Algiers until the unit was dispersed in November 1943 and reconstituted in Trincomalee in May 1944.
    10th Flotilla – re-established at Malta in January 1941(until May 1942), Alexandria (until July 1942), Malta again (until November 1943) and La Maddalena until the unit was dispersed in August 1944.
4. The 23rd Flotilla was established at Salamis in September 1941, reached a maximum strength of seven boats in December and was disbanded in April 1942; the 29th Flotilla was formed at La Spezia in December 1941, absorbed the boats of the 23rd when it was disbanded, moved to Toulon in August

1943 and ceased to exist in September 1944. It also operated boats out of Marseilles and Pola and continued to use Salamis as a base even after the 23rd Flotilla ceased operations.

5. Cf. *Niestlé*, p 219. This number includes boats destroyed while in port, scuttled to avoid capture and a couple of questionable losses which might have occurred elsewhere.

6. Seventeen Italian submarines, three U-boats and one Royal Navy submarine were lost to other submarines.

7. Between the wars, there was much disagreement in almost every navy as to whether to air-condition boats or not. The arguments in favour were strong, in that condensation build-up in boats brought with it a constant danger of electrical shorts; air-conditioning not only has the ability to cool the air but also has the critical benefit of reducing moisture levels. Navies that operated boats in hot climates also tended to favour air-conditioning because it made living conditions inside boats more tolerable over long patrols. The main argument against was that it was a complex and fragile system added to boats already the most complex in most navies. Nevertheless, the US Navy was an early adopter; beginning with the *Porpoise* class of 1933, all US submarines were air conditioned. The Germans, on the other hand, were very late adopters: only their very late war designs, such as the Type XXI, were air-conditioned. The Italians built their 600-type boats with air-conditioning, but this was not without its problems. The refrigerant they used, methylchloride, is a known toxin, causing nerve damage when inhaled even at low levels.

8. Massaua is the Italian spelling of the port of Massawa in present-day Eritrea.

9. The material on Wanklyn and *Upholder* comes from a variety of sources, the best of which is *Gray2*, p 210–12.

10. In all, nine VCs would be awarded to submariners in the Second World War.

11. The one source to give an exact number (*Rastelli*) states that 1,441 soldiers and sailors were killed.

12. These were the near sisters *Neptunia* and *Oceania*, each of approximately 19,500 GRT. Considering the number of soldiers on board the two transports – over 5,800 – the loss of life was relatively light, less than 400.

13. Not to take anything away from Wanklyn or any other of the 10th Flotilla's captains, but the frequent encounters with large, juicy targets was hardly co-incidental. By 1941, the British were regularly reading German radio traffic. The so-called ULTRA intercepts included orders for the routing and timing of Mediterranean convoys. The only fear was that the Royal Navy would get too effective at intercepting these convoys and lead the Germans to change their codes. In November 1941, fully 63 per cent of convoy traffic between Italy and Africa was sunk by RN activity. They were careful always to fly reconnaissance flights over the convoys before the submarines struck. To this day, some histories still credit British success in the Mediterranean to extra-ordinarily effective aerial reconnaissance.

14. The designed range was 19,000nm; the designed duration was six months. The one boat that was actually used as intended, *Ammiraglio Cagni*, went on two long patrols from La Maddalena and Bordeaux. Her first patrol, into the Indian Ocean, lasted 136 days. Her second mission was to Singapore, but while in the Indian Ocean on the outward passage, she received orders to surrender to the British and turned back to be interned at Durban, South Africa on 20 September 1943, after 85 days at sea.

15. Now known as Bardiyah or Al Bardiyah, it is a minor port on the Libyan coast very close to the Egyptian border. It dates back to Roman times, when it was known as Petras Maior.

16. Derna is another small port on the Libyan coast, now known as Darnah.

Benghazi is a major Libyan city and port on the eastern coast of the Gulf of Sirte, sometimes now rendered as Banghazi.
17. Tripoli is now officially called Tarabulus; it is the capital of Libya and its largest city.
18. Captain Simpson was formerly CO of HMS/M *Porpoise*. Cf. Chapter 10, Note 6 and Chapter 20.
19. British 'U' class submarines only had bow tubes.
20. A 'snap shot' in Second World War parlance was a torpedo fired without the normal elaborate set-up procedures. By the Second World War, torpedoes were no longer simple projectiles that ran in a straight line from the tube to the target. Without even considering the several anti-convoy or anti-escort torpedoes developed by the Germans during the war, all torpedoes of this era had the ability to make at least one course change, so that a torpedo could be fired by a submarine not pointed at the target. Even with the primitive analog targeting computers available at the time, the variables of torpedo speed, depth, distance to target, angle to target, angle of target, speed of target, length of run before turning, etc., were complex and took time to enter into the computer (called a TCC – Torpedo Control Calculator – on Royal Navy submarines of the time) and then more time for the physical gears of the computer to align and still more time for the data to be entered manually at the torpedo tube(s). A 'snap shot' reverted back to the earlier days when a captain pointed his boat at the place he thought the target would be at the end of a torpedo's run and fired his torpedo in a straight line.
21. I am speculating more than a little as to the events on *Saint Bon*, as the available sources give very little information. I have tried to construct a scenario that explains Miniero's decisions in a way that makes him neither suicidal nor crazy. For example, while I do not know for certain that *Saint Bon* carried no torpedoes on the night of 5 January, it is known that other Italian submarines making cargo runs to Africa landed their torpedoes in order to save weight and used the tubes as extra storage space.
    It is, of course, possible that Miniero simply made a rash choice, perhaps frustrated that he and his new, very capable boat had been assigned menial tasks, but I have no reason to believe this to be true and have chosen to assume otherwise.
22. The other credible theory of *Upholder*'s sinking is that she was sunk in a minefield near Tripoli. This is considered unlikely by most historians as this minefield was well-known to the British.
23. There is a good deal of disagreement in the available sources as to exactly how many tons of shipping and how many warships Wanklyn actually sank. The total for shipping varies between a low of 97,000 GRT and a high of 129,500 GRT. Likewise his warship totals are in some dispute. It is agreed that he sank two Italian destroyers and an armed trawler, but he claimed to have sunk a third submarine which is now generally discounted. He claimed to have sunk the submarine *Tembien* on 2 August 1941 near Malta, but that sinking is now credited to the destroyer HMS *Hermione*.

Chapter 14: The Gunfighters – HMS/M *Triad* and R.SMG *Enrico Toti*

1. Cf., Chapter 12.
2. I have used several sources for this chapter, including *Evans*, pp 262–6. Evans' account, along with most other accounts written before the late 1980s, assumes that *Toti*'s encounter was with HMS/M *Rainbow*, which disappeared in the Mediterranean about the same time as *Triad*. Recent research indicates that *Rainbow* was almost certainly sunk on 4 October 1940 when she was apparently rammed. *Rainbow* and her sister *Regent* left

Alexandria on 23 August to patrol in the Gulf of Taranto. However, on 3 October, before *Triad* left Malta, the two boats were redirected to the southern Adriatic where they were to operate against the traffic between Bari and Durazzo (now Durrës, Albania). *Rainbow* had the more easterly sector. On 7 October, *Rainbow* was again ordered to move, this time to a point off Capo Rizzuto on the Calabrian coast, not far from where *Triad* was later sunk. Finally, on 13 October, she was ordered home. She was reported overdue and probably lost at the end of October. *Rainbow* had responded to none of these orders, but that was standard procedure, so that gives no clue as to when she was sunk. However, a freighter in a small Italian convoy sailing from Durazzo to Bari early on 4 October reported striking an underwater object, approximately 60nm from Bari, followed immediately by a strong shudder, as if from a large underwater explosion. The impact and subsequent shock sprang plates on the freighter's underside, so that she was docked after reaching Bari. Examination showed deep scrapes on the ship's bottom, as if she had struck a large metal object. The consensus of researchers is now that the freighter, *Antonietta Costa*, hit *Rainbow*, causing her loss on 4 October, and that the boat that then encountered *Toti* on 15 October was *Triad*.

3. *U-120* was a UE-II boat, part of a successful series of large minelayers with a range of 12,500nm, four torpedo tubes, a 150mm deck gun and two aft-pointing mine tubes capable of holding a total of forty-two mines. They were completed too late to see much, if any, war service.

4. Again, I am indulging in some speculation here because it is hard to understand why two submarine captains would commit to a surface engagement when they had the ability to submerge and avoid the manifest dangers of a gun duel. The account reproduced in *Evans* is a translation of a report written at the time by Giovanni Cunsolo, *Toti*'s first officer, for popular consumption in the Fascist press. Cunsolo states that the decision to engage in a surface action had been agreed upon the evening before in discussion with staff officers, before *Toti* left port, should the circumstances arise. To this author, this sounds like retrospective justification for what must have been considered, at best, questionable decision-making on Bandini's part.

5. The gun mount on British 'T' class submarines was unusual. It was an open tub faired into the conning tower that rotated with the gun as it was aimed. The tub was shallow, coming up only a little above the waist on a man of average height, and was of thin, mild steel, so it provided, at best, protection only against waves and small-calibre gunfire.

6. These machine guns were in twin retractable mounts positioned in tandem behind the periscopes on the bridge. The Breda Model 1931 13.2mm machine gun compared favourably with the ubiquitous Browning M2 .50 cal machine gun, firing a slightly heavier round at a slightly slower rate. It was an effective weapon at the ranges involved in this fight.

7. Even without the need to obtain an attack solution from the targeting computer, preparing a torpedo to fire a snap shot still required that the torpedo's gyroscope be started and allowed to stabilise and the outer tube doors be opened to flood the tube. Depending on the boat and the crew, this process could take anywhere from one to a few minutes.

8. The best explanation for this is that the first shells fired from *Toti*'s gun had been affected by moisture from having been stored too long on the boat, so that their fuses did not set properly when they were fired. Artillery rounds are stored on boats in a safe state, so they will not explode if they should be thrown about by rough weather or enemy action, such as depth charging. As they are fired, the fuses 'set' through the combined effects of the sudden

acceleration and the rapid rotation caused by the rifling of the gun barrel. If there is moisture in the fuse mechanism, this can cause a fuse to fail to set and thus not explode on striking a target. Obviously, the shells fired later had been less affected and detonated properly.

Chapter 15: Trouble in Paradise – HMS/M *Clyde, U-67, U-68* and *U-111*

1. Santo Antão was the westernmost habitable island in the Cape Verde chain. In the various documents quoted in this chapter, it is also called San Antao and San Antonio. 'Tarrafal' is consistently spelled with one 'r' by the Germans.
2. The oddity that *U-111* was of an earlier type and was launched earlier than *U-67* or *U-68* can be explained by the piecemeal nature of orders for U-boats that came as war approached. The series *U-64–U-68* had been ordered as Type IXBs in 1937. Then, in 1938, the series *U-103–U-111* was ordered, also as IXBs, as a result of the increased tonnage allowed by the revised Anglo-German Naval Agreement. This second series was given a higher priority. Construction continued on the earlier series, but at a slower pace. Thus, when the improved 'C' subtype was approved, the last of the second series, *U-111*, had already been started as a 'B', but three boats of the earlier series, *U-66–U-68*, had not yet been laid down, so they were built as improved Type IXCs.
3. Cf., *U-111*. Because Kleinschmidt did not survive the sinking of his boat, but many of his crew did, this Interrogation Report includes extremely candid and uncomplimentary accounts of his behaviour under fire.
4. Very nearly in the middle of the South Atlantic, this is a group of a dozen tiny rocky islands, peaks in the Mid-Atlantic Ridge, on a line between the easternmost part of Brazil and the westernmost tip of Africa at Dakar, Senegal. Uninhabited except by lighthouse keepers and researchers, they belong to Brazil and are known officially as *Penedos de São Pedro e São Paulo*.
5. The one significant difference between the 'B' and 'C' subtypes was fuel capacity. *U-111* could hold 165t of fuel and had a range of 8,100nm; *U-67* and *U-68* could hold 208t of fuel, which gave a range of 11,000nm. *U-111* had fired nine torpedoes during this patrol, out of the eighteen she had been carrying. (This U-boat could carry twenty-two torpedoes, but *U-111*, p 9 clearly states the boat left port on her second patrol with eighteen torpedoes.) That left her with nine torpedoes; four of those were in external storage containers built into the deck casing. It was those that were transferred to *U-68*.
6. This was code-named *Alberich*. It was a 4mm thick tile made of synthetic rubber with a pattern of cavities designed to reduce the returned sound of a sonar 'ping' to as little as 15 per cent of the original strength. It was remarkably successful for such an early experiment with a revolutionary technology. There were surprisingly few problems, but those were serious. One was that the tiles' effectiveness varied considerably at different depths. More serious were the facts that they were very difficult to attach to the steel hull of a submarine and that they used a scarce resource, namely oil-based synthetic rubber. *U-67* left Kiel with a full coating of tiles, but arrived at Lorient with only about 40 per cent still attached. After the war, the Americans looked at this technology, but dismissed it as being not worth following up. They changed their minds in the 1950s, when the Soviets began coating their submarines with similar tiles. Today, all modern military submarines use some derivative of the *Alberich* technology.
7. *U-111*, p 16; *Axis*, p 66.

8. *BdU KTB*, PG 30297, p 168. Those grid co-ordinates included Tarrafal Bay. The mention of acoustic torpedoes is clearly anachronistic, as the first operational models of the T4 acoustic torpedo were not issued to the fleet until February 1943. This must be a translation error; Dönitz was certainly referring to the extra torpedoes *U-111* had in her external storage containers. These were always G7a steam-powered torpedoes; electric torpedoes could not be carried externally because their batteries required daily maintenance.
9. This was the process that allowed medium-range Type VII boats to operate with success off the coast of North America after Pearl Harbor.
10. As the focus of the U-boat war shifted from the waters around the British Isles to the open ocean from Greenland to Cape Town, Dönitz moved his headquarters closer to the ports from which his U-boats sailed. From November 1940, Dönitz established his command post at Kernéval near Lorient on the French coast.
11. *BdU KTB*, PG 30297, p 170. Note that it was the report, not the explosions themselves, that occurred at 0630 on 28 September.
12. The following excerpts are from *U-68 KTB*, *U-67 KTB* and *U-111*. I will try to make it clear where each citation comes from.
13. The full last name of *U-67*'s captain was Müller-Stockheim, but all these documents, including *U-67 KTB*, omit the second half of his hyphenated last name and I will as well in the rest of this chapter.
14. *Clyde* was a *Thames* class (or 'River' class) boat built in 1932. They were designed for extremely high surface speed and long range with the idea that they would be able to operate with the battle fleet, but even with a recorded speed of over 22 knots, they were too slow to stay with newer battleships or cruisers capable of much greater speed.
15. Cf., *Enigma*, p 173.
16. Not terribly surprisingly, given Nazi racial propaganda, the rower's skin colour was noted by the survivor. Most Cape Verdeans are mixed-race descendants of Portuguese settlers and African slaves. Merten's log refers to the locals in the boat as '*Kanakker*', a derogatory slang expression no less offensive than 'Lascar' or 'Nigger'.
17. The 'Rösing' mentioned here was *Oberleutnant zur See* Friedrich Wilhelm Rösing, *U-111*'s IWO.
18. *U-111*, p 10. *Clyde* was, in fact, painted an extremely light gray, which accounts for her 'snow-white' appearance. Cf., *Enigma*, p 174.
19. The account of *Clyde*'s actions that follows is from *U-111* and *Enigma*, p 174.
20. As has happened before in these stories, *Clyde*'s clock and the Germans' were off by an hour. By *Clyde*'s reckoning, the moon set at 0024.
21. *U-111*, pp 10–11.
22. Ibid, p 10. It is a little hard to understand why noise would be an issue when an enemy submarine is bearing down with intent to ram.
23. Ibid, pp 10–11.
24. Merten's log states that *U-68* turned south (to a course of 170°) at 0130, but this is almost certainly a mistake, as the next line states that *U-111* was still visible at a bearing of 10–20° and, for that to be true, *U-68* would have had to be on a course of approximately 300°.
25. It would appear that it was at this point, approximately 0138, that *U-68* made her turn to 170°, 8 minutes later than noted in her log. This kind of discrepancy in the writing of a log hours after the event is certainly understandable.
26. *U-111*, p 11. 'H.E.' stood for 'Hydrophone Effect', the British term for sound detection with passive sonar.
27. Ibid, p 11. 800 fathoms is approximately 440m.

28. These excerpts are from *U-67 KTB*. For some unknown reason, Müller's log shows times as two hours later than *U-68* and three hours later than *Clyde*. Equally inexplicably, Müller has the two detonations 26 minutes apart, while all other sources report them occurring between one and three minutes apart. This is not a transcription error, as the same time gap appears again later in the log, when Müller records his radio message to Dönitz.
29. Porto Grande is the large commercial port, also known as Mindelo, on São Vicente, the next island east of Santo Antão.
30. In the *Kriegsmarine*, as in all other navies, there were never enough doctors to put one on every vessel, especially the numerous smaller ones. On surface ships, this is not an issue because they tend to head back to port regularly or operate with larger ships, where the available doctors tended to be posted. Type VII U-boats were judged to be too small to accommodate a doctor even had one been available (though later in the war some exceptions were made); Type IX boats on extended patrols that could last three or more months carried doctors on the basis of one doctor for every second or third boat. The idea was that if a medical emergency occurred on a boat that did not have a doctor aboard, another boat that did would probably not be far away. For all other boats, a radioman (*Funker*) with a few weeks' basic medical training had to suffice.
31. Just to keep the times straight: 0215 by *Clyde*'s reckoning was 0315 on *U-68* (and in this narrative) and 0515 on *U-67*.
32. *U-111*, p 11.
33. Ibid.
34. The Germans were fanatical in their belief that the highest thing on a submarine should be the lookouts' eyes. Most other combatants in the Second World War designed submarines with built-up periscope supports (or shears), which sometimes towered over the lookouts' heads.
35. All references the author has consulted consistently state that the 'River' class submarines only had six torpedo tubes, all forward. The mention here of tube No. 7 and a previous mention in this source of 'stern tubes', seems to indicate that tubes were added aft after the boats were built. It appears from context that tube No. 7 was external and at the aft end of the deck casing.
36. *U-111*, p 12.
37. Cf., *Enigma*, pp 175–6.
38. *BdU KTB*, PG 30297, p 170.
39. Ibid.
40. The Germans did not upgrade the security of their Enigma codes for another 5 months, when they introduced a fourth rotor for the code machine; after that, for almost 11 months, Bletchley Park was unable to read their message traffic.
41. South-West Africa is now known as Namibia.
42. *BdU KTB*, PG 30301a, p 244.
43. *ULTRA*, pp 37–8.
44. *BdU KTB*, PG 30301a, p 249.
45. Ibid, p 250.
46. Ibid, p 261. The misspelling of *Enrico Tazzoli* is in the original.
47. *Lady Shirley* will show up again soon in these pages. Cf., Chapter 17.

Chapter 16: East of Gibraltar – O 21 and U-95

1. This first wave of boats, *U-75*, *U-79*, *U-97*, *U-331*, *U-371* and *U-559*, all arrived at Salamis without incident.
2. *BdU KTB*, PG 30300b, p 229 (entry for 20 November 1941):

   According to reports by agents and intercept messages one U-boat was sunk west and one east of Gibraltar. Which boats these are is at present not certain.

The next day, on same page of the *KTB*:

> According to a report 40 German prisoners were landed in Gibraltar on 17 November from the gunboat 'Spires' – coming from the West. (No information on this. Possibly *U-433*.)

In fact, this information was partially correct. *U-433* was indeed sunk just east (not west) of the Straits on 16 November. There was no other loss at that time. There were thirty-eight survivors.

3. Captains found that by running on one engine and at the most economical speed, a Type VIIC could operate off the coast of North America as far south as Cape Hatteras without refuelling. If refuelling was available, the duration and/or range of the patrol could be extended further. Cf., *Stern*, pp 57–8.
4. Cf., Chapter 13.
5. This and other quotes in this chapter are from *Moon*.
6. Jan Biesemaat, who was 76 years of age when his son, a journalist, wrote down his recollections of this event, did not remember the officer's name quite correctly. The Second Officer of *O 21* at the time was Ltz. II Frans Jan Kroesen, who later went on to command the boat during the last year-and-a-half of the war.
7. *U-431* left St-Nazaire for the Mediterranean on 16 November 1942, clearing the Straits on the night of 24/25 November, two days ahead of *U-95*. *U-557* left Lorient on the 19th and cleared Gibraltar the same night as *U-95*. *U-562* left Brest 17 November and reached the Straits the night after *U-557* and *U-95*. Thus Schreiber had good reason for his concern.
8. There were some differences, but in the dark and from a distance they would have been minor. Most noticeably, *O 21* had a rounded bow profile, while German boats had a more pointed bow.
9. We actually know a good deal about what went on inside the 'losing' boat in this case, because this was one of the rare instances when there were multiple survivors and some of them were talkative.
10. *U-95*, p 9. This was from a summation of the accounts given by several survivors.
11. With a relatively small number of boats operating out of Gibraltar, it was standard practice at the time to route and schedule boats such that no two would be in the same area at the same time.
12. Günzel was a 24-year-old who had joined the navy in 1936 and had served in submarines on and off since 1939. He joined *U-95* in March 1941. I have opted to use the phonetic rendition of 'bosun' rather than the formally correct, but ridiculously spelled, 'boatswain'.
13. The recorder of this account was British, so he used Royal Navy terminology. The 'First Lieutenant' was the IWO, in this case *Oberleutnant zur See* Egon Rudolph, described by his captors as 'an extreme Nazi, unpleasant and bloodthirsty', not the qualities to make one a popular officer on a U-boat. The 'Chief Quartermaster' was the boat's navigator (*Obersteuermann*), a position on a U-boat that carried with it responsibility for provisioning the boat.
14. Skat is a card game, popular in Germany and few other places, similar to Euchre and Whist, in that it is fast-paced, involves trumps, bidding and the taking of tricks.
15. The German overseas radio service broadcast the nightly news at 2200 Berlin time. Listening to this news broadcast was a ritual on many U-boats.
16. Once again, note the time difference between the British/Dutch account and

the German one. U-boats kept to Berlin time, regardless of their location; in this case, that put *U-95*'s clock an hour behind *O 21*'s.

17. The term 'conning tower' is used ambiguously in submarine literature. In the strictest definition, it refers to the watertight compartment above the control room. On Type VII U-boats, the attack periscope and attack computer were located in the conning tower. It also more generally means the external structure and bridge area built up around the watertight compartment, the visible tower structure that rose above the deck casing.

18. This and all further quotes from Günzel are from *U-95*, pp 9–10.

19. Torpedo tubes had hatches fore and aft that allowed torpedoes to be pulled back into the boat for servicing. Opening the outer caps was the last step before firing a torpedo. This flooded the torpedo tube. The torpedo was actually launched in a U-boat by the action of a piston at the inside end of the tube that was driven forward by high-pressure air. After a torpedo was fired and the outer cap closed, the piston was pulled into the boat so the tube could be reloaded. This process released high-pressure air into the boat, a source of some discomfort for the crew until the boat next surfaced.

20. The bosun and his mate were responsible for recording the weight and location of every item consumed on the boat, whether eaten, burned, fired or simply tossed overboard, as this figured into the LI's daily calculation of the weight of the boat. This figure, in turn, told the LI how to adjust the boat's trim.

21. The survivors' accounts agree they thought *O 21* fired both torpedoes at the same time, but the Dutch accounts all assert that there was about a minute between the two torpedoes being launched. An understandable mistake given the distractions of the moment.

22. The IIWO was *Oberleutnant zur See* Hans Harald Ipach, 24 years old. He had been seconded to the *Luftwaffe* for four years and had flown more than 100 missions with coastal units. He was described by his captors as 'arrogant'.

23. The standard bridge watch for U-boats was five men, as compared to the four-man watch described by Biesemaat. Each of the four lookouts was responsible for a quadrant of the horizon; the watch officer was there to supervise the watch and to watch the sky above the boat.

24. Literally 'Shut your trap, say nothing!'

25. Officers on the victorious boat generally tried to limit the plundering of the personal effects of prisoners, not so much out of any concern for their feelings, but rather out of concern for the possible intelligence value of any such plunder and also because allowing such activity could become a discipline problem on their own boat. It was a general rule in Allied navies that seamen were expected to hand over anything they took off prisoners to their officers. This did not always happen. And more than once there were instances when the nice watch or sweater taken off a U-boat man and handed over to an officer ended up becoming the officer's personal property.

26. *U-95*, p 5.

Chapter 17: In the Narrow Sea – HMS/M *Unbeaten*, U-374 and R.SMG *Guglielmotti*

1. Cf. Chapter 15.

2. This quote taken from an article on Woodward at the now off-line Royal Navy Submarines site, members.iinet.com.au/~eadej/index.html.

3. Cf. Chapter 15, Note 15. Also see *Padfield*, pp 167–70.

4. Homs is now known as Al Khums, Libya.

5. This was the underwater telegraphy feature of most later Second World War

sonar/ASDIC sets. Cf. Chapter 11, Note 4. This replaced the dedicated underwater communications systems developed by the British, Germans and others. It simply used the active sonar to send out Morse code using short or long 'pings' with the active sounder. It had all the disadvantages of the earlier dedicated systems and was rarely used.

6. These were *Neptunia* and *Oceania*, respectively. They were sister-ships of 19,500 GRT each. They were large, fast ocean liners, built in the early 1930s specifically for service between Italy and South America.

7. Howaldtswerke actually built one of the very early experimental submarines in Germany in 1897, but seems to have built none thereafter until getting these contracts at the start of the Second World War.

8. To get an idea of how many boats of one sub-type that was, note that the Royal Navy built forty-six 'U' class boats, their most numerous type, and the Americans built 225 boats of the combined *Gato/Balao/Tench* classes, though only 185 were delivered in time to see war service.

9. Cf. Chapter 16, Note 1. Von Fischel left *U-97* before she was assigned to the Mediterranean in September 1941.

10. One factor in von Fischel's rapid rise to command a U-boat may have been that he was the son of an Admiral, Hermann von Fischel, who had, as a *Kapitänleutnant*, commanded *U-65* during the First World War.

11. Just as the British were using ULTRA intercepts to locate Italian convoys in the Mediterranean, they were using their decryption of the German Enigma-based naval codes to read the orders Dönitz was sending his wolfpacks in order to route convoys away from the U-boats. The strategy of matching concentrations of merchant ships with concentrations of U-boats only works if the enemy is not reading your mail.

12. This was the standard method for attacking a convoy. The first boat to find a convoy trailed the target without attacking, reporting its progress, until other boats arrived. Only then was she free to attack. The following is a good record of the start of a typical convoy attack, including the inevitable 'fog of war'.

> *U-374* (committed to convoy No. 7) sighted a convoy at 1500 in BC 4172, course 50 degrees. Boat was forbidden to attack and ordered to shadow the convoy. *U-569, 38, 82, 202, 84, 203, 93* and *85* belonging to Group '*Schlagetot*' were instructed to operate against the convoy, as were *U-123* and *U-106*. These boats were combined to form Group '*Raubritter*'.
>
> ... At 2001 *U-374* reported convoy in BC 4191 course 50 degrees, speed 9 knots. Contact was lost, at 0300 again restored in BC 4133, course 20 degrees, then once more interrupted. Shadower forced to submerge.
>
> Radio Communication was extremely poor. Reports were not received here until hours later. *U-203* also reported no reception on Greenland radio service. No further reports had come in by the morning. (*BdU KTB*, PG 30300a, p 196.)

The convoy von Fischel found was SC.52, the coding indicating that it was the 52nd Slow convoy originating from Halifax, Canada. (The term 'slow' was relative, as no convoy was fast in absolute terms: the actual average speed of slow convoys was 6.5 knots, for fast convoys it was 9 knots. Cf. *Morison1*, p 18, Note 2.) Although *U-374* had no success against this convoy, other boats guided to SC.52 by her signals had better luck. Three boats (*U-569, U-202* and *U-203*) sank five ships totalling 20,413 GRT before the convoy took refuge in Belle Isle Strait on 4 November.

13. The increased oil bunkerage of the 'C' sub-type, the possession of Atlantic

bases in Norway and France and an effective system of mid-ocean refueling allowed Type VII boats, which had been designed originally to operate around the British Isle on patrols of no more than a few weeks to make month-and-a-half-long patrols to the shores of North America.

14. *BdU KTB*, PG 30301a, p 250.
15. Ibid, p 259. Von Fischel was clearly mistaken as to the grid square he was in, as CH 7441 would put him nearly 100nm east of Gibraltar when he was almost certainly still within the Straits at the time of his broadcast. The fact that he later reported sinking the two escorts off Ceuta, which is at the southeastern exit of the Straits, in grid CG 96, well west of the location he reported earlier, reinforces this assessment.
16. It was believed that attempting to get through the middle of the Straits was the most dangerous, that staying close to one or the other shoreline was the safest way through. Cf., *U-374*, p 10:

> A Chief Petty Officer from *U-581* said that it was sometimes the case that U-Boats, desirous of passing through the Straits of Gibraltar at night on the surface when unaccompanied, would lie off the Spanish-African coast until British corvettes swept the area with their searchlights. They would then imitate this process with signal lamps, pretending themselves to be British units, and then proceed at full speed through the Straits.

The author has seen no reference to this technique in German sources and it may, in fact, be an attempt at deception by the prisoner in question, but it sure makes a good story.

17. These were the patrol yacht *Rosabelle* (525t) and the trawler *Lady Shirley* (477t). The latter of these vessels we met before at the end of Chapter 16. Like *Lady Shirley*, *Rosabelle* had been a private vessel before the war, was drafted into war service, armed with a small gun and depth charges and sent out to strengthen the Gibraltar patrols.
18. Now Banghazi, Libya and Marsá Matruh, Egypt.
19. *Sokol* was one of a number of 'U' class boats turned over to Allied navies. Laid down as HMS/M *Urchin*, she was taken over by the Poles upon completion. In practical terms, it made a great deal of sense to equip the Poles, Dutch, French, etc with modern, British-built submarines, rather than trying to maintain boats from several different nationalities at a remote base like Malta.
20. Cf., *Jones*, pp 74–6 and *U-374*, p 8.
21. The 21-year-old Ploch's normal duty was 'talker' in the bow compartment, responsible for maintaining communications with the control room.
22. *U-374*, p 8.
23. Ibid.
24. Ibid, p 5 says of the veracity of the survivor:

> There was only one survivor, and he, throughout the long period of his interrogation, proved extremely security conscious, being well aware of the advantages from this point of view which his solitary position gave him.

> The extreme difficulty of interrogating him led to a number of inaccurate conclusions being drawn from time to time, chief among which was the suggestion that his boat was *U-331*, commanded by the celebrated Kapitänleutnant (Lieutenant-Commander) Freiherr von Tiesenhausen. The knowledge that this information was incorrect led to the decision to send the prisoner finally to the United Kingdom, where what is believed to be a more correct version of his story has been extracted.

25. Cf., Chapter 15, Note 7. Poisoning by leakage of methylchloride refrigerant was a constant problem. The loss of *Macallé*, which ran aground on an island near Port Sudan (now Bur Sudan) on 15 June 1940, was almost certainly due to methylchloride poisoning.
26. One of these, *Torricelli*, fought an epic 40-minute gun battle with five British surface ships, three destroyers and two sloops, in which she damaged the sloop *Shoreham* and sank the destroyer *Khartoum*, before she was lost.

Chapter 18: Fratricide IV – *U-254* and *U-221*

1. Cf., Chapter 17.
2. Cf., *Roscoe*, pp 504–6. On rare occasions, US packs contained five or six, once even seven, boats, but 90 per cent were made up of three or four boats.
3. The largest convoy in the Second World War was HX.300 in 1944, which contained 167 merchant ships.
4. This incident was by no means the only time two U-boats collided, just the only time that it happened in combat. For example, *U-983* and *U-988* collided during a training exercise in the Baltic on 8 September 1943. The former sank with the loss of five men from her crew.
5. The 'HX' designator originally stood for Halifax, Nova Scotia, but as the war progressed, most HX convoys originated in New York, picking up ships from the Canadian east coast as they headed up towards Cape Race on the Great Circle route to the North Channel and Liverpool.
6. The story of HX.217 is told in multiple sources, including *Edwards*, pp 127–33, *Morison1*, pp 325–6, *Ten*, pp 287–9 and *War*, Vol II, pp 68–9.
7. Wolfpacks were all given names. The names were typical of the names the Nazis gave their military units, in turns the names of weapons (such as '*Streitaxt*' – Battleaxe), generally militaristic or aggressive terms (such as '*Ungestüm*' – Impetuous) or, most frequently, the names of wild animals, particularly hunting animals (such as '*Luchs*' – Lynx, or '*Panter*' – Panther). Other groups were given patriotic, geographic, mythological and even meteorological names.
8. Most sources say the '*Panzer*' group was composed of six boats (*U-135*, *U-211*, *U-254*, *U-439*, *U-465* and *U-758*), but then proceed to include *U-524* as part of the group and the evidence from other sources supports this. For example, *Wynn* states in several places that the '*Panzer*' group was six boats, but shows all seven boats as having been part of the group. *BdU KTB* list all seven boats as being in the group on 6 December. That same day, the log states that *U-611* and *U-623* joined up with the group after refuelling further south.
9. The '*Draufgänger*' group was originally composed of *U-221*, *U-455*, *U-553*, *U-569*, *U-600*, *U-604*, *U-610* and *U-615*, and was joined by *U-609* on 6 December before it contacted HX.217. *U-524* is generally listed as part of this group, but more likely was part of the '*Panzer*' group. *U-373* had been part of the group, but was detached on 1 December because of a medical emergency (her IWO had become ill).
10. TBS – 'Talk Between Ships' – radio was a new type of voice radio system just coming into use in 1942. It operated at very high frequencies and at relatively low power; during the day, it could only be received by antennas within line-of-sight (LOS) of the sender, which limited its range to 30nm or less, depending on the height of the antennas involved. At night, the signal could bounce off the ionosphere and be heard, randomly and intermittently, at much greater distances. As it was voice radio, standard code techniques did not apply, so users were expected to use locally understood codewords as much as possible to disguise the meaning of the conversation.

11. *BdU KTB*, PG 30314a, p 171. 'R/T' – radio telegraphy (or in this case 'telephony') – used interchangeably with 'W/T'.
12. Night was the wolfpack's time to attack, but daylight offered far better chances of sighting a convoy.
13. This was the 8,194 GRT tanker *Empire Spenser*, hit by one torpedo at 0125 local time on 8 December 1942. The ship was left abandoned and burning out of control, but not sinking.
14. *BdU KTB*, PG 30314a, p 179.
15. Cf., Kemp, p 98. *Morison1*, p 325 and *Wynn*, Vol 1, p 178 appear to have it wrong. *Wynn* gets it right in Vol 2, p 80.
16. *BdU KTB*, PG 30314a, p 180.
17. The four new boats were *U-336*, *U-435*, *U-591* and *U-628*.
18. *U-611* was sunk on 8 December as well, by the 120 Squadron RAF Liberator that was wrongly credited with the sinking of *U-254*.

Chapter 19: The Only American Loss – USS *Corvina* and *I-176*

1. Cf., *Morison1*, p 80.
2. Cf., Chapter 20.
3. There were three sub-classes to the *Gato*-class, but the differences were minor and it would be entirely appropriate to consider them all one class. The *Balao* sub-class was made with a thicker pressure hull allowing deeper dives and were redesigned internally to facilitate faster construction. The *Tench* sub-class varied again internally and had slightly greater draught. Externally, the sub-classes were indistinguishable. Of the sub-classes, seventy-three *Gatos* were ordered and completed, all saw war duty and nineteen were lost; 132 *Balaos* were ordered, 122 completed, 101 made war patrols and ten were lost; 134 *Tench* class were ordered, thirty-one completed, eleven made war patrols and none were lost.
4. Most nations that built submarines at one time or another named their submarines after fish. Certainly no nation did this with more determination that the United States. With almost no exceptions, every US Navy submarine from the 1920s up to the late 1950s was so named. The string of fish-named US submarines started with SS 163 *Barracuda* launched in 1924 and ended only with the launch of SSBN 598 *George Washington* in 1959. Since 1960, most US Navy submarines have been named for cities, states or famous people, but as recently as 1997, a US Navy submarine, SSN 21 *Seawolf* was given a fish name. A corvina is a large food fish of the drum or croaker family found off the Pacific coast of Mexico.
5. This operation, codenamed 'Galvanic', was centred on landings on Betio Island in the Tarawa Atoll on 20 November 1943. Betio was dominated by an airfield that was critical to US plans to advance into the Marshall Islands and across the Pacific. The Gilbert Islands are now part of the Republic of Kiribati. Apamama is generally rendered Abemama today.
6. Truk (now Chuuk in the Federated States of Micronesia) was the major Japanese naval base in the Central Pacific.
7. US Navy operations based in Australia were divided between the South Pacific theatre, which covered the Coral Sea, Solomons and north as far as the Caroline Islands (now the Federated States of Micronesia), based at Brisbane on Australia's east coast, and the Southwest Pacific theatre, which covered Indonesia, Indo-China, the China coast and north to the Philippines, based at Fremantle (Perth) on Australia's west coast.
8. The Japanese found, as did the Americans, that the idea of a 'fleet' submarine, capable of the speed and range necessary to accompany the main battle fleet, was a moving target. The problem was that the fleets kept getting faster. In

the First World War, the average dreadnought battleship, which comprised the core of a battle fleet, had a maximum speed of approximately 21 knots and cruised at 15 knots or less. By the mid-1930s, fast battleships were joining these fleets with maximum speeds of anywhere from 25 to 32 knots and aircraft carriers, with very rare exceptions, all possessed speed in excess of 30 knots. Submarines like the American *Gato* class or the Japanese KD7s had maximum surface speeds in the range of 20 knots. This would have been adequate to work with a battle fleet of First World War ships, but not those of the Second World War. The idea of a fleet submarine was therefore dropped, only to be revived during the Cold War with the advent of nuclear submarines capable of sustained high speed underwater. A modern battle group includes at least one submarine to perform the kind of scouting and support missions envisaged for fleet submarines between the wars.

9. The Royal Navy transferred their 'J' class boats to the Royal Australian Navy in 1919, which caught the attention of the Japanese. The Japanese also got a chance to look at *U-139* after the war, a large, ocean-going *U-Kreuzer* which had been taken over by the French. Both of these influenced the KD2 design, in particular, which followed in 1921. *Kaidai* is Japanese for 'large gun'. The original KD1 design called for a 4.7in gun, by far the largest fitted to a Japanese boat at the time.

10. Before *I-168*, he had commanded *RO-59* between December 1941 and January 1942. The 'RO' prefix was used on smaller submarines in the Japanese fleet.

11. This detailed record of *I-176*'s movements comes from *I-176*, pp 1–6. This is an excellent resource for those of us who do not speak Japanese or have access to the original records.

12. The New Hebrides in 1942 were controlled by a unique joint British/French administration. The island group became independent as Vanuatu in 1980.

13. The Type 95 (533mm (21in)) submarine torpedo, developed by the Japanese in the 1930s, was one of a family of oxygen-driven torpedoes dubbed 'Long Lance' by the Americans; this name was never used by the Japanese. Using pure oxygen rather than compressed air to provide oxidant for the standard alcohol-burning steam-turbine motor increased power and virtually eliminated the trail of bubbles that was a disadvantage of all standard 'wet-heater' torpedoes. The Type 95 had a range of 4.86nm at 49 knots; in contrast, the standard American submarine torpedo of the Second World War, the Mk 14, had a range of 2.25nm at 46 knots.

14. The *Northampton*s were 'Treaty Cruisers', limited to 10,000 tons and 8in guns by the terms of the Washington and London naval treaties. Mounting a main battery of nine guns and machinery capable of 32 knots on a hull of 10,000 tons (actually just over 9,200 tons standard displacement) meant giving up something. In this case, it was armour protection that was sacrificed.

15. Rabaul is a large natural harbour at the northeastern tip of New Britain island in the Bismarck Archipelago, now part of Papua New Guinea. Its location just north of the Solomons chain made it an ideal staging base for Japanese activities in the South Pacific.

16. Lae is a town on the north shore of New Guinea. At the tip of the Huon Gulf, it was the centre of the Japanese occupation of eastern New Guinea. It is now a provincial capital of Papua New Guinea.

17. Baker-9 (which replaced JN-25 in May 1942) was a hand-enciphered code used by the Japanese Navy. By 1943, the Japanese were on their third version of the main codebook; the key book was updated every three to six months. The names Baker-9 and JN-25 were given to the codes by the US Navy; they were not the Japanese designations. The following is from *Budianski*, p 123:

The Japanese naval codes (and also most of the high-level Japanese army codes as well, which would be broken beginning in 1943 by Arlington Hall) were all of a type known as enciphered codes. Words, numbers, names, phrases each were assigned a unique numerical value, in the case of the Operations Code a five-digit number. A message was prepared by first translating the plaintext into a string of corresponding five-digit code groups. To each of these code groups was then added a random five-digit number. These were drawn in sequence from a book of 'additives'. The resulting 'enciphered groups' were what were then actually transmitted. The additive or 'key' book, in the case of the Operations Code, contained from 30,000 to (in later years of the war) 100,000 five-digit numbers. Both sender and recipient possessed a copy of the key book, and whenever a message was sent the sender would include within the message an 'indicator', a coded number that informed his recipient the page number and line number of the additive book from which he had begun drawing his additives. This meant that the enciphered group for, say 'Manila' might be 04729 in one message and 77204 in another, depending on the starting point in the key book that had been chosen for that particular message.

18. MAGIC was the term generally given to American intercept/deciphering of Japanese diplomatic and operational codes in the Second World War. It corresponded roughly to the ULTRA system of the British. These included intercepts of the Japanese diplomatic code 'Purple', which used an Enigma-like machine and was deciphered by a variant of the 'bombes' used at Bletchley Park, as well as army and navy operational codes, such as Baker-9.

19. Actually, the Japanese, like the Germans, though for different reasons, were resistant to the idea that their messages were being read. The Germans knew, through spies working in British diplomatic missions, that the Americans were reading some Japanese codes prior to Pearl Harbor. They informed the Japanese of this after 7 December 1941, but the Japanese changed none of their codes as a result of this warning.

20. American practice, unlike the German, was for submarines to maintain radio silence during a patrol unless specifically instructed to report in or faced with an emergency.

21. American records give 16 November as the date of *Corvina*'s loss. It is not clear if this discrepancy is due to keeping a different local time zone or if it is an effect of the International Date Line. US Navy submarines kept local time and date, but the official records were being kept in Hawaii and Washington, DC.

Chapter 20: Sister Act – *K XVI, K XVIII, I-66 (I-166),* HMS/M *Telemachus* and HMS/M *Taciturn*

1. In fact, the embargo on the sale of oil products to Japan was not total. On 31 July, FDR allowed the release of Japanese funds sufficient to allow the purchase of oil supplies up to the levels they had been buying before the 'China Incident'. At the same time, he put in place a complete embargo on high-octane fuels, which included aviation gasoline (avgas). The message to Japan was clear.

2. *Morison3*, pp 58–79. There is ample evidence that FDR wanted to avoid war with the Japanese, but not to the extent that he ever considered withdrawing the sanctions or embargoes imposed during 1941. There were several members of FDR's cabinet, particularly Secretary of State Cordell Hull, who took a harder line with the Japanese than FDR would have on his own.

3. The International Date Line rears its ugly head again, as it does repeatedly in

these stories of the war in the Pacific. Every schoolchild in America learns that Pearl Harbor was attacked on 7 December 1941, but in Japan and most of the areas covered by these chapters, it was 8 December when the war began.

4. The attack on Pearl Harbor was never the main thrust of the initial Japanese plans, which centred on the conquest of the Philippines, Hong Kong, Malaya, Singapore and the East Indies. Formosa, of course, is now known as Taiwan.

5. The Dutch submarines were organised into four divisions:

Div I	*K VII, K VIII* and *O 16*	Surabaya
Div II	*K IX, K X, K XI* and *K XII*	Surabaya
Div III	*K XIV, K XV* and *K XVI*	Tarakan (Borneo)
Div IV	*O 19* and *O 20*	Singapore (on 11 December 1941)

6. The *K XIV* class was the last class of submarines in which the Dutch distinguished between overseas 'K' boats and local defence 'O' boats.

7. Samah appears to have gone by many names over the years, but appears on most maps today as Sanya.

8. The troops that landed at Kuching were part of the same force that had captured Miri and other ports on the Sarawak and Brunei coasts the week before. They were marines of the 2nd Yokusuka Special Landing Force and troops of the Army's 124th Infantry Regiment.

9. Much of the detail, what little there is, on this sinking comes from the page on *K XVI* at www.dutchsubmarines.com.

10. The American submarines were *S-40, Pickerel, Porpoise, Saury, Spearfish* and *Sturgeon*.

11. Sources disagree whether *P 37* was damaged by *K XVIII*, by some US destroyers that raided Balikpapan harbour the night of 23/24 January 1942 or by hitting a mine.

12. Penang is an island, now called Pinang, off the west coast of the Malay Peninsula. The main port is George Town.

13. This account of the sinking of *I-166* is mostly from *Miller*, p 30 and www.combinedfleet.com/I-166.htm. These two sources agree in general but differ in many details.

14. Cf., Chapter 22.

Chapter 21: Battle at Periscope Depth – HMS/M *Venturer, U-771* and *U-864*

1. Operation 'Fortitude North' was a deception plan designed to draw attention away from the Normandy invasion and convince the Germans that an invasion of Norway was imminent. It was successful to the extent that the '*Mitte*' boats, at one time numbering sixteen, were kept in Norwegian waters rather than being directed against the invasion fleet off Normandy.

2. These aircraft were in fact from 333 Squadron RAF, a Norwegian-manned squadron flying with the RAF in operations over or near Norway.

3. Much of the information in this description comes from *Jones*, pp 190–1 and *Wynn*, Vol 2, p 160, with some correction and supplemental details coming from *Obit2*.

4. The only larger U-boats built by the Germans during the Second World War, excluding experimental boats, were the Type XB ocean-going minelayers, the Type XIV '*Milchkühe*' supply boats and the Type XXI '*Elektro*' boats. Only the latter were general-purpose attack submarines, which were that large because they carried vastly increased battery power allowing high-speed underwater propulsion of much greater duration.

5. The same victim was claimed four days later by *U-306* and that claim is considered more believable.

6. The *Schnorkel*, nicknamed '*Snort*' by the Germans, was originally a Dutch

invention. It was a system that allowed a submarine's main diesel engines to be run at periscope depth. It was basically a pair of pipes that ran from the engine compartment of the submarine to the surface, one pipe bringing in air and the other carrying away the exhaust. The Dutch version was first fitted to *O 21* (Cf., Chapters 13 and 16) in February 1940. That submarine fled to Great Britain with the *Schnorkel* still attached; the Germans captured all the records of the Dutch research when they overran the country. Thus both sides had access to this potentially revolutionary technology. The British removed the *Schnorkel* from *O 21* while completing the boat; the Germans found the idea interesting, but not worth following up. That changed in May 1943, when U-boat losses in the Atlantic suddenly skyrocketed. A modified, improved *Schnorkel* was rapidly developed by the Germans and fitted to U-boats from the spring of 1944. The *Schnorkel* improved a U-boat's chances of survival in an environment of persistent air surveillance, though by the end of the war improving radar capability made it possible to detect even something as small as a *Schnorkel* head valve from the air.

7. Farsund is a small port at the southern tip of Norway to the west of Lindesnes and Kristiansand. Much of this background information on *U-864* comes from *Jones*, pp 192–6 and *Wynn*, Vol 2, pp 177–8. Additional information from *Kemp*, pp 231–2.

8. There is almost no agreement between sources as to exactly what *U-864* was carrying. The one certainty is that she was carrying 59 tonnes (65.5 short tons) of mercury in her keel contained in 1,857 32kg steel flasks. (Some accounts claim that the mercury was mixed with uranium and/or heavy water, but no unusual levels of radiation have been found near the wreck, which would tend to discredit this part of the story.) But the mercury alone is sufficient to make the wreck an environmental hazard in prime Norwegian fishing waters. Tests have indicated toxic mercury levels in the seafloor surrounding the site. Plans to address the potential disaster, as the flasks will certainly continue to deteriorate, have included the possibility of raising the wreck, which is in two pieces at a depth of 150m. These are under discussion as this book is being written, with the intent to take some action in 2007.

9. Exactly what transpired on *U-864* after she departed Bergen is unknown, so what follows is speculation based on the experiences of other U-boats and on Launders' post-action reports.

10. *Kemp*, p 231. 'Gefuffle' is a fascinating word, a variant spelling of 'kerfuffle' which means a commotion or agitation. The reference is to the sound made by a snorkelling U-boat which was a combination of the sound of the boat's diesels, the wake noise of the mast passing through the water and the bubbling sound of the diesel's exhaust being vented beneath the surface.

11. Fejeosen island is now called Fedje. It is the northernmost of a chain of small islands forming the western side of the northern approaches to Bergen.

12. *Monthly*, p 7. The British actually believed that there might have been a previous case of one submarine sinking another while both were submerged. HMS/M *Tribune* attacked a submerged submarine while also submerged on 6 September 1940 northwest of the Hebrides. The other boat fired first and missed. *Tribune*, which had used active sonar to locate the other boat, then fired at the other boat and was rewarded with a loud explosion, after which no further trace of the boat was heard. However, no U-boat or any other submarine is known to have been lost at that time and place.

13. Target range could be determined only by estimation, based on the strength of the signal. The more experienced the operator, the better the estimation.

14. This and all subsequent excerpts are from *Monthly*, pp 5–6.

15. A Type IX U-boat had two periscopes, the 'attack' periscope and the so-called 'sky' periscope, which was used for rapid scanning of the

surroundings. The 'sky' periscope had a upper element that could be trained to look straight up to scan the sky above the boat. The 'attack' had a much narrower tube, designed to leave a much smaller wake when raised. The high-frequency radio antenna was a retractable vertical pole which could be extended above the surface from periscope depth to permit radio communication while submerged. It was much taller than either periscope.

16. Unlike the targeting computers used by Germans and Americans, the British version of this analogue computer (TCC – 'Torpedo Control Calculator', popularly known as the 'Fruit Machine') did not continuously update the angle to which torpedoes should turn to hit their target as the submarine or its target moved over time. Thus, Launders had to actually turn *Venturer* to point at *U-864* and manually fire each torpedo as the target reached each successive aiming point.

Chapter 22: One Magnificent Patrol – USS *Batfish* and two (or maybe three) Japanese submarines

1. Much of the content in this chapter is from the excellent site: www.ussbatfish.com.

2. On 31 January 1945, when sources such as *Watts*, p 341 say that *RO-115* was sunk by a group of four US Navy escorts approximately 130nm southwest of Manila, *Batfish* was scouting Yulin Bay at the southern tip of Hainan Island, all the way across the South China Sea.

3. *Batfish* had hull number SS 310. She was originally to be named *Acoupa*, but her name was changed before her keel was laid at the Portsmouth Navy Yard. A batfish is a small, very odd-looking fish native to the coast of the southern United States and Mexico. It is not known why the name was changed from *Acoupa*, except possibly because an acoupa is a variety of weakfish, perhaps not the most auspicious choice of name for a fighting boat.

4. This account is based on *DANFS*, www.history.navy.mil/danfs/b3/batfish-i.htm.

5. Cf., uboat.net. No official cause was ever assigned for the loss of *Dorado*, which occurred towards the end of the second week of October 1943 in the Caribbean. The cause is most often attributed to an attack by a 'friendly' aircraft south of Cuba on 12 October, but this is far from certain; *U-214*'s log describes two attacks by US aircraft that day in the area where *Dorado* was purportedly lost. Add to this the fact that the aircraft saw no tell-tale debris or oil slick and the possibility that *Dorado* encountered one of *U-214*'s mines approaching the Panama Canal cannot be discounted. *U-214* was reportedly attacked on 14 October by torpedo south of Hispaniola (*BdU KTB*, PG 3033, p 253), but on that date *Batfish* had not yet departed from New London.

6. Unfortunately, there is a gap in the *BdU KTB* microfilms available to the author for the second half of October 1943, so it was not possible to check on individual U-boat positions during this period.

7. *Batfish*'s official tally for this period shows her sinking the 990-GRT *Nagaragawa Maru* on 22 June and the 492t *Minesweeper No. 22* on 23 August, cf., *Roscoe*, p 529. Not all sources agree with this list. She claimed a number of additional sinkings that have not been confirmed by post-war analysis. DANFS credits her with sinking two small patrol craft, a trawler *Kamoi Maru* and a converted yacht *No. 5 Isuzugawa Maru* on 1 July.

8. This group, which carried the official designation TG 17.16, was named by the group's commander, who was the senior officer among the captains. The tradition of naming these packs began among Pacific Fleet boats operating out of Pearl Harbor. The names were always two words, the first being the

CO's name. Not all PACFLEET packs were so named, but most were. Cf., *Roscoe*, pp 504–6. SWPAC packs operating out of Fremantle appear to have never carried similar names.

9. This and all other excerpts in this chapter are from *Batfish6th*. Entry is for 17 January 1944.

10. Rumours have persisted that among the items being carried away from the Philippines was gold bullion, but that has never been substantiated.

11. While the six boats operated together in the Luzon Strait, they were now under the tactical command of Lieutenant Commander Clyde B Stevens in *Plaice*. It is not known if the group had a name for that period, but when *Plaice*, *Scabbardfish* and *Sea Poacher* were detached on 10 February, Fyfe specifically notes that the original three boats of 'Joe's Jugheads' remained and resumed the use of the name.

12. The APR-1/AN-SPA was a radar detector, basically a broadband high-frequency receiver listening for the typical patterns of radar transmissions. A radar could be characterised by the frequency (or wavelength, which is the inverse of frequency) of its carrier wave, PRF (Pulse Repetition Frequency – the number of times a second the radar wave pulses on and off) and PW (Pulse Width – the duration in microseconds of each pulse). Based on the reported characteristics, this sounds like a Japanese Type 3 Mk 1 Mod 3 air search radar, a type known to be fitted on submarines of the *RO-100* class, which would included *RO-112*, *RO-113* and *RO-115*. According to *Tech1*, these boats were not fitted with the microwave Mark 2 Mod 2 surface-search radar. Cf., *Radar*, p 207; *Tech1*, p 8.

13. SJ was the designation of the standard late-war surface-search radar carried on US submarines.

14. 'Dope' was Second World War American slang for 'information'.

15. 'End around' was the term used in the US Navy of the era to describe the tactic of making a high-speed loop on the surface around a moving target at the limit of visibility, with the intent of submerging ahead of the target and waiting for it to approach. The term derives from a play in American football, where a player on one end of the offensive line loops behind the line, gets the ball from the quarterback and attempts to run it around the other end of the line. It is a play that calls for speed and stealth, as did the submarine manoeuvre.

16. The first operational Type XXIs, *U-2511* and *U-2513*, had left on patrol just before Germany surrendered, but were informed of the end of hostilities before they fired any shots in anger. At the end of the war, there were more than eighty Type XXIs in commission and good repair, with five of those ready for combat (*frontreife*). Six of the diminutive Type XXIIIs, built to the same general plan as the Type XXIs but carrying only two torpedoes each, actually left on a total of nine short patrols and sank four ships and damaged a fifth for the loss of none of their own, which perhaps gives an indication of the impact the Type XXIs might have had.

17. These characteristics reinforce the identification of the radar as a Type 3 Mk 1 Mod 3.

18. 'Nip' was a derogatory slang term used by Americans to refer to the Japanese, short for 'Nipponese'. Roughly equivalent to calling a German a 'Kraut'. Not the worst of insults, but definitely derogatory. Cf., Chapter 15, Note 16. Fyfe's repeated use of racist remarks concerning the Japanese was typical of the time and obviously considered perfectly acceptable for use in a formal patrol report that would be seen by his superiors. Remember, he was the product of a country that still practised racial segregation in many states and put American citizens in internment camps for the crime of having Japanese ancestry.

19. From this point to the end of this paragraph, I am greatly indebted to the Batfish Memorial web site and, in particular, to the page www.batfish.com/whichsub.html for a concise summary of the positions of various sources on this question. Any speculation about the identity of any possible victim is entirely mine.
20. Cf., *Losses*, p 139.
21. This list of four boats is from www.combinedfleet.com/RO-115.htm. Other sources give other lists.
22. Takao, Formosa is now Kaohsiung on Taiwan.
23. Taking advantage of the fact that the radar that was being intercepted seemed not to be detecting *Batfish*, it was possible, by moving through the radar beam, to identify the pattern of power peaks (lobes) and the intervening zones of low power (nulls) and thus pinpoint the source of the signal.
24. This would seem to argue in favor of *RO-55* being *Batfish*'s victim on 10 February, as she was quite a bit larger than *RO-112*, while *RO-115* was the same size as *RO-112*. Nevertheless, other evidence still points to *RO-115* most likely being *Batfish*'s first victim.
25. In each of these cases, the Japanese boats were guilty of running their radar more or less continuously, which allowed the APR-equipped *Batfish* to home in on the radar signals. It was common practice in the US Navy to leave radars warmed up, but only 'key' them for short periods. The exception to this rule was the microwave SJ radar, for which the Japanese boats apparently did not carry a radar detector.
26. The SJ radar was mounted so that its antenna was just above the periscope shears. Diving to radar depth meant running at a depth, somewhat less than periscope depth, such that the antenna would be clear of the water.
27. Formally part of the Philippines, the Batan group is actually closer to Taiwan, north of the middle of the Luzon Strait.
28. Even though the log does not state it explicitly, *Batfish* obviously surfaced at this point and headed south at high speed to gain a position ahead of the southward track of the target. It speaks volumes about the opinion US submariners held of their Japanese counterparts that Fyfe would surface his boat in the vicinity of a submerged enemy. It is unthinkable that a Royal Navy submariner, hunting a U-boat, would do that.
29. The ship was *Marion Moller* (3,827 GRT).

Chapter 23: Nearly Another Fratricide – uss *Hoe* and *Flounder* (and *U-537* too)

1. Cf., Chapter 18.
2. This and much else in this interlude are from *Roscoe*, pp 452–3.
3. *Hoe* sank *Niisho Maru* (10,526 GRT) in February 1944 and *Kohoku Maru* (2,573 GRT) in October.
4. Cf., *Hoe8th*, pp 6–7.
5. 'Jake' was the Allied codename for an Aichi E13A reconnaissance floatplane.
6. Cf., *Hoe8th*, p 7.
7. This was *Nipponkai Maru* (2,681 GRT) in June 1944.
8. The station was known as WFL 26, (*Wetterfunkgerät-Land* 26) because it was the sixth in the second series of such stations. The station was code-named '*Kurt*' after Dr Kurt Sommermeyer, who was sent along with his assistant to do the hooking-up and calibration of the instruments. The weather station continued to transmit for three months, until its batteries ran down. Some reports say the transmissions were jammed after the first few days, but all accounts agree that the Allies were completely unaware of the weather station until its existence was revealed in the 1970s by a retired

German engineer. The jamming appears to have been done inadvertently by a German radio station. The remains of the station were found, 400m inland atop a small hillock by the Canadian Coast Guard in July 1981.

9. It is quite possible that the long delay was due to the installation of a *Schnorkel*, but the author has been unable to verify this.

10. Batavia is now Jakarta, Indonesia.

11. Much of this detail comes from *Paterson*, particularly from pp 232–3.

12. In the US Navy, an officer other than the captain who had responsibility for the boat at any time was known as the 'Officer of the Deck' or OOD.

13. The US Navy's Mk 18 torpedo was a direct copy of the German G7e, several examples of which fell intact into American hands when they failed to explode after running up on the beach during the U-boat offensive off the American east coat in early 1942. The Mk 18 was very popular with US submarine commanders despite being high-maintenance and not terribly reliable. By the end of the war, more than half the torpedoes being fired by US submarines were Mk 18s.

14. Cf., *Flounder5th*, pp 19–20.

15. Both of those boats are known to have sunk themselves with their own torpedoes making circular runs. Both sinkings occurred after firing Mk 18 electric torpedoes after their introduction in 1944. However, the problems the US Navy had with torpedoes in 1944 were not limited to Mk 18 torpedoes; the torpedoes that nearly sank *Flounder* were both Mk 14s, which had been in service since 1931 and were only finally retired in 1970.

16. Cf., *Flounder5th*, pp 21–2.

17. Ibid, p 22.

18. Ibid. Spellings are as in original.

19. Because a radar is nothing other than a specially modulated form of radio, a particular model of radar shared by two boats could, and often was, used as a relatively secure form of line-of-sight communication between boats.

20. Cf., *Hoe8th*, p 7. Refo had earlier reported the interference on the SJ's frequency. Its presence and then sudden cessation, indicating that a radio source at that frequency had been switched off as opposed to fading away, was finally enough to indicate to *Hoe* that there was an another American submarine in the vicinity, probably damaged.

21. Cf., *Flounder5th*, p 23.

22. Cf., *Hoe8th*, pp 7–8.

23. This was *Shonan* (940t).

Chapter 24: The Last 'Official' Kills – USS *Besugo* and U-183; USS *Spikefish* and I-373

1. Cf., *Paterson* for an account of the '*Monsun*' boats.

2. Some of this useful detail comes from www.combinedfleet.com/RO-500.htm.

3. The *I-201* class (*Sen Taka* – high speed) submarines were designed, like the German Type XXI, which they superficially resembled, for high underwater speed and exceptional underwater endurance. The development of the *I-201* class appears to have been independent of the German programme, dating back to pre-war experiments with a prototype launched in 1938. Like the Type XXI, some *I-201* class boats were approaching operational status as the war ended. Unlike the Type XXI, the Japanese never saw this boat as a potential 'war winner' and never pursued their development with the same energy that the Germans put into their *Elektroboot* programme.

4. The return to France of *U-183* appears to have been cancelled due to the sinking of two German supply ships off the coast of East Africa in February 1944.

5. Cf., *Wynn*, Vol 1, p 138; *Geck*, pp 7–8.
6. Whether this really was a resupply mission is speculation, but sending out a U-boat unable to dive into the Java Sea in April 1945 was practically a suicide mission for which there would have to be a compelling reason.
7. '*Hinomaru*' – literally: Sun Circle – is the red disk that is still the national emblem of Japan. The Japanese national flag, flown by merchant shipping, centered the *Hinomaru* in a white field; the naval ensign was the so-called 'Rising Sun', which added red bands radiating out from the *Hinomaru* to the edge of the flag.
8. USS *Besugo* (SS 321) was named for a predatory fish of the Porgie family with a broad range throughout the tropics.
9. By this time, Japanese warships were either in ports in the Home Islands, or clustered at one or two ports near oil supplies and relatively unmolested by Allied airstrikes, such as Singapore and Surabaya. *Besugo4th* makes no mention of MAGIC, but that is understandable, given the highly classified nature of the intercepts. In all likelihood, Miller did not know the source of the information behind his orders, but he would have known that it was important and reliable.
10. This was the minesweeper *W 12* (630t).
11. *Gabilan* and *Charr* officially share credit for sinking IJN *Isuzu*. *Gabilan* hit her with one torpedo and *Charr* finished her off with three more hits.
12. The '(I)' refers to the timezone codenamed 'Item' which is 'Zulu' (GMT) plus 9.
13. The '(T)' indicates 'True' direction, meaning relative to geographic north (0° True) as opposed to magnetic north.
14. In US practice, classified materials to be disposed of are placed in a special bag, which is supposed to be burned at regular intervals by the site's security officer. The capture of a burn bag would have tremendous intelligence value.
15. Cf., *Besugo4th*, pp 20–1.
16. 'Wisniewski' is the most common spelling of his name in German sources. The misspelling by Miller is as in the original log. The other spelling common in German sources is 'Wiesniefsky'.
17. For those unfamiliar with military ranks, services traditionally distinguished between commissioned officers, who were, until quite recently, drawn solely from the highest ranks of society and sometimes were at best marginally competent at command, and warrant officers who were raised from enlisted ranks by government warrant as a reward for technical skill and command experience. Some navies, such as the *Kriegsmarine*, treated their most senior enlisted personnel as officers and expected them to take responsibilities similar to those given to junior officers in other navies.
18. Cf., *Wis*. According to *Geck*, Wisniewski confirmed that *U-183* was carrying oil in her ballast tanks and, even though he thought he might have seen *Besugo*'s periscope before the torpedo struck, he had been reluctant to order a dive, as that would have flushed the oil out of the dive tanks. In neither of the available accounts attributed to Wisniewski is there any mention of oil in the ballast tanks, but that is hardly proof that the story is untrue. Six lookouts plus the navigator were two more than would have normally been on the bridge, perhaps a concession to the boat's inability to dive.
19. Cf., *Geck*, p 8. The submarine tender was actually USS *Anthedon* (AS 24).
20. 'Snorkel' is the standard American spelling for *Schnorkel*.
21. USS *Spikefish* (SS404) was a *Balao* class submarine named for the spiked marlin found off the Pacific coast of the United States.
22. This nice detail comes from www.combinedfleet.com/I-373.htm.

Chapter 25: War by Another Name – Submarine Encounters since the Second World War

1. The common term for an anti-submarine-submarine in English is a 'hunter-killer' submarine.
2. Cf., www.britsub.net/html/r_class.htm.
3. 'ASW' is a contraction of Anti-Submarine Warfare that came into common usage only after the Second World War.
4. The captured U-boats were *U-2513* and *U-3008*. They were worked hard by the US Navy. In 1947, for example, they were at sea for a total of 204 days between the two boats, a rate of usage not much lower than would be expected in combat. Both boats were worked to exhaustion and retired by 1949. Cf., *1945*, p 23. *Cold*, p 24, mentions that the Soviets, who also tested surrendered Type XXIs, found them to be insufficiently reliable, having been built for a short service life.
5. GUPPY stood for 'Greater Underwater Propulsive Power', with the 'Y' thrown in to make the acronym easier to remember.
6. The US Navy actually built three purpose-built hunter-killers at this time, designated SSK 1 to 3, but these were not followed up in the face of a parsimonious Congress, which had the option of funding more, less-expensive SSK conversions.
7. The SSK conversions were *Grouper* (SSK 214), *Angler* (SSK 240), *Bashaw* (SSK 241), *Bluegill* (SSK 242), *Bream* (SSK 243), *Cavalla* (SSK 244) and *Croaker* (SSK 246). All were boats that had seen considerable action during the war, completing at least five war patrols each.
8. In terms of general layout and appearance, the 'Whiskey' class looked much more like the Type XXI original than the *Tang*s did. 'NATO' is the North Atlantic Treaty Organisation, a multi-national coalition of western states, mostly, but not necessarily, bordering the North Atlantic, for the express purpose of opposing the Soviet Union and its 'bloc' of Warsaw Pact states. (NATO was established in 1949; the Warsaw Pact came into existence in 1955.) NATO still exists as a military alliance long after the dissolution of the Warsaw Pact. Its current purpose, other than as a proxy for US foreign policy, is obscure. Because no-one in the West knew (or admitted knowing) the Soviet designations for their military hardware, as each new piece of equipment was identified, it was given a NATO codename, such as 'Whiskey'. Henceforth in this chapter, I will use the NATO codename for boats in the main text and give the Soviet designation only in the notes.
9. This mainly comes from *Blind*, pp 42–55.
10. CINCLANTFLT stands for Commander-in-Chief Atlantic Fleet.
11. The 'Zulu V' NATO codename was given to the four Project AV-611 boats built in 1957. Each carried two R-11FM (NATO codename 'Scud-A') ballistic missiles with a range of perhaps 75km.
12. 'Nuke' was common slang in the US Navy to designate a nuclear submarine. Various sources put the date of this event as 14 or 16 November 1969.
13. The Soviets built nuclear submarines much faster than the Americans did. This was one of the reasons why they had a much higher reported rate of reactor accidents.
14. 'Hotel' was the NATO codename given to the Project 658 submarines, eight of which were built. They carried three R-13 missiles (NATO codename 'Sark'), with a 650km range.
15. Much of this information comes from www.fas.org/nuke/guide/russia/slbm/658.htm.
16. Sources differ in details here. For example, www.fas.org states that it was a heat-exchange pump failure that caused a coolant leak that led to the radiation leak, and other sources say that only fourteen sailors died as a

result, eight immediately and six more due to radiation-caused diseases over the next few years.

17. Ballistic missile submarines, SSBNs in US Navy official parlance, were affectionately called 'boomers' in US Navy slang.

18. The primary, but by no means only way to detect Soviet submarines heading out on patrol was the SOSUS network of ocean-floor listening devices arrayed across the exits from Soviet submarine bases to the open Atlantic and Pacific. SOSUS stands for SOund SUrveillance System.

19. Operation 'Holystone' at various times went by the names 'Binnacle' and 'Bollard'. (*Hersh* says 'Pinnacle', but that is probably a typo.) Cf., *Blind*, p 70.

20. For a lot of very good reasons, it is desirable that the trailing submarine remain undetected. The main reason is that, should a shooting war start, the trailer wants to able to attack its target without the target being aware of the trailer and possibly attacking first. With modern, mostly wire-guided and/or active-homing torpedoes, very little if any set-up is necessary before firing.

21. There are many sources of noise in a submarine, but the two main ones are machinery noise – that is, the noise made by the pumps and turbines that power the boat – and cavitation – the phenomenon of bubbles forming and then collapsing as the boat's propeller moves through the water. The collapse of cavitation bubbles generates considerable noise. Cavitation can be reduced by propeller design (multiple, small propeller blades generally cause less cavitation than fewer, larger blades) and by making sure that the rate of rotation of a propeller changes only gradually.

22. Cf., *Blind*, p 400 and *Hersh*. According to *Hersh*, there was a cover-up at the time and no official announcement of the event, which was not acknowledged by the United States until many years later. Even now it is described as a minor scrape.

23. Most of the following comes from *Hersh*.

24. Scrapping nuclear submarines is a costly and dangerous business. Russia inherited a large number of often poorly built, aging nukes from the dying Soviet Union. The cash-strapped post-Soviet Russia has had little inclination to spend the limited defence roubles available on cleaning up after the former regime. The US has tried to help with the Nunn-Lugar Cooperative Threat Reduction Program, which pays for projects in the Former Soviet Union (FSU) aimed at destroying or neutralising nuclear weaponry. Some Nunn-Lugar money has gone to dismantling Russian boomers, but not nearly enough money to address every submarine, some of which are rusting in Russia's harbours ten or more years after being withdrawn from service.

25. 'Golf II' was the NATO codename for the Soviet Project 629A SSBs (ballistic missile diesel-powered submarines). They carried three R-21 (NATO codename 'Serb') missiles with a 1,400km range.

26. The American side of the story comes from *Cold*, p 111 and *Blind*, p 109.

27. There is not even complete agreement on when *K-129* sank. A number of US sources put her sinking on 11 April 1968, more than a month after the 8 March date accepted by most accounts. Nor is there agreement on the depth to which *K-129* had sunk. Most sources say just over 4km, but some put the depth at greater than 5km.

28. The propellant was a mixture of triethylamine and xylidine, both toxic and corrosive chemicals.

29. This is mainly from *Kursk*, p 1. As recently as 1999, the Russians complained formally to the United States that the Americans have not been forthcoming about their knowledge of (and involvement in) the loss of *K-129*. At that time, the Russians requested a copy of *Swordfish*'s patrol report, but that request was denied.

30. I have no idea how much of the account in this last paragraph is true as the available accounts differ in almost every detail. I have tried to piece together those elements that appear most consistently into something resembling a believable story.
31. This from the book *Red Star Rogue* by Sewell and Richmond.
32. USS *Tautog* (SS 199) was named for an edible sportfish found off the east coast of the United States. She is credited with sinking *RO-30* on 9 April 1942 and *I-28* on 17 May. The first of those sinkings is now discounted because that boat survived the war and no other Japanese submarine was lost on that day or in that area. Her war record was nothing short of extraordinary. She ended up first among US submarines in number of ships sunk (twenty-five) and eleventh in terms of tonnage sunk (over 72,000 tons).
33. 'Echo II' was the NATO codename for the Soviet Project 675 SSGN (nuclear guided missile submarine) which fired P-6 supersonic anti-ship cruise missiles (NATO codename 'Shaddock').
34. This account comes from multiple sources, mostly from *Blind*, pp 197–211 and *Deep*, p 1.
35. 'Sail' is a common term for a modern submarine's tower, a term derived from the fact that submarine towers are now essentially smoothly curved like a sailboat's sail.
36. Cf., *Kursk*, pp 3–4.
37. Underwater temperatures often do not vary directly with depth. Thermal inversion layers (also called 'thermoclines') can be caused by local current flows that cause cooler water to lay over a band of warmer water. The boundaries between such thermal layers tend to reflect sound. A submarine lying below such a boundary can be undetectable to sonar above it and vice versa.
38. There seems to be remarkably little information available on these two incidents, at least information that this author was able to find. There even appears to be disagreement as to what year the *Sceptre* incident occurred, some sources saying it took place in 1982.
39. The Northern and Pacific Fleets of the former Soviet Union naturally became the core of the new Russian navy. The Black Sea Fleet (and the Crimea where it was based) were the subject of conflicting claims between Russia and the now-independent Ukraine for many years. The Russians claim that they no longer deployed submarines anywhere in the vicinity of the US coast or kept boomers in position to hit the US after 1992.
40. 'Sierra' was the NATO codename for the Project 945 *Barrakuda* class submarines. They had titanium pressure hulls that allowed very deep (600m) diving and high speed. The *Los Angeles* class was the definitive US Cold War SSN, remaining in production for 20 years; sixty-two were built between 1976 and 1996. By this time, attack submarines on both sides carried cruise missiles capable of being launched from their regular torpedo tubes and of carrying nuclear warheads, making the distinction between boomers and attack submarines far less distinct.

   There is considerable confusion in Russian sources as to the identity of the submarine that collided with *Baton Rouge*. Most sources say it was *K-239*, but some say *K-276*. (One even says it was a third 'Sierra' class boat named *Barrakuda*, but that seems unlikely.) Most give the name *Karp*, but some say *Tula*. Most agree *Karp* was returned to service, but was then retired in 1997 or 1998 . . . or maybe not.
41. Cf., *Blind*, p 375; *Murmansk*, pp 1–5 and *Kursk*, p 4.
42. As of the most current list available at the time of this writing (a list on the US Navy's website www.navy.mil/navydata/fact_display.asp?cid=4100&tid=100&ct=4),

updated on 6 April 2006, fifty of the original sixty-two *Los Angeles*-class SSNs remain in commission.

43. 'Delta IV' was the NATO codename for the Project 667BDRM *Delfin* class SSBNs, capable of carrying sixteen RSM-54/R-29RM (NATO codename 'Skiff') liquid-fuelled SLBMs with a range of 8,300km.

44. Cf., *Kursk*, pp 4–5.

45. 'Oscar II' was the NATO codename for the Project 949A *Anteiy* class SSGNs, capable of carrying twenty-four P-700 *Granit* (NATO codename 'Shipwreck') cruise missiles.

46. Cf., *Squall*. The principle behind a supercavitating torpedo is basically simple. (Cf., Note 21 for more on cavitation.) A torpedo-like device is boosted rapidly by a large rocket engine to a speed at which a cavity of water vapour of a size sufficient to envelop the entire device is created, after which it can 'cruise' in this cavity with its speed sustained by a much smaller rocket.

47. Cf., *Kursk*, pp 6–7.

Sources

It should be noted that, given the research resources available at the beginning of the twenty-first century, some sources I have used exist only in cyberspace. In these cases, I have given the hyperlink to the source rather than the more traditional publisher information. It is a characteristic of such sources that they are more ephemeral than paper-and-ink sources. When the site that serves the pages is changed or ceases to exist, the effect can be as if every copy of a book was instantly vaporised. All links listed here were active and available at the time this manuscript was written.

Not all of these sources are directly referenced in my notes, but those that are may be identified by the short name given in the first column below.

Primary Sources

Note on *KTB* translations: The US National Archives maintains copies of individual German U-boat war diaries (*Kriegstagebücher*) from both the First and Second World Wars in microfilm form, as well as the war diaries of various U-boat commands, including *BdU*. (A two-volume 'Guide' to these records was produced by the US National Archives in 1984–5, which are themselves very useful documents and are included below in the list of uncredited secondary sources.) The *BdU* war diary was translated immediately after the Second World War and may be found in English (see below). The remaining diaries are copies of the original documents, meaning that they are in German and, in the case of many First World War diaries, in handwritten form. The copies vary in readability, based on the handwriting of the crewman taking down the day's events or the newness of the typewriter ribbon he used, as well as the skill of the post-war microfilm crew. Where parts of a document were unreadable, I have so noted in the translation. All translations of these documents were done by the author and I am solely responsible for the accuracy of the translations.

> Biesemaat, Ton, *Battle by Moonlight: The Dutch O 21 versus the German U 95*, www.dutchsubmarines.com. (This is an eyewitness account as related by the author's father, Jan Biesemaat, who served on *O 21*.)
>
> Dönitz, Karl, *The Sinking of U.B.68* (1918).

O'Neill, Gerry, *Favourable Winds: The Memoirs of Gerry O'Neill*, www.tallrite.com/oneill/chapter65.pdf.

Auszug   *Auszug aus dem Kriegstagebuch des Kommandos S.M.Unterseeboot 'U.27'*, US National Archives Publication T1022, Roll 33, Item PG61556. (The original of this *KTB* was handwritten and unreadable by this author. This must have been true for some contemporaries as well, as the excerpt (*Auszug*) was typewritten and then signed by Wegener.)

Gefechts   *Gefechtsbericht über die Vernichtung des italienischen U-Bootes Medusa (Action Report on the Destruction of the Italian Submarine Medusa)*, US National Archives Publication T1022, Roll 64, Item PG61749. (This report was included with the *KTB* of *UB-15*.)

Gutachten   *Gutachten des Flottillenchefs zu den Verhandlung über den Untergang von 'U 7' (Investigation by the Flotilla Chief into the Circumstances of the Sinking of U 7)*, US National Archives Publication T1022, Roll 24, Item PG61540. (This report was included with the *KTB* of *U-22*.)

Tech2   *Japanese Antennae: 'Intelligence Targets Japan' (DNI) of 4 Sept. 1945, Fascicle E-1, Target E-16*, US Naval Technical Mission to Japan, December 1945. (This excellent document is available at www.fischer-tropsch.org.)

Tech1   *Japanese Submarine and Shipborne Radar: 'Intelligence Targets Japan' (DNI) of 4 Sept. 1945, Fascicle E-1, Target E-01*, US Naval Technical Mission to Japan, December 1945. (This excellent document is available at www.fischer-tropsch.org.)

BdU KTB   *Kriegstagebuch des Befehlshaber der Unterseeboote*, US National Archives Publication T1022. (This is a microfilm record of an English translation of Dönitz's daily logs from August 1939 to January 1945. It is subdivided into half-monthly sections, each with a different 'PG' code. All citations of this document give 'PG' record and page number(s). This document is being made available online at www.uboatarchive.net.)

U-4 KTB   *Kriegstagebuch 'U 4'*, US National Archives Publication T1022, Roll 3027, Item PG30003/4. (This records *U-4*'s fourth patrol between 4 April 1940 and 14 April 1940.)

U-9 KTB   *Kriegstagebuch 'U 9'*, US National Archives Publication T1022, Roll 2928, Item PG30006/6. (This records *U-9*'s sixth patrol between 5 May 1940 and 15 May 1940.)

U-34 KTB   *Kriegstagebuch 'U 34'*, US National Archives Publication T1022, Roll 3039, Item PG30031/4. (This records the second half of *U-34*'s sixth patrol between 19 July 1940 and 3 August 1940.)

UB-14 KTB   *Kriegstagebuch des Kommandos S.M.Unterseeboot 'U B 14' vom 5. November 1915*, US National Archives Publication T1022, Roll 64, Item PG61748. (This covers the one-day patrol on which HMS/M *E.20* was sunk.)

UC-22 KTB   *Kriegstagebuch des Kommandos S.M.Unterseeboot 'U C 22'*, US National Archives Publication T1022, Roll 70, Item PG61928. (This covers the patrol on which *Ariane* was sunk.)

U-67 KTB   *Kriegstagebuch des Unterseebootes 'U 67'- 2. Unternehmung*, US National Archives Publication T1022, Roll 3030, Item PG30064/2. (This records *U-67*'s second patrol between 2 August 1941 and 25 December 1941.)

U-68 KTB   *Kriegstagebuch des Unterseebootes 'U 68'- 2. Unternehmung*, US National Archives Publication T1022, Roll 3030-1, Item PG30065/2. (This records *U-68*'s second patrol between 14 September 1941 and 16 October 1941.)

Monthly   *Monthly Anti-Submarine Report – February 1945*, C.B. 04050/45 (2), Anti-U-Boat Division of the Naval Staff, 15 March 1945.

Wis   *Report of the sole survivor Karl Wiesniefsky*, www.deutscheuboote.de/dieboote/u0183.html

The Sinking of UB72, 12 May 1918, www.gwpda.org/naval/ub72.htm. (This brief account is transcribed from a document of unknown attribution in the collection of the RN Submarine Museum.)

U-95   *'U 95' Interrogation of Survivors*, C.B. 405I (35), Naval Intelligence Division, N.I.D. 0197/42, January 1942. (This document is available from the British National Archives, Kew, Richmond, Surrey TW9 4DU. There is an excellent website that explains how to obtain copies of these reports at ubootwaffe.net/research/reports.cgi?a=1;p=1.)

U-111   *'U 111' Interrogation of Survivors*, C.B. 405I (32), Naval Intelligence Division, N.I.D. 2778/41, November 1941. (See above note.)

U-374   *'U 374' Interrogation of Sole Survivor*, C.B. 405I (44), Naval Intelligence Division, N.I.D. 03373/42, August 1942. (See above note.)

Batfish6th   *USS Batfish (SS310), Report of Sixth War Patrol*. (Available at www.ussbatfish.com/patrol-6.html.)

Besugo4th   *USS Besugo (SS321), Report of Fourth War Patrol.* (Obtained from the US Navy Submarine Force Library and Museum, Groton, Connecticut.)

Flounder5th *USS Flounder – Report of War Patrol Number Five.* (Obtained from the US Navy Submarine Force Library and Museum, Groton, Connecticut.)

Hoe8th   *USS Hoe, Report of War Patrol Number Eight.* (Obtained from the US Navy Submarine Force Library & Museum, Groton, Connecticut.)

Geck   Geck, John, *USS Besugo*, www.subvetpaul.com/Geck2.htm. (This article recounts the experiences of Geck, an EN1 1/C (SS) on *Besugo* for all five of her war patrols.)

Secondary Sources (author known)

Kursk   Aleksin, Valery, 'The *Kursk* Must Have Been Rammed by a Foreign Submarine', *Nezavisimaya Gazeta*, 12–13 September 2000. (Found at www.wps.ru/en/pp/kursk/2000/09/12/1.html. An interesting Russian take on a number of Cold War incidents. It is not clear to what extent the facts brought forth in this article are substantiated or are believed by a significant number of Russians.)

             Bagnasco, Erminio, *Submarines of World War Two* (Arms & Armour Press, Lionel Leventhal Ltd., London: 1977).

             Bañón Verdú, Jorge, *La Intervención Alemana*, www.submarinos.net/articulos.php?idArticulo=2.

Blair   Blair, Clay, Jr, *Silent Victory* (Bantam Books, New York: 1975).

Losses   Brown, David, *Warship Losses of World War Two* (Arms & Armour Press, London: 1990).

Budianski   Budianski, Stephen, 'Closing the Book on Pearl Harbor', in *Cryptologia*, Vol XXIV, No 2, April 2000. http://www.dean.usma.edu/math/pubs/cryptologia/ClassicArticleReprints/V24N2PP119-130Budiansky.PDF.

             Coder, LCDR Barbara J, USN, *Q-Ships of the Great War* (Air University, Maxwell AFB, AL: 2000).

             De la Vega, Julio, *'Operation Ursula' and the sinking of the submarine C-3*, uboat.net/articles/?article=59.

Ten   Dönitz, Karl, *Memoirs: Ten Years and Twenty Days* (Greenhill Books, Lionel Leventhal Ltd. London: 1990).

Deep   Drew, Christopher, Michael L Millenson and Robert Becker, 'A

Cold War Fought Deep', *The Chicago Tribune* (6 January 1991). (Note that Drew is also the co-author, with Sherry Sontag, of *Blind Man's Bluff,* cited later.)

Edwards   Edwards, Bernard, *Dönitz and the Wolf Packs* (Arms & Armour Press, London: 1996).

Evans   Evans, A S, *Beneath the Waves: A History of HM Submarine Losses 1904–1971* (William Kimber & Co, London: 1986).

Radar   Friedman, Norman, *Naval Radar* (Naval Institute Press, Annapolis, MD: 1981).

Since   Friedman, Norman, *U.S. Submarines since 1945* (Naval Institute Press, Annapolis, MD: 1994).

Goebel, Greg, *The First Battle of the Atlantic,* http://www.vectorsite.net/twsub2_1.html.

Gray1   Gray, Edwyn, *The Underwater War: Submarines 1914–1918* (Charles Scribner's Sons, New York, NY: 1971).

Gray2   Gray, Edwyn, *Captains of War* (Leo Cooper Ltd, London: 1988).

Gray3   Gray, Edwyn, *The Killing Time: The German U-boats 1914–1918* (Charles Scribner's Sons, New York, NY: 1972).

I-176   Hackett, Bob, and Sander Kingsepp, *HIJMS Submarine I-176: Tabular Record of Movement,* http://www.combinedfleet.com/I-176.htm.

Hersh   Hersh, Seymour M, 'A False Navy Report Alleged in Sub Crash' in *The New York Times* (6 July 1975), p 1.

Jane, Fred T (ed), *Jane's Fighting Ships 1914* (Sampson Low Marston Ltd., London: 1914. Reprinted in 1969 by Arco Publishing Co, Inc, New York).

Jones   Jones, Geoffrey P, *Submarines versus U-Boats* (William Kimber & Co. Ltd., London: 1986).

Kemp   Kemp, Paul, *U-Boats Destroyed: German Submarine Losses in the World Wars* (Arms & Armour Press, London: 1997).

Mars, Alastair, *British Submarines at War 1939–1945* (Naval Institute Press, Annapolis, MD: 1971).

Maulini, Robert L, *R.SMG. Enrico Toti,* www.regiamarina.net/subs/submarines/toti/toti_us.htm.

Messimer, Dwight R, *Verschollen: World War I U-Boat Losses* (Naval Institute Press, Annapolis, MD: 2002).

Murmansk   Miasnikov, Eugene, *Submarine Collision off Murmansk: A Look from Afar*, www.armscontrol.ru/subs/collisions/db080693.htm.

Miller   Miller, Vernon J, *Japanese Submarine Losses to Allied Submarines in World War II*, Monograph 56 (Merriam Press, Bennington, VT: 2003).

Morison1   Morison, Samuel Eliot, *History of United States Naval Operations in World War II: Vol I – The Battle of the Atlantic September 1939–May 1943* (Little, Brown and Co, Boston, MA: 1947).

Morison3   Morison, Samuel Eliot, *History of United States Naval Operations in World War II: Vol. III – The Rising Sun in the Pacific 1931–April 1942*, (Little, Brown and Co, Boston, MA: 1955).

Morison2   Morison, Samuel Eliot, *History of United States Naval Operations in World War II: Vol V – The Struggle for Guadalcanal August 1942–February 1943* (Little, Brown and Co, Boston, MA: 1948).

Mollá   Mollá Ayuso, Capt de Cor Luis and Capt de Cor José A Portolés Sanjuán, *La Historia del Submarino C-3, Revista General de Marina*, Nov 1998, Ministerio de Defensa, Spain. Available online at www.memoriahistorica.org.

Niestlé   Niestlé, Axel, *German U-Boat Losses during World War II: Details of Destruction* (Naval Institute Press, Annapolis, MD: 1998).

Padfield   Padfield, Peter, *War Beneath the Sea: Submarine Conflict during World War II* (John Wiley & Sons, Inc, Chichester: 1995).

Paterson   Paterson, Lawrence, *Hitler's Grey Wolves: U-Boats in the Indian Ocean* (Greenhill Books, London: 2004).

Cold   Polmar, Norman, and K J Moore, *Cold War Submarines* (Brassey's Inc, Dulles, VA: 2004).

Ranieri, Adm (ret) Attilio Duilio, *R.SMG. Gemma*, www.regiamarina.net/subs/submarines/gemma/gemma_us.htm.

Ranieri, Adm (ret) Attilio Duilio, *R.SMG. Ammiraglio Saint Bon*, www.regiamarina.net/subs/submarines/saintbon/saintbon_us.htm.

Rastelli   Rastelli, Achille, *The Italian Merchant Marine during WW II*, www.regiamarina.net/merchant/troops/troops_us.htm.

Axis   Rohwer, Jürgen, *Axis Submarine Successes 1939–1945* (Naval Institute Press, Annapolis, MD: 1983).

Roscoe   Roscoe, Theodore, *United States Submarine Operations in World War II*, (Naval Institute Press, Annapolis, MD: 1949).

Schwarz, Eric R, *Special: Submarine vs Submarine*, www.dutchsubmarines.com.

Enigma   Sebag-Montefiore, Hugh, *Enigma: The Battle for the Code* (John Wiley & Sons, Inc, Hoboken, NJ: 2000).

Sieche, Edwin, *The Austro-Hungarian Submarine Force*, www.gwpda.org/naval/ahsubs.htm.

Siegel, Adam B, 'International Naval Cooperation during the Spanish Civil War', *Joint Force Quarterly* (National Defense University, Washington, DC: Autumn–Winter 2001-2), pp 82–90.

Blind   Sontag, Sherry, and Christopher Drew, *Blind Man's Bluff: The Untold Story of American Submarine Espionage* (HarperCollins, New York: 1998).

Stern   Stern, Robert C, *Type VII U-boats* (Arms & Armour Press, London: 1991).

Tarrant, V E, *The U-Boat Offensive 1914–1945* (Arms & Armour Press, London: 1989).

Taylor, John C, *German Warships of World War I* (Doubleday & Co, Garden City, NY: 1970).

Wilk   Varvounis, Miltiades, Saiva Ziogate and Bob Baird, *The Wilk Case*, www.dutchsubmarines.com, 2000. (This article is in two parts, both of which are accessible under the 'Specials' link at the cited site.)

Watts   Watts, A J, and B G Gordon, *The Imperial Japanese Navy* (Doubleday & Co, Inc, Garden City, NY: 1971).

ULTRA   Winton, John, *ULTRA at Sea* (William Morrow & Co, Inc, New York, 1988).

Wynn   Wynn, Kenneth, *U-Boat Operations of the Second World War* (Chatham Publishing, London: 1997). (This work, in two volumes, is a boat-by-boat compilation of every U-boat, listing patrols, successes and fates.)

Secondary Sources (author unknown/uncredited)

'Codebreaking and Secret Weapons in World War II', *Nautical Brass Magazine*. home.earthlink.net/~nbrass1/enigma.htm. (A very useful multi-part account of Allied codebreaking before and during the Second World War.)

DANFS   *Dictionary of American Naval Fighting Ships*, Naval Historical Center, US Department of the Navy, Washington, DC, www.history.navy.mil/danfs/index.html. (Just as the print edition has long been a work in progress, so is the online version.)

Guides to the Microfilmed Records of the German Navy, 1850–1945: No 1 – U-Boats and T-Boats 1914–1918, National Archives and Records Service, Washington, DC, 1984. (Besides being an invaluable index into the holdings at the US National Archives, this document contains extremely useful cross-indices between boats, commanders and units.)

Guides to the Microfilmed Records of the German Navy, 1850–1945: No 2 – Records Relating to U-boat Warfare 1939–1945, National Archives and Records Service, Washington, DC, 1985. (Companion volume to the above covering the Second World War.)

Le 8 Mai 1940: Perte de la Doris, www.defense.gouv.fr/portal_repository/1521856251 0001/fichier/getData. (French government site recounting the story of the loss of *Doris*.)

Loss of HM Schooner 'First Prize', qships.freeserver.com/LossofPrize.htm. (This is in part an English translation of sections of a longer article available in French at multisites.phpnet.org/alaurent/marine/qship/prize.html.)

Loss of the Royal Edward, www.geocities.com/Heartland/Acres/5564/royaledward.html.

Obit1   *Obituary of Tom Martin Moore*, archiver.rootsweb.com/th/read/ENGLISH-OBITS/2005-08/1125411106. This is a copy of an obituary of the coxswain of HMS/M *Clyde* that ran in *The Daily Telegraph*, filed 7 September 2004.

Obit2   *Obituary of Lt Cdr Andy Chalmers,*
              http://www.telegraph.co.uk/news/main.jhtml?view=DETAILS&
              grid=&xml=/news/2005/11/24/db2402.xml. This is the obituary
              of the first lieutenant of HMS/M *Venturer* that ran in *The Daily
              Telegraph*, filed 24 November 2005.

              Russian & Soviet Peacetime Submarine Losses,
              www.lostsubs.com/Soviet.htm. (Excellent, concise summary of
              Russian submarine losses.)

              Stealth Beneath the Sea: The 'Wet Cold War', www.sid-
              hill.com/history/wcwvfw.htm. (This reportedly was an article
              originally published in April 1997 in the online magazine of the
              American VFW (Veterans of Foreign Wars).)

              The Saltzwedel Flotilla in Spain, www.uboatwar.net/spain.htm.

Squall   *The Storm over the Squall,* diodon349.com/Kursk-
              Memorial/storm_over_the_squall.htm.

War   *The U-Boat War in the Atlantic 1939–1945,* Ministry of
              Defence (Navy), (HMSO, London: 1989). (In fact, the authors
              of this work are known, simply not credited. The work was
              written by Dönitz's son-in-law, Günther Hessler, with the
              assistance of Alfred Hoschatt and Jürgen Rohwer, during the
              immediate post-war period, at the behest of the Royal Navy.)

Losses   *United States Submarine Losses – World War II,* US
              Government Printing Office, Washington, DC, 1963. (This
              document had its origin as a classified study commissioned by
              Commander, Submarine Force, US Pacific Fleet (COMSUBPAC)
              in 1946. It was declassified in 1955 and published by the US
              Navy's Division of Naval History in 1963.)

General Resources

The following sites are mostly, but not entirely, in English:

www.uboat.net – Excellent overall source for data on German U-boats of both
world wars.

www.britsub.net – Good source for British submarines of all eras.

web.ukonline.co.uk/chalcraft/sm/ww2sm2.html – Another good site for Royal
Navy submarine histories.

www.regiamarina.net/subs/index.htm – Good source for Italian submarines of
the Second World War. Easily the most useful government-run naval history
site.

www.battleships-cruisers.co.uk/submarines.htm – Despite the site name, a very
good source of general information on Royal Navy submarines.

www.turkishnavy.net/submarine/hist1.htm – Useful history of submarines in Turkish service.

www.geocities.com/~orion47/ – A site named *Axis Biographical Research*, it has some detailed career resumés of selected German naval officers.

www.dutchsubmarines.com – An excellent site detailing the development and actions of Dutch submarines.

www.combinedfleet.com – An excellent general resource on the Japanese Navy of the Second World War; of particular interest to those researching submarines is www.combinedfleet.com/sensuikan.htm by Bob Hackett and Sander Kingsepp.

www.submarinos.net – A general history site for Spanish submarines. Many of the pages are available in English.

www.wlb-stuttgart.de/seekrieg/ – This link is to an index of pages of day-by-day lists (in German) of German naval activities maintained by the *Württembergische Landesbibliothek (WLB)-Stuttgart*.

homepage.ntlworld.com/andrew.etherington/ – A day-by-day chronology of the Second World War. Extraordinarily detailed and useful.

www.polishnavy.pl/ships/submarines/ – This link is to an index of English-language articles on Polish submarines of the Second World War.

chrito.users1.50megs.com/daily.htm – A work-in-progress, daily reports of German naval and other military activities in the Second World War. Appears to be complete up to April 1941.

www.ussbatfish.com – a site maintained by the Batfish Memorial Foundation in Muskogee, OK.

www.fas.org – a site maintained by the Federation of American Scientists that has excellent current material on nuclear-related issues.

Sadly, one additional site I used, members.iinet.com.au/~eadej/index.html, a very good site for information on Royal Navy submarines, seems to have gone off-line during the time I was writing this book.

Index